MYTHS IN ISRAELI CULTURE

Parkes–Wiener Series on Jewish Studies
Series Editors: David Cesarani and Tony Kushner
ISSN 1368-5449

The field of Jewish Studies is one of the youngest, but fastest growing and most exciting areas of scholarship in the academic world today. Named after James Parkes and Alfred Wiener and recognising the co-operative relationship between the Parkes Centre at the University of Southampton and the Wiener Library in London, this series aims to publish new research in the field and student materials for use in the seminar room, to disseminate the latest work of established scholars and to re-issue classic studies which are currently out of print.

The selection of publications reflects the international character and diversity of Jewish Studies; it ranges over Jewish history from Abraham to modern Zionism, and Jewish culture from Moses to post-modernism. The series also reflects the inter-disciplinary approach inherent in Jewish Studies and at the cutting edge of contemporary scholarship, and provides an outlet for innovative work on the interface between Judaism and ethnicity, popular culture, gender, class, space and memory.

Other Books in the Series

Holocaust Literature: Schulz, Levi, Spiegelman and the Memory of the Offence
Gillian Banner

Remembering Cable Street: Fascism and Anti-Fascism in British Society
Edited by Tony Kushner and Nadia Valman

Sir Sidney Hamburger and Manchester Jewry: Religion, City and Community
Bill Williams

The Making of Manchester Jewry 1740–1875 (Revised Edition)
Bill Williams

Anglo-Jewry in Changing Times: Studies in Diversity 1840-1914
Israel Finestein

Double Jeopardy: Gender and the Holocaust
Judith Tydor Baumel

Cultures of Ambivalence and Contempt: Studies in Jewish–Non-Jewish Relations
Edited by Siân Jones, Tony Kushner and Sarah Pearce

Alfred Wiener and the Making of the Wiener Library
Ben Barkow

The Berlin Haskalah and German Religious Thought: Orphans of Knowledge
David Sorkin

Myths in Israeli Culture: Captives of a Dream
Nurith Gertz

The Jewish Immigrant in England 1870–1914 (Third Edition)
Lloyd P. Gartner

MYTHS IN ISRAELI CULTURE

Captives of a Dream

NURITH GERTZ

VALLENTINE MITCHELL
LONDON • PORTLAND, OR

First published in 2000 in Great Britain by
VALLENTINE MITCHELL
Newbury House, 900 Eastern Avenue
London IG2 7HH

and in the United States of America by
VALLENTINE MITCHELL
c/o ISBS
5804 N.E. Hassalo Street
Portland, Oregon 97213-3644

Website: www.vmbooks.com

British Library Cataloguing in Publication Data

Gertz, Nurith
Myths in Israeli culture: captives of a dream. –
(Parkes–Wiener series on Jewish studies)
1. Jews – Israel 2. Israeli literature 3. Israel –
Civilization 4. Israel – Politics and government
I. Title
956.9'405

ISBN 0 85303 386 2 (cloth)
ISBN 0 85303 383 8 (paper)
ISSN 1368-5449

Library of Congress Cataloging-in-Publication Data

Gertz, Nurith.
Myths in Israeli culture: captives of a dream / Nurith Gertz.
p. cm. – (Parkes–Wiener series on Jewish studies)
Includes bibliographical references (p.) and index.
ISBN 0-85303-386-2 (cloth) – ISBN 0-85303-383-8 (pbk.)
1.National characteristics, Israeli. 2. Memory–Social aspects.
3 . Memory–Political aspects. 4. Jews–Israel–Identity.
5. Self-perception–Israel. 6. Heroes–Mythology–Israel.
I. Title. II. Series.
DS113.3.G47 2000
956.94–dc21 00-032104

Printed in Great Britain by
Creative Print and Design (Wales), Ebbw Vale

CONTENTS

To Shlomzion and Rona

INTRODUCTION

This book attempts to present different aspects of the rapidly changing Israeli culture through various texts written before and after the establishment of the state of Israel. By analysing and comparing these texts, selected from the spheres of *belles-lettres*, journalism, politics, cinema and television, lights from different directions are cast on chapters of the modern history of Israel.

The texts studied were taken from the political system (party leaders' speeches, leaflets and posters, election propaganda), the media (newspaper and television), *belle-lettres* and the cinema, and from street signs and graffiti. An analysis of these texts reveals that, despite their dissimilar forms and styles, they are based and constructed upon identical narratives that appear and reappear in variations according to the specific events taking place at a given time and the system in which they occur. These might be called master narratives in the sense Lyotard has given to this term – all-encompassing models by which people are asked to think, live and die.[1] They might just as well be called myths, for they transmit ideological messages that, although not formulated directly, can be discerned in the subtexts.

Whatever we call them, narratives or myths, they articulate the common and shared worldview of a given society, provide legitimacy to its social order, foster integration between its members, and lead them to action. In order to do this, they often construct imaginary views of the world.[2] One of the main functions of such narratives is to preserve and prolong the existing social order by embellishing historical facts and specific conditions with an aura of eternal and immutable phenomena.

The narratives discussed in this book deal with the image of the Israeli-Jewish society in Israel. They present its existence as a struggle between opposing forces – the few against the many, West versus East, 'sons of light' versus 'sons of darkness', and 'a people that dwells alone' against 'the family of nations'. These narratives are all closely intertwined with universal humanism, Zionist-socialism, and various other ideologies, all of which can be found in texts dating from well before the state of Israel was declared. The status, circulation and position of each of these narratives in Israel's cultural hierarchy has risen or fallen at different times, and their structure and even content were often altered to suit the systems in which they appeared.

As the years went by – with the state of Israel being established and going through several wars, with its long-standing leftist Labor government being replaced by a coalition of its arch-rival rightist parties, and with Israel's status in the world changing – the hierarchy, content and structures of these narratives also changed. These permutations bear witness to the changing history of the Israeli culture. The descriptions of the metamorphoses of the narratives, and of the constantly changing relationships between them, are based on the view that a culture is a totality composed of the systems operating within it, all struggling for power, prestige and hegemony. The texts formed in – and by – a society are weapons used in these struggles. Thus, texts that were central in one period are shunted to the sidelines in another, and vice versa. In this process, the narratives embedded in the texts go through greater or lesser adjustments in content and structure to adapt them to their new status.[3]

Rather than trace each and every stage of all of the changing narratives, the descriptions focus on the changes that occurred during crucial periods of political upheaval. In the Israeli context, such periods are usually those in which a war took place or the party in power was replaced by the opposition party. Selected for discussion in this book are 'The Disturbances' (the Arab rebellion against the British which lasted from 1936 to 1939 and was accompanied by attacks on the Jewish population of the country), and several wars or near-wars – Independence (1947–49), Six Day (1967), Yom Kippur (1973), Lebanon (1982–83), *Intifada* (1987–94), and the Gulf War (1991). The changes in the Zionist narratives that occurred when the government changed in 1977, after almost 30 years of Labor hegemony, will also be studied.

In each of these periods some of the voices that were heard articulated the dominant views of their time. These voices were heard in political speeches, party banners and election posters, in newspapers and in advertising, and even in certain types of literature and cinema. But beyond the voices expressing these views there were always others – now quietly whispered, now loudly shouted – the voices of those who expressed doubt in the justice, truth or strength of the dominant narratives. These voices of doubt were often heard between the pages of books or in darkened theatres.

'When the king and his armies have gone to sleep, it is the turn of the court jester to have his say' is how the role of literature and the arts has been described.[4] This role was filled by the stories of Haim Hazaz and S. Yizhar, by the writings of Amos Oz, A. B. Yehoshua, David Grossman and others and, since the early 1980s, by many Israeli films. The art forms of *belle-lettres* and cinema have blurred the lines constructed in the ideological narratives to delineate the few from the many, West from East, and the 'Jewish People' from the 'Nations of the World'. They have divested their protagonists of their national identities, presenting their Jewish-Israeli distress and anguish as universal emotions, and have separated the nation's history into discrete scenes in a pageant of existential moments. By doing this, the *belle-lettres* and the cinema have forced Israeli society to re-examine its Zionist narratives in order to discern and understand the contradictions within them and between them and reality.

In many cases the dominant narratives absorbed the voices of doubt expressed in *belle-lettres* and the cinema, and used them as a source of moral justification. The voices of doubt, however, could not ignore the dominant narratives; they assimilated them, but transformed them in order to serve their own purposes. The two 'sides' were thus locked in a complex network of tensions within which they interacted and struggled, but from which they also nourished each other. In some instances a message enunciated in a literary work or in the cinema was echoed in other texts, even years later when the historical conditions had changed, and was used to create a new dominant narrative. This, perhaps, was the case with regard to the Gulf War, which opened a gap between the old narrative used by the country's leadership and the new reality. The narrative of 'a people that dwells apart' surrounded by adversarial 'forces of darkness' did not fit a war in which Israel was part of a large coalition of 'enlightened' nations. This disparity quickened the pace at which a new, individualistic 'post-Zionist' narrative penetrated the cultural and political centres.

Vehement disputation has been a characteristic of the Israeli culture both prior to and following Israel's establishment, in peacetime as well as in wartime. The polemics break through the boundaries that set apart left from right, *belles-lettres* from politics, minority from majority, and the nation from the individual. The subjects debated concern the identity of Israeli society, its moral principles, and its place among the other nations of the world. It is this overarching polemic, in its many forms and shades, that the present book attempts to delineate and clarify.

NOTES

1. J. Lyotard, 1984.
2. R. Barthes, 1982. See also L. Althuser, 1971 and M. Angenot, 1984, 1988.
3. See I. Even-Zohar, 1990; B. Even-Zohar, 1988; P. Bourdieu, 1980.
4. By Angenot, in a lecture on literature and society, Tel Aviv University, 1994.

1

THE FEW AGAINST THE MANY: Jewish-Hebrew Culture in the 1930s

INTRODUCTION

One of the central narratives in Zionist culture depicts the Jewish–Arab conflict as a 'war of the few against the many'. The few were those who emulated the historic freedom fighters of ancient Israel; the many were the modern embodiment of various ancient oppressors. The Jewish struggle against the Arabs was thus perceived as a modern re-enactment of such ancient battles and wars as David's slaying of Goliath, the Hasmonean (Maccabean) uprising against ancient Greece, the Jewish war against the Romans that ended in AD 73 with the Zealots' last stand at Masada, and the Bar-Kokhba revolt 65 years later. Thus it was depicted as a war of the few – isolated, degraded and despised – who, driven by their faith and will, bravely resisted a stronger enemy.[1]

The few-against-the-many narrative is widespread in western culture, appearing in numerous variations, up to, and including, American westerns. Since the nineteenth century, Jewish historiographic literature has based its version of this narrative on biblical and historical accounts of the conquest of the Land of Israel. For example, from the Book of Maccabees:

> It is not on the size of the army that victory depends, but strength comes from Heaven. They come against us in great pride and lawlessness to destroy us and our wives and our children, and to despoil us; but we fight for our lives and our laws.... Do not fear their numbers or be afraid when they charge. Remember how our fathers were saved at the Red Sea when Pharaoh with his forces pursued them.[2]

The modern Zionist culture adopted these sources and interpreted them in the light of current needs, turning religious faith into secular ideology, God's commands into social mores, and heavenly given heroism into earthly human valour. In all other aspects the ancient story is retained: the few overcome the many by virtue of their absolute faith and the inspiration of past victories. In both past and present versions the struggle leads to victory, and the victory changes the status of the Jewish people, who are now recognised and honoured by all other peoples.

In many texts written by the modern Jews of the *Yishuv* in Palestine[3] in the first decades of the twentieth century this narrative does not appear on the surface but is concealed in the subtext and overshadowed by apparently neutral documentary details and descriptions. In this mode the narrative appears as a permanent pattern in texts that deal with totally different topics, evoking again and again, although in variations, the eternal cosmic drama of the few versus the many. The pattern can be detected even in descriptions of struggles in which the Jews were not a minority or in which their righteousness or faith was not the motivating force. The need to cast these events into the mythic die is especially conspicuous in the accounts of struggles that ended in defeat and destruction but are nevertheless depicted as victories. In such cases the facts are interpreted to suit the narrative: failure becomes heroic death, and heroic death a triumph in the eyes of posterity, of the enemy, or of God. As in the biblical and historical sources, such a triumph is often phrased in end-of-days terms, a vision of a time when all the nations of the world will 'ascend the Mountain of the Lord' to behold the 'light emanating from Zion'.

This narrative expresses the Zionist culture's efforts to secure the re-establishment of the Jewish people in the Land of Israel. It was shared by all sectors of the *Yishuv*, although in each of the cultural systems it was affected by different constraints, such as the character of the target audience, the structure of the system, and its relationship with other systems. Thus, in different cultural systems the narrative appears with somewhat different attributes and structures.

An analytic study of the manifestations of this narrative in the 1930s will enable us to understand the culture of the period both as an integrated totality and as a set of schisms and contradictions between social trends and constraints. Examined in this chapter, through various different texts, are the political, literary and journalistic systems. The analysis of the three systems will reveal how the content shunted aside in one system is brought to the fore in another.

The political texts include party leaders' speeches and the election propaganda that was disseminated in those years through leaflets and on placards as well as in newspapers. Leaflets distributed to the public and placards posted on walls and bulletin boards were the prevailing means for communicating propaganda to the broad public. The *Yishuv*, which then numbered about 200,000, comprised a broad stratum of bourgeois and working-class intelligentsia. They constituted an enthusiastic readership of newspapers and placards, as well as of *belles-lettres* and literary magazines, although the latter were less popular.

THE POLITICAL SYSTEM

Most of the questions facing the *Yishuv* in pre-state Israel led to vehement disputes between the large political blocs, but they were also vigorously argued within the different factions that constituted each bloc. This dispute, concerning the nature of the nascent Jewish national entity, the area it was to inhabit, and methods to be used in fighting against the British and the Arabs, almost led to civil war in the 1930s. It was expressed in a fiercely contended struggle between the left (the Labor movement bloc headed by the ruling Mapai Party) and the right (the Revisionist movement). The trend in the Revisionist movement was to solve the Jewish–Arab conflict by force, to achieve complete Jewish sovereignty over Palestine, on both sides of the Jordan River, and to stress, beyond the fundamental principles of democracy, the importance of the authority of the party's leadership. In the Labor movement, where opinions about these issues varied greatly and were constantly thrashed out in heated arguments, the overall tendency was to view Jewish settlement in Palestine as a necessarily long and gradual process, to recognise the limits of national activism, to take a strong stand for a democratic approach, and to agree to a reduced Jewish area, albeit temporarily, in order to ensure Jewish sovereignty in at least part of the country.

Despite the ardour of these disputes, the various factions and blocs agreed on several basic Zionist precepts, among them the immutable attachment of the Jewish people to the Land of Israel (*Eretz Yisrael*) and the establishment of an independent society with a decisively Jewish majority in that land. These and other commonly held precepts were given prominence in the political and propagandistic texts of both parties in two ways – articulation in the light of each party's ideology, and appropriation by each party in order to describe its struggles as national struggles and its members as national heroes.

The Zionist narratives were exceptionally well suited to such use because they carried an accepted and shared meaning that was not explicitly conceptualised. In many cases these narratives aroused an irrational identification with the speaker's ideology and a similarly irrational rejection of that of the opponent. The 'few against the many' was the most prominent of these narratives, appearing in the leaflets and placards of both the Labor movement and the Revisionist Party. The narrative started with a description of the nation's distress caused by the *Yishuv*'s utter isolation while confronting the danger of larger and stronger evil forces. The left: 'Difficult days are upon us, days of distress, starvation and retribution.' The right: 'We are in the midst of days of historical ordeal, unparalleled perhaps since the destruction of the Second Temple.' The *Yishuv*, according to the left, faced 'the danger of a rift in the land of Israel', while the right warned of the Jewish land being 'torn asunder'.[4]

The 'difficult days' and the 'historical ordeal' in these examples refer to 'The Disturbances' – the Arab rebellion against the British which lasted for some three years, from 1936 to 1939, and was inevitably accompanied by widespread attacks on the Jewish population of the country. Similar descriptions appear, however, during periods of quiet as well. A 1931 Mapai Party leaflet speaks of an 'hour of crisis for the nation's great endeavour ... in the Land [of Israel] and ... in the Diaspora', while a 1935 Revisionist leaflet exhorts that 'the moment is a moment of crisis ... the hour in which the Jewish People of the world have reached the brink of the abyss'. The same 'terrible abyss' was also used in Mapai placards to describe the situation of European Jewry in the 1930s.[5]

The Jewish people was seen by both parties as 'oppressed, disgraced and denigrated ... detached from the land, lacking bread, deprived of honour, divested of rights', and as having accepted 'suffering and bitterness with love' (the words 'disgraced' and 'denigrated' were not used by mere chance: they evoke the Suffering Servant of God described in Isaiah). The ability of the *Yishuv* to withstand such suffering and survive is portrayed in both cases as the result of the nation's profound faith: 'Our confidence in the final victory shall never be weakened for there is no other way for a people rotting in poverty and persecution.'[6]

The narrative now enters its second stage. In the texts of both parties the people's faith must lead to action. This is a crucial stage, both because the purpose of the leaflets and placards was to spur their readers to action, and because the modern Zionist pioneers' action was thought of as a major character trait – and the complete opposite of the traditional passivity of the Jews of the Exile. Both parties recognised and proclaimed the need for action, but they disagreed, often violently, as to its nature. For the left, action meant a strengthening of the effort to establish new settlements despite enemy attacks, while for the right, action meant war and vengeance. Thus, in a Mapai leaflet we find:

> We remain at the forefront of construction and creation of life. ...We shall not cease to build in our Land. The transport on the roads will not cease. ...The fields and orchards have not been abandoned. Not a single position has been relinquished not a settlement abandoned. ... And, moreover, from our ranks forces have arisen and gone out to make new conquests, to establish new outposts, and to discover new goals in construction and settlement.

Leaflets of the right, on the other hand, called for 'a war of conquest and momentum ... many-sided retaliation ... vengeance by force of arms [because] in blood and in fire Judea fell; in blood and in fire Judea shall rise'.[7] While the words repeatedly found in the placards of the Labor movement are 'build', 'plant' and 'create', the key terms in the Revisionist placards include 'courage for war', 'armed resistance to the oppressors' and 'conquest'. Even when the word 'conquest' appears in placards of the left, it refers to the 'conquest of labour' and not to military conquest.

Although these terms obviously imply very different modes of action, the differences are subsumed, for both parties harness time and space to the common Zionist cause in similar ways. For both, 'past-time' is as vital as the present, and from it confidence in the future success of the Zionist endeavour is drawn. The strife of the Maccabean and Second Temple periods, the Bar-Kokhba rebellion and the generation of the first Zionist pioneers are invoked as evidence of the people's one-time strength, assurance for the future and a command for today's fighters: 'Memorise this and remind others: the idea of redeeming the People of Israel is not the legacy of our generation alone; we received it from previous generations and bear the responsibility of fulfilling it for posterity' (from a leaflet of the right).

The heroes of biblical and Jewish history are accordingly defined as links in a chain that continues to the present: 'In the same breath as [we say] the names of Samson, Joab, Judah Maccabee ... Bar-Kokhba ... we may also say the name of the esteemed Yosef the Galilean.'[8] Heroes and martyrs of the Diaspora are added to those of the past, especially in leaflets of the right:

> The People of Israel have been drenched in their own blood during two thousand years of Exile, have leapt into the flames of martyrdom, have been the victims of beasts of prey, and have fallen as sacrifices at the hands of murderers and enemies of Israel in seventy lands of Exile – but have never veered from their ways ... nor lost their eternal hope that they will come back to live freely in a Hebrew State in the Land of Israel.[9]

The parties engaged in bitter ideological controversy over the borders of this soon-to-be-realised Hebrew state. The right dreams of, and urges, the 'establishment of national independence within [its] historical borders ... between the sea and the desert', while the left is willing to accept a country with a smaller territory. However, both sides address the land issue in terms that mute specific disagreement. The right: 'This land is ours in its entirety, from end to end; we shall never relinquish an inch.' The left: 'We have clung to this land and have forged an eternal covenant with it.' A placard of Betar (the youth movement of the Revisionist Party) urges 'a vision of complete Hebrew redemption' while a poster of the left calls for a 'Zionist vision of redemption'.[10] Both also invoke 'the entire world', 'heaven and earth', and 'one end of the universe to the other' to attest to the suffering of the Jews and the justice of their cause.[11]

The posters of both sides depict the struggle as an ascent to the peak of a high mountain, leading to the third stage – victory – in which the summit is conquered and an absolute bond with the land is ensured. Future time is transformed in this case from historical to supra-historical, an eternal epoch in which the people of Israel 'dwells securely in its Land ... building and planting' (a poster of the left) and 'not relinquishing an inch' (the right). At this stage all the peoples of the world gather in wonder at the greatness of Israel and at 'the day-to-day heroism of the settler-peasant' (the left) and the 'tenacious fighting Jew' (the right). The utopian panorama portrayed in these texts disregards the salient historical fact that most of the Jews' past struggles for freedom had ended in failure, and often in death. They eschew this demoralising fact and refer only to the victory that will surely be attained.[12]

A central topic in their leaflets, the parties' bitter political controversy, is based on accusations and denunciations, defamation and scorn. However, both parties used the same expressions in this controversy, as both were inspired by the same historical associations and by a common cultural background that transcended the accusations and scorn themselves. The context of biblical religious wars is thus utilised in Revisionist placards that label Mapai followers 'sacrificers of the dead' and 'the faithless ... dancing around the golden calf of materialism', and in Mapai posters that revile the Revisionists who 'offer our life endeavour ... to a false god'. Past persecutions of Jews constitute the background for Revisionist descriptions of Mapai members as 'spreaders of blood libels' (about the Revisionists) and for Mapai descriptions of the Revisionists as 'instigators of pogroms' (against the Labor movement). Even the national and international consensus regarding Nazi Germany serves as an underlying theme for both parties. The Mapai leadership is accused of having 'neither ideals nor faith' and of behaving 'like the Hitlerites in Germany', while the Revisionists are called 'Hitlerites' and 'enemies of constructive Zionism [who cooperated with the] malignant fascism'.[13]

Both parties use the ideological narrative to emphasise their common Zionist values, while controversial issues are presented as part of the national consensus. Both also utilise the tactic of appropriating the national narrative and converting it into a party possession. Although this is very conspicuous in their posters, our inquiry is also based on speeches made by leaders of the two parties. In these, each movement is portrayed as a tiny minority forced to contend with a multitude of enemies both at home and abroad. In order to transform the national narrative into a movement narrative, the two dominant leaders, Ze'ev Jabotinsky of the right, and David Ben-Gurion of the left, equated their respective movements with the nation: for Jabotinsky, the Revisionism of the right-wing bloc was the sole national standard; for Ben-Gurion, only Labor Zionism was true Zionism.

To this end, both Jabotinsky and Ben-Gurion adopted the elemental figure of the *halutz*, the suffering, self-sacrificing Zionist pioneer. Jabotinsky declared: 'in all Palestine there is one small group of individuals, called "Betarists", who have said to themselves, "If I come to Eretz Israel as a *halutz*, then I must suffer".' Ben-Gurion expressed a similar thought: 'The Zionism of the working class in *Eretz Israel*, from the very beginning of our movement to the present, is a Zionism that demands of each adherent everything he has – all his time, his life, his future and destiny, his longings and exertions, unconditionally.'[14] Both leaders described their members as those who 'sacrificed their lives defending their country' (Betar poster), and who 'heroically dedicated their souls to the Land' (Mapai poster).[15]

To drive home the identity of the movement and the Jewish people, each of the leaders appropriates the nation's past and turns it, too, into its own movement's 'past'. The heroes of the past are thus portrayed as the vanguard of their respective movements. For example, Theodore Herzl, prophet of the Jewish state and founder of Zionism, is depicted both as the pioneer of the right and as a trailblazer of the left by leaders of the respective parties. A fierce argument evolves around Yosef Trumpeldor, a Jewish settler-guard who was killed in 1921 defending the isolated pioneering farm Tel-Hai, after which both sides claimed him as one of their own. Jabotinsky, in a World Trumpeldor Covenant poster, makes a call to 'realise Trumpeldor's prophecy', and Mapai, in an election poster, exhorts: 'Don't allow the name of Tel-Hai to be profaned! Don't allow the name of Trumpeldor to be taken in vain! Be faithful to the banner of the defenders and saviours of the Galilee! Vote for the Labor Party.'[16]

After the movement has been equated with the nation and given a national past, a national saga can be constructed. In this saga members of the right/left stand alone – shunned, abused and scorned since the dawn of Zionist history. 'When Herzl spoke of political Zionism', Jabotinsky declares, 'we were mocked. They called Zionism a movement in which the clever Jews would send the fools to the Land of Israel'; while Ben-Gurion states:

> in the history of the labour movement there is not a single act that did not first meet with a blank wall, a lack of understanding, or even opposition and strife against various circles in Zionism.... The labourer began his work in the country completely alone – alone in Zionism and alone in the *Yishuv*.[17]

The scorned and isolated few, be they left-wing Labor Zionists or right-wing Revisionists, neither give up nor give in; guided by their faith, they remain steadfast. They believe in their goal, are confident that it is attainable, and are able to carry out their mission even as their opponents mock them: 'You're sick. Go see a doctor' (Jabotinsky). Despite the many difficulties in going against the mainstream, their faith will carry them through. Where Ben-Gurion, in reference to the members of his party, asserts that 'the road is rough, the way is strewn with obstacles and paved with suffering … no one comes to their aid and no one understands them [but] they know it is their task to work a miracle, to build a state', Jabotinsky claims that his followers will 'turn hardship into a banner and privation into a memorial [for] they are builders of a nation through sadness and suffering'.[18]

The third stage – victory – is the inevitable culmination of the struggle. For the left, which was in power at this time, the victory has already been achieved, as proletarian values had become indelible tenets of the Zionist movement. For the right, it is postponed, and viewed in end-of-days terms, when all the nations of the world will acknowledge the Isaiah-inspired Servant of God, who epitomises the men of the right: 'You will yet see – the people in the Jezreel Valley [that is, of the left] will soon awaken, stand up, and bow their heads before us' (Jabotinsky).[19]

In both instances, the few-versus-many narrative is combined with the Servant-of-God figure in order to communicate a single message – the isolated and shunned few will be sustained in their struggle against the many by their spiritual values and will attain the height of the mountain, to which all others (movements and parties) will make pilgrimage. Thus, the national drama of Zionism was the same for both parties; the heroes and anti-heroes alone were different. This common basis enabled them to mute their specific positions and to address the public in the name of a common consensus.

The political manifestations of the few-versus-many paradigm illustrate the *Yishuv*'s conformity to shared values and its confidence in the justice and ultimate triumph of its cause. This confidence is not drawn from rational historical arguments but from twin analogies rooted in myths of the past – that the suffering of Jews is evidence of their righteousness, and that this suffering and righteousness will lead to victory. According to this narrative, 'the few' who suffer are always right and always emerge victorious. However, the new narrative ascribes supreme importance to action, a recent addition to the paradigm. Action, in this new context, is central because it attests to the Hebrew-Israeli activism that has replaced the exilic Jew's historical passivity.

THE LITERARY SYSTEM

In the pre-state period, particularly during the Disturbances of the 1920s and 1930s, the political system exerted strong pressure on writers to articulate the Zionist pioneers' life and faith optimistically in order to bolster their spirits. Not only did this also answer the demands of the reading public, composed largely of workers and *halutz* (pioneer) settlers, it was consistent with the writers' own tendencies to praise and glorify the pioneers' activity. And yet, the Hebrew literary circles of the *Yishuv*, which by this time had a relatively long tradition of autonomy, were also sensitive to pure literary values and believed in their right to articulate positions which were not necessarily nationalistic or Zionist.

Writers were affected to varying degrees by these two types of constraints, one originating in the social system and the other in the literary circles themselves. The authors dominating the centre of the literary system – those who were accepted by its institutions, praised by the critics, and read by the elite and the wider public, and whose writings were taught in the country's schools – were usually older and more faithful to the traditions of literary autonomy. They had been able to free themselves of the social dictates. Some of the younger writers followed in their footsteps. There were, on the other hand, writers on the periphery of the literary system who were not accepted by the literary institutions but were read by a small, faithful public. Their writings were published in small literary publications such as *Gilionoth* and *Gazit* and in the literary section of the daily *Davar*, which was the newspaper of the left.[20] These writers tended to respond to the socio-political dictates, as can be seen in the different ways in which they used the few-versus-many narrative.

Literature of the Periphery

The stories based on the few-versus-many narrative tend to describe the act of pioneering settlement at great length, inflating this stage of events to mythical, timeless and absolute dimensions. The ensuing accounts of threats to this toehold are tersely and briefly related, after which the long-winded narrative is resumed up to the stage of victory.[21] This framework enabled the stories to fulfil the functions with which the literature of the period was charged, namely, both to strengthen the pioneers' confidence in the success of their endeavours and to bolster their faith.

The stories usually combine two literary models to restructure the narrative. One is the idyll, expressed in lengthy descriptions of a peaceful Jewish-Israeli existence. The other is a literary device, well-known in European novels, in which the protagonist's heroic death serves as an harmonic final link in the chain of developments and events. They are thus constructed with excessively long expositions composed mainly of bucolic landscapes that reshape time and space into timeless, absolute dimensions. Horizon-to-horizon landscapes are portrayed as if viewed from a central point of observation, from which their every dimension is absorbed, as if to attest to intimate familiarity and the ability to dominate: 'Wherever you turn your gaze – to the south or the north, to the east or to the west – the entire expanse of uncultivated fields has suddenly girded itself with the sharp daggers of thistles' (Shmeterling, 'Sights of Summer'). And, similarly, 'The silence grows and deepens, it descends oppressively, conquering everything as it spreads in every direction and to every height and depth' (Arikha, 'Paths in the Upper Galilee').

Despite its vastness the landscape does not threaten. It is safe and secure because the horizon envelops the earth gracefully and lovingly, and sky and land are woven together into a closed and protected space. Although the protagonist who moves within this space is generally a lone wanderer, tractor driver or farmer, the setting and the protagonist's awareness that throughout its length and breadth there are others like him, impart ease and confidence. The others are usually only suggested by the lights of distant tractors or faraway settlements, or remote but familiar sounds. Their existence attests to the fact that the lonely *halutz*, the representative of the tenacious 'few', is only one of many others like him:

> At eventide, as the Carmel turns blue and the red edges of the sky meet the deepening shadow of the earth, Uri, seated on the tractor, drives down from the settlement for a night of ploughing in a distant field. [Although he is alone in the field, he is not lonely because] from the slopes above the valley dots of light float and move about. The lights of tractors from the neighbouring villages find their way in the furrows of their fields. (Rabinov, 'The Night Ploughman')

Time, too, is given absolute dimensions. Although the action of the stories takes place within only a few hours or days, innumerable memories of the distant past and thoughts of an assured future expand their duration. The past is presented in recollections of the settlement's first days, as in Rabinov's 'The Night Ploughman', or in envisioned memories of ancient settlements, as in Arikha's 'Paths in the Upper Galilee': 'This pageant of the night is taking shape here as in years gone by, in the primitive bosom of this same nature.' The future is revealed in the scenery itself, as cypress trees seem like 'a huge rampart marching into tomorrow' ('The Night Ploughman') or through the narrator's confidence that this night is 'the same as the nights of tomorrow and the next day' (Bass, 'Last Stop in Canaan'). Tomorrow is a time of hope, when the seeds planted in the soil today will sprout and a 'new life will begin' ('The Night Ploughman'). In many cases the historical continuity leads from ancient times to an end-of-days future; present moments 'like drops of dew reflect both the past and the future' (Bass, 'Great Moments') and historical time becomes eternity. Time that 'began in the distant past' (Bass, 'The Farmer from Motsa') will flow 'beyond all generations' (Bass, 'Winds of August in Jerusalem').

The first stage in the structure of these stories is thus far from the misery and suffering described in contemporaneous political texts. Instead, it depicts the settlers' deep attachment to the soil. It is this attachment, rather than the action which was so essential an element in the placards and speeches, that is reinforced mythically by being expanded into infinite time and space. The great importance of this phase is emphasised in page after page of descriptive prose, which the stories appear reluctant to interrupt for the sake of creating the dynamic unfolding of the plot.

The second stage consists of a severely truncated account of attackers who pounce from ambush upon the unaccompanied protagonist. Overwhelming him in numbers and strength, in most cases they injure or kill him. Although the familiar narrative form is thus adhered to, only a few lines are devoted to the description of the disastrous event, whose importance is thus lessened and virtually glossed over. In Rabinov's 'The Night Ploughman', for example, a two-page description of the landscape is followed by six lines that describe the shot fired from ambush and the death of the hero, while in Yosef Hanani's 'Three Fingers', three pages of landscape precede the single page in which the shot, the agony and the death of the hero are described. Yehuda Ya'ari's short story 'The Bird's Nest' contains only descriptions of the hierarchy and organisation of a camp of *halutz* road builders, and its very last lines alone describe the death of the protagonist.

In these and similar stories, the disproportion between the very long idyllic exposition and the very briefly described tragic aftermath serves an important function – it portrays permanence and stability as crucial factors that no one-time occurrence can negate. The pain and tragedy of the attack are assuaged and its significance minimised in three ways: very little space is devoted to it; the literary convention which views death as an harmonic culmination of life rather than a violent shattering of it is invoked; and it serves as a brief and rapid transition to the last phase of the story – victory – in which the hero's values achieve immortality.

Thus, for example, in 'The Night Ploughman' the morning star, Venus, rises 'from an harmonious chorus of lights' just as the hero, Uri, dies. At the moment of death he feels that he is the very centre of creation. Despite Uri's death, the world around him is still portrayed as broad and secure, full of 'joyful but soundless [lights] sparkling in the distant settlements'. A similar sense of attachment to the soil and the world at the very moment of death is also evoked in 'Three Fingers' and in other stories. Death crowns the protagonist Yonah with a 'hero's wreath' (Yehuda Ya'ari, 'The Hero') and Mishka's entire life is infused with light and beauty (Ya'ari, 'The Bird's Nest'), as attested by the hero's last words or by his comrades' eulogies.

Not only is the hero's death briefly and quickly dealt with, it is transformed into its very opposite – the way to eternal life. The new Hebrew culture perceives the deaths of the Masada and Bar-Kokhba warriors in a similar light, although these events actually culminated in the almost total devastation of the Jewish people, loss of its independence, and the exile of its survivors (as mentioned above). Their modern renderings, however, describe them as heroic victories and vestibules to the timeless (albeit future) life of the people in its land.

The problem in stories of this type lies not only in the disproportion between their expository and event sections but also in their distorted causality. The bullet whizzes from the ambush like a *deus ex machina* whose only purpose is to cut short the hero's exaltation. Neither reason nor explanation for this bullet is provided, for the Arab who fired it lacks one. He does not and cannot appear earlier in the story because the Israeli-Jewish hero occupies the entirety of eternal Jewish time and space. The Arab's sudden appearance and his attack on the hero are non-causal; it is a demonic *ex nihilo* event.

Both the constraints and the possibilities of the literary system enabled it to stress several elements that the political system subsumed. Stressing these elements, however, was precisely what allowed deep contradictions in the collective social conscience of the community to emerge. The community's awareness of its virtual state of war with the Arabs, its fervent willingness to act, and its absolute faith in victory (as articulated in the political texts) overshadowed a strong concomitant tendency to sink into a static and serene state and to ignore the Arabs' existence.

The literary and the political systems appealed to the same community, the basically homogeneous *Yishuv*, and both employed the narrative to conceal the historical factors underlying the Jewish–Arab conflict. Thus, both portrayed it as a universal phenomenon which therefore needed neither cause nor explanation. The political system, however, stressed the readiness of the leaders and the nation to fight and win, while the literature, by ignoring the Arabs and the conflict with them, exposed the somewhat incomplete nature of this readiness. The *Yishuv* was indeed completely surprised in 1936 when the Disturbances broke out. An analysis of texts written at this time might explain this.

Literature of the Centre

The literature described above, although popular enough, was not the central component of the literary system. At its centre was a model that had become established in Europe at the beginning of the century and was recognised and accepted by both the literary establishment and the general readership of the time. This literature is epitomised by writers such as Jacob Fichman, Jacob Steinberg, Rabi Benyamin, Gershon Shoffman and Shai Agnon; it was later continued by younger writers, such as Haim Hazaz and S. Yizhar, who were recognised either immediately, or in the course of time. These writers were less yielding to the socio-national dictates of the period and more intent on preserving the tradition of literary autonomy. Nevertheless, since they could not ignore the ideological narratives so common in general and literary circles, they manipulated them in such ways that their essential character underwent a complete metamorphosis. This phenomenon can be observed in stories that deal with contemporaneous events, especially the Disturbances.

Hazaz, for example, juxtaposed variations of action and passivity in such ways that they simultaneously affirmed and negated each other; he revealed that hidden in the passivity of the Jewish Exile is the potential for action, and that in Zionist action there is the potential for passsivity. These two elements, the action that characterised political texts and the passivity that was assimilated into literary writings, were inseparably intertwined in Hazaz's stories.[22]

At first glance, Hazaz's story 'The Great Sojourner' seems to scorn those passive Jews who 'deliver themselves up to the nations to do to them as they will'. As the story progresses, however, the force of this initial scorn weakens. Its protagonist, Reb Meshel Yeshel, is exalted as he rises into a sublime spiritual world dedicated to the study of the Torah, and it is seen that Jewish passivity may be lofty and noble rather than humiliating and shameful. This is especially prominent when Reb Meshel's passsivity is compared with the action and dynamism of his donkey, the allegorical personification of the materiality and corporeality of physical life. Although action and dynamism are shown to be a way of life, while passivity is depicted as a type of death (Reb Meshel is described as 'neither alive amongst the living nor dead amongst the dead'), action is shown to lead to death when the donkey goes wild and dies. It is thus Reb Meshel's passivity that is seen to be the source of life – the life of the spirit.

In another story by Hazaz, 'Drabkin', Zionist allusions are used to dissever concepts that are linked to each other in the original narrative. In the stories of the periphery, for example, dimensions of time and space were melded together and into the Israeli landscape, where they symbolise the perpetuity of Jewish-Israeli life in the Land of Israel. In 'Drabkin' these dimensions are disengaged in such a way as to raise the question of whether living in a Jewish land is preferable to Jewish life in exile. Drabkin claims that,

> [In our Exile,] we existed elevated above place, in the depths of time, in generations past, in life everlasting ... a measure of eternity in this passing and ephemeral world ... but here [in the Land of Israel] we are only like the [other] peoples ... here we are of this world and of this place.[23]

'This place' is ridiculed in the story by being described in overt literary clichés. The scenes of the Land of Israel that Drabkin dreams about are not based on reality but are quoted directly and profusely from both Zionist publications and the widely-read fiction written in Palestine. Thus, Drabkin's dream-landscapes are broad and pastoral, its inhabitants sowing and planting in scattered groups. The hero is at centre-stage, as it were, surrounded by 'the length and the breadth' of this vastness 'from Dan to Be'er Sheva'. He is part and parcel of the landscape and of the multitude of people that inhabit it, for they are similar to him and live and work as he does:

> Here is Ekron, a pleasant and pretty colony, and very respectable, with a well of sweet water in it and well-built houses ... whose farmers, one-time teachers, shopkeepers and peddlars do their work with wonderful industry and vigorous

> diligence. … Here is Rosh Pinna in the Galilee, where springs of cold and crystal-clear water flow from the high hills of Naphtali to water it and make it fertile. At the moment that one is privileged to enter the Land of Israel, immediately the whole country is stirred and comes out to meet you.[24]

Generally, in Hazaz's stories, belief in the justice of the struggle for the Land of Israel is juxtaposed with the realisation that the struggle is in vain, and attachment to the Land of Israel is juxtaposed with the premise that the place of the Jew is in the Exile where Jewish spiritual values blossomed. This play of contradictions allows the stories to both articulate and negate the narrative at one and the same time. Hazaz's plots also tend to place the narratives in unsuitable contexts, thus stripping them of their relevance and meaning. The story 'The Great Sojourner' makes use of the prevalent narrative to describe the death, at the hands of Arabs, of its protagonist. Reb Meshel's donkey dies along the way and he buries it in a nearby field. Years later, after the grave has become known as that of a holy Jewish *tzaddik* (pious man), it is appropriated by Arabs as that of a Muslim holy man. The story ends when Reb Meshel arrives at the site many years later and unthinkingly tells the pilgrims there that the grave is not that of a holy man, but that of his donkey. Upon hearing this the pilgrims kill him; his revelation of the truth costs him his life.

The Arabs' appropriation of the supposed grave of the Jewish holy man is related thus: 'A great number of people gathered and set upon the celebrants, pelted them with stones and beat them with swords.' As in the mythical stories of the periphery, no plausible explanation is given for this act, and it is described solely as the result of what are seen as the inveterate negative traits of Arabs:

> These slothful and shiftless Arabs are envious of all they see. They toil not nor labour nor travail and they have only what they can take from others; they see a sown field and take possession of it, they see a planted orchard and take it by force.[25]

Arabs' deeds and Arab character are described here according to the familiar narrative, but because their rationality is lost in the context in which the events take place, the original narrative is blurred beyond recognition. On the one hand, the Jews portrayed in this story are those of the 'old' *Yishuv* of Palestine who neither sow fields nor plant orchards, their main occupation being religious study. On the other hand, at the end of the story Reb Meshel Yeshel is murdered not because of any dispute between Jews and Arabs, or between the few and the many, but because he has besmirched the sanctity of a holy man's grave.

S. Yizhar, one of the most prominent writers of the 1940s and 1950s, published two of his earliest stories, 'Paths in the Fields' and 'A Night Without Gunfire', at the end of the 1930s. In these stories he articulated the contemporaneous ideological narrative, as in the literature of the periphery, but at the same time shattered and distorted it, as in that of the centre.[26] Yizhar's descriptions of landscape, like those of the stories of the periphery, are presented from horizon to horizon and from mountain peaks to valleys. However, not only is this landscape depicted as mere platitude, it also reflects the subjective moods of the protagonist. Thus the description of timeless landscapes that appear in the other stories are deprived of their objectivity in those of Yizhar. In his moments of serenity and joy the protagonist discerns the conventional characteristics of this landscape; he feels he is in the very middle of a broad open space enclosed on all sides and senses a feeling of security. Even the horizon surrounds him, in such moments, with a yellow light 'that whisks up bubbles of mist'. But when the protagonist's mood is one of loneliness and estrangement this same enclosedness suffocates him and blocks his way to other spaces. At these moments of isolation and alienation the very openness of the landscape evokes a sense of perdition rather than magnitude.

The horizon now threatens, the 'desolate road is swallowed and is lost immediately without an echo' and the valleys and heights look unfamiliar; the entire 'broad space looks like a shadowy and black abyss'. At moments like these the protagonist is 'abandoned [and] alone … in the very heart of distant fields' rather than secure and safe in the middle of the scene. His feeling of loss is expressed also by a sensation of blindness; the objects in the 'broad space' seem to be vanishing into the horizon but he, dazed by the heat and the sun, cannot see them in any case.

The protagonist's changing moods also determine the perception of time in the story. At the plot's outward level he has come, as a Zionist *halutz*, to a new village for a life of hard work. Thus, as in other stories of this kind, he has chosen to realise a dynamic continuity of time which progresses towards a national future. At the plot's internal level, expressed in the protagonist's deep thoughts, he withdraws and clings to the past as he tries 'for but one moment, small and fleeting though it may be' to rise above himself and be more in accord with the world. In this way, the progression of time of the outward level is accompanied by a halt or withdrawal of time at its internal level. This contradiction between the two is expressed in the protagonist's desire 'to go back, to return, to go back' – just as he arrives at the new village where he is to settle down and begin his future.

The structure of the plots of these two stories by Yizhar also both reconstruct and destroy the narrative presented in the other contemporaneous stories. In 'A Night Without Gunfire', for example, the middle stage is omitted altogether. After the usual very long exposition during which the expectation of gunfire from ambush is built up, nothing happens; the Arab attacker fails to appear and thus does not fulfil his mythic role: it is a 'night without gunshots'. In 'Paths in the Fields', on the other hand, the causal links that were severed in other stories are reconstructed, but are set in an unconventional level: a shot is fired from ambush two different times, but is given a new and completely unfamiliar explanation each time. The first bullet is fired at the protagonist, Yitzchak, as a result of his romantic yearnings, which have led him to walk at night in the dark fields, carelessly unmindful of the dangers. His death is interpreted by the second protagonist of the story, Avner, as one that has given Yitzchak's life a most harmonic completion, just as he reaches that peak of exaltation from which there is no return. Similar romantic yearnings also draw Avner to wander in the fields at night, and he too draws fire from Arabs hiding in ambush. His awakened awareness of the inescapable end forces him to re-examine his emotions and values, and to choose a new way of life. Thus, an event that had been given no cause in the other stories has now been given one. However, it is not to be found in the political reality of the time – the natural place to seek it – but in the existential reality of the protagonist.

In a more general sense, the narrative is parodied when it is integrated into either universal or completely individual issues and problems, thus taking on a secondary and highly marginal role in the story. By addressing the narrative to individual or universal themes, Yizhar's stories strip it of significance and reveal its virtual inability to explain the distress or dilemmas that are not purely national in nature. Thus, for example, the anguish of a handful of isolated settlers is equated with that of modern man who, having lost all faith, must continue to live in this world with neither purpose nor reason. Existentialist doctrine in this setting provides a new explanation for the settlers' anguish and thus casts the mythic account in an ironic light.

The Narrative in Literary Periodicals

All of the stories discussed above were first published in *Gilionoth*, *Moznayim* and *Gazit*, the literary journals of the time, and in the weekly literary section of *Davar*. Literary activity in the 1930s centred largely around these periodicals, in which stories and poems, as well as articles on *belles-lettres*, society and politics were published. As mentioned above, the political system exerted great pressure on the literary system to take an active role in the national struggle by depicting the Zionist endeavour in an optimistic light. The literary works published in these journals did this only to a limited extent, while the political articles were more responsive and expressed, repeatedly and in various ways, the conventional Zionist ideology. These articles, however, were part of the literary system and followed the conventions expressed in literary works. The fact that they wavered between the literary style that described stability and security and the political style that expressed the need to struggle for them can apparently be explained by the fact that they played a part in both systems.

In many cases the publicistic articles avoid dealing with the contradiction between the two types of writing by turning their attention to generalities regarding the character and deeds of the adversaries rather than to those of the *Yishuv* Jews. To do this they used an old Orthodox-Jewish narrative (that would become pivotal only several years later) which describes unremitting hatred towards Jews. These articles were written mostly by the older generation, writers who had grown up in Europe during a period of anti-Semitism and persecutions. Usually constructed in the form of a passage that moves from the specific to the universal, they open with an account of an attack on a Jewish settlement. At first, as in the stories, the attack seems causeless. Subsequently, however, the cause is presented. Sometimes, at this point, the reason is still a specific or 'local' one, such as the 'unsavoury nature' of Arabs: 'We dwell among desert people who find it convenient to accept the beneficence we shower [on them] to this very day, and thrust their daggers murderously at innocent passersby.'[27] In other cases, however, the causality shifts to a universal level. It is based on the Orthodox-Jewish narrative which asserts that there is an unbridgeable gap between Jews and non-Jews:

> Has that same atmosphere of enmity ... that united front of foes and evil-wishers ... not changed since the days of the First and Second Temples? During the Enlightenment we were

> sure that if we improved our ways and devoted ourselves to fruitful labour they would look upon us graciously, and the word 'Jew' would never again be used as an epithet. But they do not want us to improve our ways at all.... From the hooligan nursed on hatred of Jews to the *effendi* whose rest is disturbed by our construction work ... they all shudder at anything positive we do.... Their enmity for the builder-Jew is seven times greater than their enmity for the idler-Jew.

The articles tend to depict this enmity as 'a latent, constant intrigue that connives to uproot the hope of the handful assembled here in this tiny parcel of land'.[28]

By focusing on the adversary, the topical articles uncover additional, mythic, reasons for phenomena that the literature tends to describe as causeless, thereby revealing further contradictions in the national consciousness: the Arab, who has no place in the time and space of this literature – and therefore enters the stories like a genie out of a bottle – now evolves into a figure with a timeless existence in history and a boundless existence in space, a figure which personifies eternal hatred towards the Jew. The result is a further manifestation of the tendency to convert the Arab into a mythic persona by ignoring him as a real entity.

Preoccupation with 'eternal hatred for an eternal people' led to the discovery of another characteristic of the national mind, one that both the proclamations of action in the leaflets and posters and the idyllic depictions in the literature had concealed. It reveals that behind the heroic Zionist effort to build a new national society in Palestine, an old Jewish anxiety was lurking: if hatred for Jews is mythic and timeless, the fate of the Jews is predestined, and neither Zionist activism nor the peaceful development of farms will change it. The fact that these accounts relied so heavily on anti-Semitism reveals that conviction in the Zionist endeavour was less than absolute. While this lack of faith is subsumed in the texts, it continued to flicker behind the contradictions and beneath the attempts to reconcile them. It will flare up and become increasingly evident as the narrative that expresses it goes on to occupy a more central place in Israeli society.

NOTES

1. For an analysis of this myth and other myths, see Y. Zerubavel, 1995 and C. Liebman and E. Don Yehiya, 1983.
2. Maccabees 3:19-21 and 4:8-9, The Holy Bible: Containing the Old and New Testaments with the Apocrypha/Deutercanonical Books, Revised Standard Version (New York, Glasgow and Toronto: Collins, 1973).
3. The *Yishuv* is the term used for the Jewish Zionist community living in Palestine before the establishment of the state of Israel on 15 May 1948. Although the country's name, Israel, came into use only after this date, it is often used in this book to designate the country before this date in order to distinguish between the *Yishuv* and Jewish communities living outside it, that is, the Diaspora or, in some contexts, the Exile.
4. Revisionist Zionist Organisation Steering Committee leaflet, 1932; 'In View of the Decrees', Mapai leaflet prepared for the 20th Zionist Congress, 1937; leaflet of Betar (the youth movement of the Revisionist Party) on the subject of the (British) Partition Plan, 1937. And compare the following: 'A year of siege and bloodshed has befallen us. We have held firm in the battle against the wild black forces of Arab reaction seeking to destroy us, against incited violent mobs which have given themselves the right to participate in acts of destruction and cravings for murder' (Mapai May Day leaflet, 1937), and 'For more than two years your blood has been spilt in Zion. Hundreds of guiltless victims have fallen. Hundreds have been disabled for the rest of their lives. Thousands of refugees have been left without homes. Tens of thousands of planted [trees] have been uprooted' (Revisionist leaflet, addressed to 'The House of Israel', against 'self-restraint' (*havlagah*) which was the policy of Mapai during the Disturbances, 1938).
5. Mapai leaflet before elections to the Council of the Elected (*Asefat Ha-nivharim*), 1931; Betar leaflet, 1935; Mapai leaflet prepared for the 19th Zionist Congress, 1935; respectively.
6. Mapai leaflet for the 19th Zionist Congress, 1935; Betar leaflet, 1937; Mapai leaflet for the 20th Zionist Congress, 1937; Mapai May Day leaflet, 1937; respectively.
7. Mapai May Day leaflet, 1937; Betar leaflet, 1937; 'Only Thus', Revisionist military organ (*Irgun Tzvai Leumi* – Etzel), leaflet; respectively. The closing sentence of the last leaflet, which appears in many Betar publications, is taken from a poem by Ya'akov Cohen.
8. Yosef the Galilean is Yosef Trumpeldor.
9. Betar leaflet, 1937; Irgun Tzvai Leumi in Eretz Israel leaflet, 1939; Betar leaflet, 1937; Betar leaflet, 1936, respectively.
10. Irgun Tzvai Leumi in Eretz Israel leaflet, 1939; Betar leaflet, 1937; Mapai leaflet entitled 'The *Emek* [Jezreel Valley] for the People of Israel', n.d.; Betar leaflet, 1937; Mapai leaflet for the 19th Zionist Congress, 1935; respectively.
11. 'The nation, heaven and earth, and the conscience of mankind are witnesses that our demands are justice and our aspirations truth. … The desire for freedom and deliverance of the masses of our persecuted nation – whose bitter cry is heard from one end of the world to the other', Betar leaflet, 1937.
12. This phenomenon is discussed in greater detail in Chapter 2.
13. Betar leaflet, 1934; Mapai leaflet, 1935; Mapai leaflet, 1935; Ha-Tzohar (Revisionist Zionist Organisation) Workers and Betar leaflet, n.d.; Mapai leaflet for the 18th Zionist Congress, n.d.; respectively.
14. Ze'ev Jabotinsky, in H. Ben-Yeruham, 1976: 1005; David Ben-Gurion, 1933: 300; respectively.
15. Commission of Betar in Eretz Israel leaflet, n.d.; Mapai, Jerusalem Branch, leaflet before elections to Council of the Elected (*Asefat Ha-nivharim*), 1931.

16. Leaflet of Hatzohar (Revisionist Zionist Organisation), 1935; Mapai, Jerusalem Branch, leaflet, 1931.
17. Jabotinsky, in H. Ben-Yeruham, 1976: 1005; Ben-Gurion, 1933: 246; respectively.
18. Jabotinsky, in H. Ben-Yeruham, 1976: 1002, 1003; Ben-Gurion, 1933: 265; Ben-Gurion, 1933: 245; Ben-Gurion, 1933: 246; Jabotinsky, in H. Ben-Yerucham, 1976: 1005; Ben-Gurion, 1933: 246; Ben-Gurion, 1933: 265; Ben-Gurion, 1933: 246; Jabotinsky, in H. Ben-Yerucham, 1976: 1005; respectively.
19. Ben-Gurion, 1933: 246; Jabotinsky, in H. Ben-Yeruham, 1976: 1000; respectively.
20. *Davar* was the daily newspaper of the *Histadrut*, the national federation of Jewish workers in Palestine. The federation led the workers in trade union-type struggles, organised and managed cultural activities, and established a health care system. From 1930 the main party active in the *Histadrut* was Mapai.
21. For examples of different types, see Shmeterling, 1935; Y. Arikha, 1936; Y. Rabinov, 1936; S. Bass, 1934; Y. Hanani, 1937; Y. Ya'ari, 1933, 1934.
22. See H. Hazaz, 1938a, 1938b.
23. H. Hazaz, 1938(a): 392.
24. Ibid., 1938(a): 183.
25. Ibid., 1938(b): 297.
26. S. Yizhar, 1938, 1940. For a thorough analysis of Yizhar's stories, see G. Shaked, 1971, 1992 and D. Miron, 1975.
27. Y. Fichman, 1934. This description is based on the twin dichotomies of East and West, desert and civilisation. The use of these dichotomies, common during the period of modern Jewish settlement in the country, became prevalent during the War of Independence. It is discussed in Chapter 2.
28. See also Peli (Y. Fichman), 1937; Y. Fichman, 1934; Steinman, 1937. The narrative of 'a people that dwells apart' is discussed in Chapter 3.

2

AMONG THE NATIONS OF THE WORLD: The War of Independence, 1948–1949

INTRODUCTION

On 29 November 1947 the United Nations General Assembly resolved by a majority vote to partition Palestine into two separate states, a Jewish one and an Arab one. Seven months later, on 15 May 1948, 30 years of British mandatory rule over Palestine came to its official end and the state of Israel was declared. The next day, the forces of five surrounding Arab countries invaded the former Palestine and the war, called in Israel the 'War of Independence', began. The Jews of Israel, then numbering 600,000, spent the entire year-and-a-half war period in geographical isolation and suffered exceedingly heavy casualties. And yet, a study of the journalistic war reports reveals absolute confidence that the human and material efforts invested in the struggle would lead to victory.

The rhetoric of these reports was shaped by ideological narratives originating in both recent European culture and in ancient Hebrew traditions. Particularly influential were descriptions of the Allies' struggle against Germany in the Second World War and accounts of ancient Hebrew struggles. These narratives were selected from the repertoire available to the nascent Israeli culture not because they were so suitable for an accurate articulation of the historical events, but because they coincided with the country's perception of itself and its relations with the surrounding peoples on the one hand, and stood in opposition to Orthodox-Jewish streams of thought and the image of Judaism as perceived by the Zionist community on the other. The image being negated was one of a passive culture that not only kept itself apart from the peoples within which it lived, but existed outside of reality, a culture that held a worldview based on a-historical, metaphysical concepts of destruction and redemption.[1] The narratives that took shape in response to these perceptions served as the ideological foundations upon which the new image of the emerging Israeli society was built. This image had an effect on determining the fate of the war, for it fostered optimism in the besieged country and helped it to persevere even when the situation seemed hopeless.

Two ideological narratives can be discerned in the journalistic reports of the War of Independence in Israel – the few-versus-the-many narrative that had been dominant in the 1920s and 1930s, and the Europe-versus-Asia narrative which was then only peripheral. During the war the status of these narratives went through a gradual transformation: the previously central few-versus-many narrative was relegated to the periphery while the formerly marginal Europe-versus-Asia one became dominant. Both, however, can be found in various forms in war reports that appeared during May, June and July 1948 in newspapers and periodicals. Some of these publications were associated with the main political parties and therefore had considerable cultural status (for example, *Al Ha-mishmar*, *Davar* and, to a certain extent, the army monthly *Ba-mahane*, in which the writers of the generation that fought in the War of Independence frequently published stories and articles) while others (for example, *Ma'ariv*, *Ha-boqer* and *Ha-mashqif*) were associated with marginal parties and therefore played only a secondary role.[2] The impact on Israeli culture of the narratives expressed in these publications can best be understood by comparing them with the way in which contemporaneous literary works coped with them.

THE FEW VERSUS THE MANY

The few-versus-the-many narrative which had been so prominent in texts of the 1920s and 1930s, during the Disturbances, did not appear frequently in journalistic reportage during the War of Independence itself. It is then found in articles written by older journalists who tended to describe Israel's struggle as that of an isolated people surrounded by hostile adversaries. These consisted equally of German, British and Arab figures: 'St George, the Koran and Fritz of Hamburg – a world fighting against the untrained hands of youth whose strength has been spent in struggles and in longings.'[3] The relative marginality of this narrative (that even when used was not a central theme) can be explained in terms of the propagandistic function of the press at that time. When the War of Independence began, the Arab armies outnumbered that of Israel and were far better equipped. In May 1948, chosen as the first month for analysis of the articles, Israel's situation appeared precarious enough. On 16 May, when the Arab armies invaded the country, the road to Jerusalem was engulfed in desperate battles and five outlying settlements (the Etzion Bloc) fell, several Jewish settlements elsewhere were evacuated, and others stood singly against well-equipped forces. In the early stages of the invasion, five brigade-level counter-offensives failed (three against Latrun in May, one against Jenin on 1 June, and one against Ashdod on 2 June). One month after the invasion began the toll on the Jewish side was 1,200 dead and thousands wounded, this in addition to 2,000 Jewish military and civilian casualties suffered in actions that had taken place before the invasion itself.

At the beginning of the war Israel was isolated not only in the region but in the world as well. British policy remained hostile and the United States, after retreating at the end of March from the United Nations' partition plan in favour of an imposed trusteeship, even announced (in early May, before Israel declared its independence) that it would not offer Israel military assistance if it became involved in a serious war with its neighbours. Even the Israeli leadership was far from optimistic at this time. Just before independence was declared, experts in the *Haganah* (the forerunner of the country's army, the Israel Defence Forces) admitted at a meeting that the Arab armies were far superior to Israel's, that the odds were even at best, and that the morale of many on the Israeli side was not high.[4]

This being the state of affairs, the press was mobilised, either by explicit order or by the journalists' own volition, to emphasise the strengths of the Israeli community and to play down its scanty might and mass. For this, the narrative of 'the few against the many' was too dangerously close to reality. It was not suitable for meeting the desperate need to portray complete and unquestioned confidence in victory at a time when such a victory could hardly be taken for granted. A more tenable narrative was needed, and was indeed found.

EUROPE VERSUS ASIA

Most of the journalistic reports written during the first three months of the war portray the determined Israeli fighter as the representative of a broad coalition of European nations in confrontation with a cruel and primitive eastern/Asian world. One reason for the predominant use of this narrative was its ability to extricate the Israeli fighters from their isolation by depicting them as soldiers belonging to a great army – that of the Allies – and describing the Arabs, the reputedly brave warriors, as an isolated, weak enemy. The Allies' triumph in the Second World War, still fresh in the collective memory, could serve in this situation as a guarantee of success in the present war.

Being partners in a broad front fighting for western, European values also released the Israelis from their 'Jewish fate' of being a despised and persecuted minority. This was particularly important in view of the impact of the Holocaust on the Israeli populace. As members of the great European family the Israelis were turned into the successors of the Allies in their struggle against the Nazis (that is, of the Russians in their struggle at Leningrad or the British in their stand during the blitz).[5] Moreover, they were depicted as fighting to preserve European civilisation, along with its secular and religious values. The Israelis thus embodied the very opposite of the familiar image of the Jew as one dissociated from his surroundings.[6]

The authors attest to their connection with Christian civilisation by expressing distress about 'the shrines of Christianity … placed under the highly dubious care of the Muslims'.[7] The connection is depicted as a bilateral alliance:

> We are not alone in our struggle against desecration, against the breaking of promises. We have found allies. The Christian clergy here, already sitting amidst the ruins of their churches, wail and cry for deliverance from the evil and the insult being perpetrated against their shrines.[8]

This alliance is both secular and religious, and is based on energetic activity by both sides:

> While the representatives of the enlightened Christian countries tried to rescue from the risk of destruction at least this ancient and hallowed section of Jerusalem, [the Jewish fighters were helping them by] driving back their assailants [or by] protecting other Christian sites from the Arab artillery, from Kaukji's guerrillas.[9]

In all these cases, the Jewish–European alliance is targeted against the East, whose traditional attributes undergo a transformation. In the early years of modern Jewish settlement the East is often portrayed as the embodiment of authenticity, youthful vigour and strength – the opposite of the abstract Jewish culture and of the exhausted, declining civilisation of the West.[10] During the War of Independence it is precisely the negative and disparaging image of the East that surfaces. Admittedly, this image had appeared in previous years, most frequently during the Disturbances at the end of the 1920s and again at the end of the 1930s, but had not played a central role at those times. Now the roles were reversed – an abstract, rootless and ancient Arab civilisation is portrayed as the culture of the desert, and is contrasted with that of Europe, now depicted as a culture of building and planting that embodies human and national values and strength: 'A civilisation of life and faith in man and the future is fighting for its life against the desert tempest … [a civilisation built through] arduous toil and love …' (from a description of a battle at Kibbutz Yad Mordechai). A civilisation that 'expresses the spirit of man, tempered in the heart of the desert' is now 'pitted against forces of destruction' (from a description of Kibbutz Beit Yosef).[11]

The struggle between Europe and Asia – between East and West – is also a struggle between the country's contrasting landscapes:

> To your right you see the parched mountains, projecting upon you and upon all the green profusion around you the hate harboured by the desert for this oasis of a flourishing, settled community.… The very moment you turn into the narrow road to Negba, you observe the malicious caprice of the hand of the desert, wielded with hatred against the first conquests of civilisation.[12]

While some of these descriptions were written about Jewish settlements established in the desert and destroyed by the Arabs (for example, Yad Mordechai and Negba), others invoke the desert for metaphorical reasons only (Kibbutz Beit Yosef, for example, is in the well-watered and fertile Jordan Valley, not in the desert).

To arrange Jewish–Arab relations within the civilisation–desert dichotomy, the writings describe even the *fellahin*, the Arab subsistence farmers, as sons-of-the-desert Bedouin:

> The Hebron mountain people, about 20,000 bloodthirsty desert savages cunning as snakes, will not, despite all their attacks, overwhelm the handful of Jewish heroes who have settled in the mountain area, ended its desolation, and revived its soil.[13]

The wish to characterise the Arabs as sons of the desert is particularly noticeable when, within an article or even a single sentence, a poor and simple Arab dirt farmer becomes a desert savage and his cultivated land becomes a wilderness:

> Not only did the Arabs leave, but they also bequeathed a vast legacy in the form of planted fields and orchards and, above all, in the form of the dearest of all – land.... The Arabs' barren fields will be harvested, their bounty satiating a Hebrew population in town and vineyard.... Under no circumstances will they deprive the Jewish settler of the Arab land, into which he has now driven his stake. He is attached to those goodly acres with the mighty yearning of the peasant for his land. He will not return it to the desert savage, even if Prime Minister Ben-Gurion himself so orders.[14]

It is this overarching framework, the tension between desert and civilisation, that now determines the way in which the abandoned Arab villages are described. The ruins of these villages are contrasted with the plants and blossoms in the Jewish settlements. They are thus viewed not as the outcome of the war but of the desert-versus-civilisation dichotomy, that is, of neglect and desolation versus planting and building:

> Facing the ruins of the Arab villages, Be'er Toviyya and Kfar Warburg stand out all the more, their well-tended carpets of green vegetation adorning the desolation.... Below me is a deserted Arab village, all its houses destroyed, with nothing but dogs picking their way among its ruins ... the forested hills all around are turning green and yellow with the vegetation of late spring.[15]

In certain cases the Arab villagers' unsavoury nature is mentioned in order to obfuscate the aesthetic, attractive picture that may arise from the description of their well-tended fields. Usually it is the flourishing vineyards and fields of the Israeli villages alone that are noted, while the Arab villages are characterised as desert-like. When exceptions are made, the articles create a contrast between a fertile Arab landscape and its cruel inhabitants, thereby providing justification for depriving them of their right to it:

> [The soldiers] follow the commander's remarks intently, as he explains tersely and clearly the details of the mission. Here's the village with its houses, vineyards, and fields, standing out wonderfully against the backdrop of the military map.... Here are the gullies, the puddles, and the rest of the weak spots of the notorious village. Incidentally, Beit Darras has earned itself a reputation. When an Arab wishes to define someone negatively, he says: 'The guy's a Darrasawi' [that is, from Beit Darras].[16]

The Israelis' attachment to the civilised, European side of this East–West equation is reinforced by foreign observers such as British soldiers, journalists and American diplomats who admire and support their behaviour and actions: 'The foreign journalists, most of them experienced from the World War, were highly impressed by the Jewish strike force. "They look just like a British paratroop battalion," one British writer exclaimed.' And, elsewhere:

> An Australian journalist who recently visited the kibbutz [Negba] couldn't grasp something. He asked Kobi, the regional commander, to be so kind as to explain 'how the people of a ruined village such as this held its ground, how it goes on living and producing and does not seek a new home elsewhere'.

In all cases, partnership in the European community is acquired by proof of resolute struggle leading to victory: 'Major Fielding Eliot, the renowned American military commentator who reached Jerusalem just a few hours ago … handed the first wreath of flowers to the young Jewish commander.'[17] By integrating the Israeli fighting force into the European front, the newspaper articles strengthened the foundations of the country's national existence. In doing this, however, a new dichotomy was created between the (new) state of Israel as a member of the western world and the (old) Jewish Exile as 'a people that dwells alone'.

The reaction to the image of the passive Jew of the Exile is strengthened when this image, negated and rejected by the new Israeli Jew, is applied to the Arab. The Arabs are the ones who fail to fight, who have no roots in this land, and who are not a people 'like all other peoples'. The Israelis, by contrast, are active, fighting and firmly rooted – integral members of the world community of nations.

The Arab had always constituted a 'partner' of sorts in the definition of the Jewish-Israeli identity. In the early years of modern

Jewish settlement – mainly the years before the Disturbances when Jewish–Arab relations had, for the most part, been tranquil – the tendency, as stated previously, was to use the Arab as a positive model in constructing the prototype of the active and tenacious 'new Hebrew'.[18] The Arab was then described not only as a son of 'the ascendant East', a noble savage, but was also viewed as a primordial Hebrew cast in the mould of the biblical patriarchs. The Disturbances before Israel's independence had caused this image to erode, but during the war, and especially after it, when the Arabs had been defeated and their weakness revealed, the Arab exemplar used in defining the Hebrew identity was less frequently invoked. Instead, he became the embodiment of a negative figure, of the Exilic Jew. Therefore, in contrast to the fighting, active Israeli who clings to his land, controls his surroundings and toils with his own hands, the Arab is now portrayed as a passive, frightened refugee:[19]

> Entire villages, miserable columns of people carrying their belongings on their backs, are moving out.... Waves, torrents are moving in all directions.... This stubborn, topsy-turvy, barren-fertile, soft-hard land ... moves and eludes whenever it isn't held by the fingernails.[20] [...] We have read that nearly 700,000 Arabs have fled Palestine during this war. We have not read, however, that as many as 100 Jews have done so.[21]

The manner in which Arab refugees are described rests on familiar accounts of 'the wandering Jew' in Hebrew literature. In many cases the Arabs even bear explicit Jewish markers: 'From being court-protected Jews, we have become the conquerors by storm of Canaan, who dominate court-protected Arabs.' These labels become especially blatant when the writer tests the Israeli–Jewish dichotomy by directly inserting it into an Israeli–Arab one. In such instances the Israeli, who looks like a *yeshiva* (rabbinical seminary) student with 'the glasses of a Russian student [and a] placid, almost melodious elocution', turns out to be a valorous soldier, whereas the Arab, who looks like a valorous soldier, proves to behave like a frightened Jew.[22] In other cases the writer explicitly reverses their roles:

> We do not intend to die. It is not immutable law that we must forever clutch the wanderer's staff. Now you have learned to clutch it. We are capable of turning this staff into a weapon of war and battle.[23]

As in the previous examples, the significant point is not the denigrating descriptions of the Palestinian Arabs, but rather the narrative chosen to present them. In it, their role is to define the new Israeli identity as the antithesis of the old Jewish one. Like the Israel–West alliance, the Israeli–Arab dichotomy provides a way to define and confirm this identity. Often occurring in tandem, these pairs are used to support each other: the rejection of passivity on the one hand and of Jewish isolation on the other are interrelated. In this way the firmly rooted, active Israeli earns his acceptance as a full-fledged member of the community of nations.

UNIVERSAL HUMANISM VERSUS NATIONAL HUMANISM

Humanism, the heritage of European ideologies of the nineteenth century, has invariably been considered an integral value of Judaism and a central element in Zionism. In the socialist left it was part of the ideology that espoused the brotherhood of nations and races, while the moderate right saw in it the nexus between nationalism and liberalism. During the 1930s, modernist streams in Hebrew literature, for example the poet Avraham Shlonsky and his journal *Turim*, were drawn to universal ideas of morality and justice above and beyond national goals, and to the cardinal importance of relations between people as individuals above and beyond those between peoples as nations. Many of the literary texts published in *Turim* went so far as to present humanism as antithetical to Judaism, which was in turn perceived as a culture divorced from the world and insulated from its surroundings.

While the humanistic narrative was undoubtedly dominant in the Zionist culture before the War of Independence, during the fighting it became marginal, appearing only occasionally, in but a few newspapers, and in language that did not necessarily articulate firm commitment. The authors tended to make broad statements about the importance of ethical awareness in the Israeli army, and to speak in general terms against those who 'attempt to educate [the soldiers of Israel] to learn from the Arab his manner of waging war, his cruelty, his methods of abusing the wounded', and so on.[24] However, statements such as these reveal a strong belief in Israel's superiority above and beyond their underlying humanism. The statements also lost much of their potency in descriptions of the battles themselves. In these one fails to discern moral sensitivity to or compassion for the physical suffering of the Arabs. This is especially noticeable in the socialist newspaper *Al Ha-mishmar*, in which statements affirming the belief in brotherhood between nations and peoples contradict graphic battlefield descriptions, such as 'large bloodstains inside the house, on the floor, and on the walls confirm that our defenders had aimed their bullets well',[25] in a report from El Arish, and, elsewhere:

> At sunrise – and what a beautiful sunrise it was – the residents of Beit Darras began to flee en masse, trying their luck to reach Ashdod. But the marksman, positioned on the structure covering the Arab well, had other ideas. His well-aimed bursts of fire forced them to retrace their steps.[26]

These news reports were written in the very midst of the battles. Despite the reassuring descriptions, the Israeli army had actually suffered a serious setback in Tel Arish and Beit Darras had been captured by Egyptian forces as they advanced north towards the heartland of Israel. A successful Arab offensive had also severed the Arab town of Acre and the entire region of Galilee, which included many Israeli settlements, from the rest of the country. The conquest of Ramle had yet to be carried out, and thus lift the Arab threat from Tel Aviv and its environs and open a corridor from the coastal plain to Jerusalem. The fierce battles and frequent defeats might explain the writers' insensitivity to their adversaries' plight. In some cases this is expressed explicitly:

> Our hearts do not bleed at the sight of thousands of refugees straggling through the streets.... They had stoned us and shot at our heads; they had rampaged, and had vowed to drive us into the sea. Our annihilation was their favourite dream. Our pooled blood whetted their appetites. Here ... this is their reward![27]

HISTORICAL PAST AND FUTURE

Along with the image of the new Israeli, the writings introduce a new historical perspective that is the antithesis of the ahistorical, metaphysical Jewish perception of time. This is manifested both in the detailed descriptive writing style and in the causal, dynamic plots in which the resolute Israeli fighter dictates the pace of events. Although both these elements were adopted from the realist literature of the nineteenth and twentieth centuries, their ideological function becomes especially conspicuous when they are entwined with other components serving the same function. Together, they make it clear that resolute human action is one of the characteristics of the new Israeli reality. Activism of this kind is counterpoised against the perception of history as a metaphysical interplay of destruction and redemption driven by supernatural forces.

Contemporaneous newspaper articles present history as a causal continuum that connects the present to specific events selected from the past. The conquest and settlement of the land during the time of Joshua, the revolt of the Maccabees and the last stand at Masada thus lead to modern immigration to Israel and to the then very recent struggle against the British (especially in writings based on the few-versus-many narrative).[28] This linking of present and past is a major element in the dynamic, causal plot; the present war is thus dictated and justified by past events, and will lead to the desired results in the future.[29]

In many cases the concatenation between the two periods is made through a compound sentence that integrates different historical eras within a single, strong chain: 'Thousands of hearts pounded on the night that the new State of Israel was established, anxious for the fate of the Jewish Quarter that harboured the last remnants of the ancient Kingdom of Israel.'[30] The existence of an historical bond as tight as this may explain the ease with which the articles switch, within one or several sentences, from present to recent past to more distant past, with sorties into a future that includes the inevitable 'happy end', and then back to the present, where the entire process begins again.[31] Such transitions in time also express the belief that historical events can be guided and modified. They also explain the reluctance to declare past events as 'over and done with', describing them instead as on-going processes. Room is thus left for many options, reinforcing the impression of a process that may still be shaped, modified or influenced – one that has not yet been sealed into the historical past:

> It is doubtful that the [Arab] Legion … could have conquered the city by storming it from the outside. Had it succeeded … such a victory would have been achieved at great cost, perhaps even the total destruction of the Legion and [the death of] its commander.… Meanwhile, however, the war continues on our territory.… If we lose, we will have suffered a great loss, and the fighting will return to the alleys of Jerusalem.… However,

> if the Arabs suffer a crushing defeat here, this defeat will mark the destruction of the Legion.[32]

The continuum of events in the narrative present, that is during the on-going war, is presented as part of the chain of history. Like the entire chain, the continuum is structured causally, thus establishing significant links between the plan of the battle, its course and the final victory. Each of these stages is the inevitable outcome of the previous one: the military operation follows the plan, and the victory is a result of the military operation. In all cases victory is inevitable. It is thus frequently mentioned at both the beginning and the end of an article, and even when the victory does not occur, it is described as a hope, a possibility, or even a moral triumph:

> Militarily speaking, the loss of the Old City is not a real loss, not even a battle lost. On the contrary, the magnificent stand of two hundred fighters ... bolstered the morale of the Jewish people, not only in Jerusalem, but on all fronts, and throughout Israel.... The Arabs made no progress in the war with this victory. In fact, it is the only victory the Arabs have gained this week, and it is an illusory one at that.[33]

This description refers to the fall of the Old City of Jerusalem on 28 June 1948. And yet, during that same week, two Israeli attacks at Latrun (26 June and 30 June) were repulsed. In addition, although earlier in June the Egyptian army was checked at Ashdod on the coast and at Kibbutz Ramat Rahel immediately south of Jerusalem, two offensives against the Egyptian forces (1 June and 5 June) had failed, and a week before these, on 24 May, Kibbutz Yad Mordechai in the south had been evacuated.

The articles discussed here fail to mention any of these defeats. The fact that they had occurred is overshadowed by accounts of actual victories or plans for future victories. Similarly, the surrender of two settlements in the Jordan Valley is mentioned only after an emphatic declaration of the fact that the Jordan Valley had withstood attacks in the past and would continue do so in the future:

> The Jordan Valley mounted an exemplary resistance during the initial stages of the war. The enemy was unable to capture a single position. And it will again have an opportunity to mount an exemplary resistance in the future.... But war is war.

> In war a position may fall even if it is bravely defended. Thus two positions in the Jordan Valley – Masada and Sha'ar HaGolan – have, for the time being, fallen into enemy hands.[34]

The outcome of the fighting at Kibbutz Yad Mordechai is also described mainly as a victory, followed by the information that the kibbutz had actually been evacuated:

> It was a war of flesh and spirit against iron.... The champions of armour retreated in shame and disgrace against the young warriors who resisted them with their bare fists and their anger.... Our young men who were left behind ... isolated from the rest of the country ... chose to leave the site.[35]

It is significant that the articles rarely describe death. Where the dead are mentioned, the reference is parenthetical, made in the course of describing the battle: 'By day and by night they watched the water tower, so riddled by bullets as to resemble a sieve ... and although some fell, the rest carried on.'[36] Death is often subordinated within a lengthy, run-on sentence, or glossed over in a detailed account of victory and conquest, thereby representing but one more stage on the road to victory:

> The village we are approaching at breakneck speed – the same village where Yehiam Weitz and his comrades fell on the Night of the Bridges – was captured by the Haganah just one day before Israel's independence was declared, in Operation Ben-Ami, named after the battalion commander who fell heroically among the victims of the convoy to Yehiam. The entire area was occupied on the same day.[37]

Death is never the main subject in a sentence; it is a secondary issue and is overshadowed by the struggle or the victory, which are the true subjects of the text.

Like the panoramic historical process, the causal continuum that dictates the general structure of the plots is reflected in small units composed of specific goals and actions. The causal bond in these small units strengthens the overall structure of the plot, which leads from goals to victories, but also adheres to the slow, stubborn, rational process that underlies this structure. This causal bond is often sharpened by conjunctions of contrast:

> They approached in 30 waves ... but our soldiers met them with all the weapons they had.... The infantry beat a hasty retreat, but the tanks advanced and knocked out two of our positions.... Our soldiers seized new strongholds.... A tank broke through the barrier; it approached the outermost house but was repelled. Another tank, bearing the commander's Egyptian flag ... suffered engine damage but was towed away.[38]

This entire account is structured as a step-by-step process which proceeds from initial plan through actions and counteractions, and then to the final result.

The causal, dynamic structure of plot was a central norm during the War of Independence and it dominated many of the texts of the time. It was well suited to the dynamics of the events for it corresponded to the need to describe these events as they occurred, at a time when anything was possible. Nevertheless, this particular structure was selected from the many possibilities that the culture offered, not only because it reflected reality but also because it answered several immediate needs, mainly the imperative to boost morale and strengthen belief in victory. Moreover, it helped to fashion a dynamic and rational Israeli existence anchored in the history of the country and carrying it forward towards its future goals. Such an existence was the antithesis of the abstract universe considered typical of the Exile, one driven by supernatural forces and ahistorical upheavals. These functions are clearly revealed both in the superstructure of the reports and in each link within them; the unbroken progression of history guided by human activity is reflected in the plot as a whole and in each specific event. The causal perception of history is thus embedded in the description of every event and every battle.

This plot-structured model was predominant in the newspapers of the centre (*Davar, Al Ha-mishmar* and *Ba-mahane*). In the peripheral newspapers (*Ha-boqer*, *Ma'ariv*, *Ha-mashqif* and, to some extent, the private newspaper *Ha-aretz*), most of the articles concentrated on descriptions of the settings of the events, their inhabitants and their recent and more distant histories, a manner of presentation reminiscent of the literature of the 1930s. The settings are described as if viewed by someone from a central vantage point and thoroughly familiar with them. The author proves this by pointing out familiar details and by describing vast spaces that are nevertheless closed and sheltered – the land below, the sky above, the colour of the hills, the scent of the trees

– while the actual battle is summarised only at the end and in the briefest of terms: 'The area commander told us that Rosh Ha'ayin had been liberated, and then we walked up to the Institute', or 'We entered the building and drove the Arabs away', and 'The battle lasted a whole day, at the end of which the entire village was abandoned'.[39]

In the limited number of battles that are described in reports of this type the initiators are generally Arabs, not Jews. This is borne out by the use of active verbs to describe Arab actions, and the passive or gerund to describe Israeli ones: 'The main advance was achieved by storming the printing house and pounding Arab positions.'[40] In some of the reports the focus is exclusively on the Arabs. In these the transition from active to passive verbs signals a transition from the Arab action to the ways in which they suffered the consequences of the Israeli response, while the Israeli action is not mentioned at all: 'First the Arabs began to retreat. Two of their infantry companies were caught in an ambush.... Eight Egyptians were killed.... Their weapons were destroyed.'[41] Not only does the article open with a description of the Egyptian retreat without mentioning the Israeli action that precipitated it, it then continues in the same vein, so that the action appears to have been perpetrated by the Arabs, not the Israelis. In certain cases, the transition from passive to active verbs suggests an internecine struggle amongst Arabs rather than an engagement with the Israeli enemy:

> The Arabs tried to push through to the northern entrance of Jerusalem but were repulsed.... They attacked the Sheikh Jarrah neighbourhood but were repulsed.... They assaulted the police station during the night ... captured it, but were forced once again to withdraw.[42]

The writers of these reports appear to be reluctant to describe an active, Jewish fighter. Thus, although they had also helped fashion the image of the new Israeli as the antithesis of the passive Jew of the Exile, the contrast was created mainly by showing the Israeli's rootedness in the land rather than in his actions as a soldier. The literary model of the 1930s, that seemed to have been abandoned during the 1940s in both literary and other texts, still flickers in the periphery of the culture. There, it continued to testify to a reluctance to express any heroic activity which, during the years of exile, had characterised the 'Goy', the gentile, and not the Jew.

THE ENCOUNTER BETWEEN THE NARRATIVES OF THE PRESS AND THE *BELLES-LETTRES* OF THE WAR OF INDEPENDENCE

The *belles-lettres* of the War of Independence availed itself of the same repertoire of ideological narratives as did the press. It, too, was subject to national constraints in selecting from this repertoire, such as the need to profess confidence in the justice of the national struggle and in Israel's ability to achieve victory, and in the necessity of fashioning an Israeli identity counterposed to the old Jewish one. However, the authors of *belles-lettres* also had an individualistic, existentialist literary heritage and were less willing than the press to accept social dictates. Even when the country became involved in the war, and these literary concerns were subdued in order to make way for a national heroic literature, they continued to be used in order to question blind faith in the justice and eventual success of the struggle. While national heroism predominates in some of the literary writings, in others an ambivalent scepticism is expressed. In all of them, however, the conflict between the two trends is apparent.

The similarities between the literary and the journalistic writings are indicative of the shared *zeitgeist* that prevailed during this period. The differences between them can shed light on how heterogeneous the Hebrew culture was even when 'the entire nation was a battlefront'. The interface between the country's *belles-lettres* and its journalism illuminates how the Israeli culture, while contending with the accepted norms, was at the same time weakening their foundations. In doing this, it prepared the scene for the models that would be dominant in the future.[43]

The National Heroic Literature

The few-versus-many narrative that had virtually disappeared from reportage during the War of Independence made its comeback, after the fighting ceased, in Israeli culture and in the national *belles-lettres*. In many stories the motivating theme is the desperation of an isolated small group, surrounded and with no safe way of escape. Thus, in Yig'al Mossinsohn's story 'Blue Jeep', messengers of a surrounded unit get to the command headquarters to request reinforcements only to find the headquarters also surrounded and to discover that there is apparently no way for either of them to escape. In many cases the encirclement is broadened and the beseigers consist of all the nations of the world, past, present and future – 'Ammonites, Syrians, Kaukji's bands, Poles, Yugoslavs, mercenaries and despicable Germans'[44] – all are fighting in a broad frontline against the Jewish people.

Descriptions such as these, which had appeared only occasionally in newspaper writings, are found repeatedly in literary ones and, somewhat later, in the cinema as well. They focus on a heinous alliance between the Arabs and the Nazis, as in the film *Exodus* (Otto Preminger, 1967) in which Nazis incite the Arabs to fight the Jews, or in *Hill Twenty-four Doesn't Answer* (T. Dickenson, 1954/55) in which an Arab soldier turns out to be a Nazi in disguise. This alliance between Arabs and Nazis sustains two narratives simultaneously: it presents the war of the Israeli few against a broad coalition of enemies, and allows the Israeli fighters to participate, as it were, in the Allied armies' war against the Axis powers. In both these narratives the Israeli's new identity as a brave fighter is proved. By fighting alone and heroically against the Nazis, he avenges all the evil perpetrated in the past, thus proving that he has changed, in both character and role, from being a victim of war and has become a warrior in it.

The stories invariably end in either victory or vengeance, during which, even as the heroes exclaim that 'Masada shall not fall again', the Masada myth is turned into an anti-Masada myth. Even those stories that end in suicidal acts relate to a Samson-like heroism rather than to the staunch valour of the fighters on Masada; the suicides are deeds of action that result in a semblance of physical victory rather than acts of passive, albeit courageous, acceptance of fate. In Moshe Shamir's 'Leazar's Little Girl', for example, the heroes, beseiged by larger and stronger forces, choose heroic deaths, 'to die with the Philistines' in Samson's words; in their deaths they bring defeat upon their enemy.[45]

Although this narrative dominates the story lines, the *belles-lettres* remain faithful to their sceptical, critical tradition and attempt to both parody it and contrast it with other perspectives. Such attempts, however, are rather half-hearted and in many instances the narrative emerges more strongly than all the sceptical criticism that was brought to refute it. In Abba Kovner's 'Face to Face', the commander complains that 'reports brought to him by the units [always refer to] our fighters in the singular', whereas the enemy is described as a 'multitude'. When he himself joins the battle, however, he finds that the enemy is indeed a multitude, and the Jewish fighters are but a few weak and isolated individuals.[46]

The isolation of the Israeli forces is contrasted in the national literature, as in its journalism, with the perspective of Israel as a partner in a broad European front engaged in a battle against the primitive, cruel Orient and the passive and discredited Arab, the latter now bearing Jewish marks of disgrace. The authors, aware that these models are stereotypical and contradictory, often introduce and validate them, and then go on to undermine them. The literary critic Dan Miron describes the contradiction the poet Natan Alterman faced in having to depict the Israelis as partners in the Allied struggle even after having been abandoned by them. Alterman resolves the contradiction, Miron says, by showing that by standing firm against the enemy, the Israeli community had become 'more British than the British'.[47] Haim Guri, in a monograph that can be placed in the grey area between journalism and literature, invokes standard stereotypes of Arabs as 'Oriental' – but follows this immediately with an entirely different tone:

> [The Arabs] have a constant companion – destruction. They'll rape your sisters and abuse your mother. They'll turn your mansions and houses into stables for their horses. They are Egyptian curs, plagued with boils and syphilis. They will tyrannise you and everything you've got.... The oil barons will stride over the rubble – the priests of blood and Mammon will saunter along haughtily as your children walk around naked, hungry, begging for alms [but] by night you will come across people you have never seen before – simple, poor people, fathers of children, an errant, misled flock ... human fear flickering across their swarthy features.[48]

The stereotyped description which associates the Arab with wild animals, disease, cruelty, murder and destruction is immediately followed by a more humane depiction. Guri thus portrays the Arab on the one hand as a desert nomad who digs his claws into 'our land', while on the other he believes that harming this Arab brands the Israeli with a Cain-like mark of disgrace. He regards the Arab as an enemy, but also as a human being. The contradiction is allowed to stand; the narrative is thus confirmed and negated at one and the same time.

Historical Past and Future

The dynamic, causal, historical continuum used in the press is the cornerstone of the literature of the War of Independence[49] and is characteristic not only of journalistic and literary writing, but even of military orders-of-the-day, public announcements, slogans, political speeches and election propaganda.[50] That this causal continuum is the common denominator of such different text types is an indication of how closely the different systems were interrelated, but also testifies to their common and shared sources (such as the then popular socialist-realist literature and the realistic literature of the nineteenth century). Moreover, it testifies to the shared ideology focused around the 'secular' image of the Israeli who takes an active part in the historical events that befall him.

In this respect, too, the *belles-lettres* literature is more complex than the other texts as it tends – simultaneously – to both shape and undermine the narrative. Confidence in the historical, plot-like continuum, and in the dynamism of the protagonist fashioning it, indeed underlies the literary works, but this framework must at times withstand anxieties and doubts, or pointed observations on a reality that does not always match it. In the 'national-heroic' literature, however, the conventional narrative is restored even after it has been refuted, and it is sometimes even reinvigorated by its 'dispute' with its 'challengers'. For example, Natan Shaham's story 'Queuing' expresses a fatalistic consciousness in its opening segments as its protagonists acknowledge that it is not their heroism that will save them but rather the vicissitudes of fortune, which are expressions of nihilisim and existentialism.[51] This and other stories present harsh descriptions of death and fear of death, and of defeat and failure, articulating feelings and facts that the press had neglected to address. In the end, however, all these stories vindicate anew the virtues of the fighter, the justice of the goals for which he acts, and confidence that even death and failure are mere steps along the road to final victory. They thus reconfirm the narrative that they had ostensibly rejected.

The picture arising from the poetry of the period is sometimes even more complex. Natan Alterman's poem 'The Silver Platter', as analysed by Dan Miron,[52] is an example of this. It opens, as do newspaper reports and many stories, with the future tense: 'And the land shall rest' (*Ve-ha-aretz tishqot*). This future perspective evokes the historic past – the 'resting' of the land in the hinted-at biblical sense of 40 years of tranquillity after a period of turbulence. It is intended to express assurance of the happy outcome of present events. But, according to Miron, faith in this continuum of events is abruptly shaken, for even in the anticipated post-war 'rest', the heavens are still 'streaked with red' and young people are still 'dressed in khaki and wearing bandoleers'. The biblical past which is meant to support the present fails to do this; the young people shedding blood in the present are forging a link with the past, rather than the other way around.

In an article on Haim Guri, Miron describes a similar phenomenon of ambivalence.[53] Guri's heroes exhibit elements of dynamism and vigour: 'Let us get up and sally forth again, as we did then, / and let us come back to life / because everything is still alive inside us, / flowing and blazing.' These lines, however, are uttered by young soldiers killed in battle who are lying prostrate and no longer breathing 'in a long, long row [their eyes] glazed in death'. They are thus certainly no longer able to 'sally forth' again.

DEFYING THE CONVENTIONAL MODELS: S. YIZHAR

The conventional narratives dominated most of the literary works of this period and attempts to question or denigrate them were marginal and weak. In only a few works were they actually defied. Most prominent among these is S. Yizhar's story 'Hirbet Hiza'a'.[54] The story takes place on a hot summer day as an Israeli squad prepares to drive the inhabitants of an Arab village, Hirbet Hiza'a, out of their homes. The ostensible theme – the Jewish–Arab conflict, camouflages the real theme: a conflict between what the Israeli culture of the War of Independence period allowed to be revealed, and what it suppressed. Viewed in terms of rhetoric, structures and intended meaning, 'Hirbet Hiza'a' may be described mainly as a debate with the national narratives in general and those of the War of Independence reportage in particular.[55]

Humanistic Nationalism

The eviction of the inhabitants of Hirbet Hiza'a is described from a humanistic viewpoint, one that had been somewhat overtaken in Israeli culture during the war. It is from this perspective that the protagonist of 'Hirbet Hiza'a' urges himself to forfeit the secure shelter of the military collective in order to help the adversaries, the Palestinian Arabs. However, the story also addresses itself to the prevalent perspective that was reflected by the press during the war. It attacks this perspective, contrasting it with humanistic Judaism based on the teachings of the prophets and the heritage of Jewish thought.[56]

The belief in a moral ethic and in human equality affects how the events are described and determines the point of view from which they are presented. Contrary to journalistic and literary conventions, these viewpoints transcend the insular vision of the Israeli. The Palestinian point of view, too, is considered and is at times actually reported in his own words, clearly disclosing his feelings and suffering: 'Even the boy would emit a kind of tight-lipped "what-have-you-done-to-us" wail ... it was as if a scream had shouted from their tracks, a kind of hateful "Accursed-be-you"'.[57]

In 'Hirbet Hiza'a' the 'disputation' with the conventional narratives is perceptible when the narrator begins his account from the familiar point of view of the Israeli soldier. At times corresponding journalistic texts are quoted almost verbatim, and then gradually shift to the standpoint of the Arab villager. The reality viewed through the villager's eyes exposes the insularity of the Israeli point of view, which utterly fails to acknowledge the Arab reality. For example, a newspaper description of Arabs fleeing from their village reveals an attitude of alienation and contempt:

> At sunrise – and what a beautiful sunrise it was – the residents of Beit Darras began to flee en masse, trying their luck to reach Ashdod. But the marksman, positioned on the structure covering the Arab well, had other ideas. His well-aimed bursts of fire forced them to retrace their steps.[58]

The description of the Arab flight from Hirbet Hiza'a begins in much the same vein:

> A volley of gunfire rained down at once ... among the trees that the sun had begun to wash.... 'Ahalan!', Shmulik cried suddenly, as the great dustcloud that he had caused dispersed. 'Look, they're already running away over there!... Running away ... without even a single shot, the bastards! Hit 'em!', cried Shmulik in growing agitation. Gabi tilted the machine gun and released several bursts.

Although in 'Hirbet Hiza'a' the soldiers maintain the same distance and alienation that is presented in the newspaper article, this estranged account is followed by that of the protagonist-narrator, who identifies with the fleeing Arabs and describes the gunfire through their eyes:

> At once, evidently in the same context, a precise and certain portrayal was presented: how in the same house, with its bluish-white paint and its green shutters, someone now looms over something with abrupt anxiety, how someone in the

> mud-brick hovel stopped eating, how someone in the group of houses to the right broke into the conversation in mid-sentence: 'Gunfire!'[59]

This underlying disputation becomes more explicit when the soldiers in the story voice the highly familiar rationales that appeared in the press on innumerable occasions to explain military actions. These explanations seem flimsy when viewed against the terrible reality described and the blatant injustice perpetrated against the inhabitants of the village. Their flimsiness is further underscored when they are uttered by the soldiers in their colourless, laconic elocution:

> So what do you do to them? Kill them? Better to transfer them to their side. Let them sit there and wait. And that's very nice on our part. Nowhere else in the world would they be treated that way. Besides, no one asked them to start up.[60]

This is immediately contrasted with the position taken by the narrator, who communicates the humanistic values of the entire story.

The Few versus the Many: Europe versus Asia

The soldiers in 'Hirbet Hiza'a' behave as if they are fighting a few-versus-the-many war: 'What are we here, one jeep and a few men capturing an entire village.... Look how many they are.... If they wanted to, they could finish us off just by spitting.'[61] The few-versus-many narrative in this case consists of a group of soldiers capturing and evacuating an entire village. But the village is inhabited only by women and children, and some old men, which makes the whole narrative somewhat ridiculous. In another story by Yizhar, 'The Prisoner', the same narrative is mocked when a group of Israeli soldiers continue to prod a prisoner, who obviously does not know anything, for details on a large and threatening unit of British and Arab forces operating against the Israelis from a tranquil village. In both stories the side presented as cut off from assistance and facing an overwhelmingly strong hostile front is the Arab side. The Arabs are the ones who are betrayed and abandoned (by the Egyptians and the British), and they are the ones who must alone face a merciless enemy – the Israelis.[62]

As noted, the few-versus-many narrative found its place in the journalistic reports alongside the East-versus-West narrative, which drew an analogy between Jewish–Arab relations and Europe–Asia relations. This narrative is given full expression in 'Hirbet Hiza'a'. Like the other narratives, however, it is used here in order to serve as the target of biting criticism and parody.

In principle, the story 'Hirbet Hiza'a' maintains the same dichotomy as that presented in the journalistic reports – physical and spiritual desolation on the one hand, blossoming nature and flourishing civilisation on the other. In some instances the narrative even utilises the rhetoric of the press reports to describe the two worlds. In this story, however, these worlds are switched: desolation is typical of the Jewish side; nature and civilisation are portrayed as characteristic of the Arab side.

The description of landscape in the story follows the conventional forms used in the Hebrew literature of the 1930s and in the peripheral newspapers during the War of Independence. The protagonist-narrator climbs a hill from which he can take the measure of the entire area; he scans it as far as the horizon, and takes it all in with his gaze. His sense of comfort in this landscape is revealed when he describes it as familiar and well known. It envelops him protectively as the earth and sky meet on the horizon and enclose the vast expanse:

> And here are the squares of the fields ploughed and profuse with greenery, the parcels of orchards with their many shadows, the ditches partitioning the territory into forms that retreat soothingly into the distance, and the various hills, now obstructing and then revealing distant bluish horizons.[63]

This rich landscape, however, is not an Israeli one, and the protagonist's contemplation of it does not suggest any possibility that the Israeli will sink roots in it. It is a landscape planted, cultivated and harvested by the Arabs, and steeped in generations of Arab history. The Israelis, of all people, are the ones who will turn these cultivated fields into a wilderness, who will destroy and savage the land and the historical continuity that it embodies. 'The well-tended carpets of green that embellish the desolation' are Arab now, whereas the 'desert tempest', the 'fallow fields' and the 'parched mountains waylaying … all the plentitude of greenery around you' are creations of the Israelis:

> Beyond all these, the melancholy of orphanhood, an opaque veil, descends on them: fields that will not be harvested, orchards that will not be irrigated, paths that will be deserted … a kind of tapestry of thorns and thistles blanketing

> everything, along with a desolate goldenness and the howling open fields.[64]

In 'Hirbet Hiza'a', as in the newspaper articles, negative characteristics of Arabs are mentioned in order to blur the aesthetic and positive impression that the description of their fields may evoke. Here, however, it is the soldiers of the squad who, in laconic, crude army-talk, express this attitude by making strongly derogatory remarks. This attitude is contrasted by the narrator-protagonist who, after summarising the squad commander's instructions, reveals their true meaning:

> That is how it became apparent that the handful of houses visible in the folds of another hill were this Hirbet Hiza'a, that the orchards and fields all around belonged to the village, and that throughout its long history the good land and superb crops had given the village a reputation almost as much as did its inhabitants, who are, they say, scoundrels who aid the enemy, willing to perpetrate any evil.[65]

The squad commander has actually restated a formulation used pervasively by the press. One example was the bucolic description of the houses, vineyards and fields of Beit Darras, which was followed immediately by the clarification that this village was 'notorious' for the villainous character of its inhabitants.[66] In Hirbet Hiza'a, however, the seemingly innocuous connection between the goodness of the fields and the maliciousness of the residents is revealed: the Israelis, who covet the Arabs' fertile fields and wish to justify their occupation, find justification in the disreputable personalities of its Arab inhabitants. The narrator makes this point explicitly by mentioning plans to resettle the village with Israelis.

By vacillating between his own opinions and those of the squad, the protagonist-narrator reshapes the convention that regards Arab landscapes as wastelands, and then exposes and shatters it. He begins by articulating the collective voice:

> All these filthy Arabs, infiltrating in order to restore their desiccated souls in their empty villages, have made us fed up, fed up to the point of anger. What dispute have we with them? What issue exists between us, our young lives and our passing days, and their flea-infested, desolate, suffocating villages?

Then he speaks in his own voice, disclosing the painful reason for this desolation and filth, a reason not mentioned in the journalistic reports:

> Suddenly, in mid- or late-afternoon, the village, just a heap of desolate huts a moment ago, opens up – and then shuts up like an orphan, a harsh silence, and emits a heart-shaking dirge. This large, gloomy village opens its mouth and sings a song of dead yearnings … a song of tidings of sudden, crushing disaster.[67]

Another conventional dichotomy is reversed in 'Hirbet Hiza'a'– that of youth as a symbol of power, potency, and hope of Israeli existence, versus the senescence and exhaustion of the Arab world. The dichotomy is first presented at the beginning of the story in the form of encounters between the Israeli soldiers and the old people of the village. The narrator, too, addresses this issue directly by complaining about the need to waste 'our young lives' in miserable Arab villages. Near the end, however, the promise of hope and youth emanates – but from the Arab village of all places. It appears in the symbolic figure of a colt which breaks free from his fastening and gallops away, and in the weeping and hatred of the village children. At first the narrator recalls: 'We saw how something was happening in that kid's heart, so that when he grows up he won't be able to be anything but a venomous snake, that kid crying so helplessly now.'[68] But he then goes on to experience a stupefying reaction:

> I knew just one thing, and it hit me like a hammered nail. The fact that you can't accept any of this – not as long as there are tears in the eyes of a child crying as he goes out to exile with his mother, her anger restraining her silent tears. [And he] takes with him as he goes a roar decrying the wrong done him, and a scream so shattering that someday someone in this world will have to gather it up.[69]

In all these examples the story reverses the East–West dichotomy, but it does not build anything new. Instead, it restores the perceptions that had prevailed in the Israeli culture before the Disturbances and the War of Independence, perceptions of the Arabs as the genuine inhabitants of the country, and as the bearers of a young and vibrant civilisation.

The Israeli–Jew Dichotomy

The sharpest reversal of convention in 'Hirbet Hiza'a' is connected with the Israeli–Jew dichotomy. The conventional journalistic attitude attributed negative and disgraceful 'Jewish characteristics' to the Arabs, whom they then viewed as the opposite of the Hebrew-Israelis. In 'Hirbet Hiza'a' this dichotomy, like other themes, is expressed by the soldiers in terse and uncouth clichés, and is negated by reality itself.[70] The soldiers articulate their conventional attitudes by ridiculing the Arabs' alleged cowardice and their contemptible lack of military prowess – 'they're running away … they're not even trying to fight' – which is unjustified in view of the description of the villagers as a handful of women, children, and old men.[71]

Other Jewish characteristics of the Arab villagers are introduced by echoing familiar literary accounts of the Jewish exile. The Arabs are led like 'frightened, obedient sheep' who accept their fate without resisting. They give the impression of being a group of Jewish beggars: 'All that's missing is the wailing of Lamentations and the Yom Kippur breast-beating.' They even look Jewish, with 'a white beard' or 'a small skullcap'.[72]

This portrayal, however, is turned upside-down both because the description reverberates with strong allusions to the depiction of a pogrom in Haim Nahman Bialik's well-known poem 'In the City of Death'[73] and because it evokes the protagonist's feelings about the Jewish exile and arouses strong sympathy with the Arab:

> I was never in exile, I told myself. I never knew what it was like.… But they spoke with me, told me, taught me; they repeated it time and again. In every corner, book, and newspaper, everywhere: Exile. They played it on my every string. Our people's challenge to the world: Exile! I seem to have imbibed it along with my mother's milk. What, indeed, have we perpetrated here today?

It is now the Arab who, having assumed the role of the Israeli's Jewish shadow, reminds the hero of his biblical heritage:

> I passed among them all.… I wanted to find out whether there was a mourning or a burning Jeremiah among these people who, his voice choking over the clatter of the wagons of exile … and with burning rage in his heart, was calling out to the old-man god.

The repugnant figure now is the new Israeli, whose image is that of the anti-Jewish gentile, the agent of expulsion and exile.[74]

Historical Past and Future

Beyond its dispute with respect to the expulsion itself, 'Hirbet Hiza'a' conducts a penetrating dialogue with the various time continuums used in the journalistic writings. Each of these is used in the story, examined on its own merits, and is compared with the reality described in the narrative and with the others. As this is done, fissures appear in the causal progression of history, a progression that the journalistic and other texts in the culture had used with much confidence. The Israeli has neither past nor future; his actions have neither purpose nor reason; he exists within a closed, repetitive cycle of time. This kind of time is familiar to us through existentialist literature, especially the writings of Albert Camus and Jean-Paul Sartre. The writings of Camus, in particular *The Stranger* (1941) and *The Myth of Sisyphus* (1940), seem to have strongly influenced Yizhar, who used similar themes in 'Hirbet Hiza'a' in order to criticise a society that, having abandoned its values, beliefs and aspirations, has therefore lost the possibility of progressing along the continuums of historical or natural time.

In every description of the Israeli squad's behaviour or action in 'Hirbet Hiza'a' time stands still. The soldiers are immersed in seemingly endless boredom and inertia and in a protracted anticipation of 'something' that will happen, that will materialise 'all at once'. Even when progress in time does occur, it is merely comical. It appears that something is on the verge of occurring when, for example, the narrator begins a paragraph with the statement 'And when it was noon', but the sentence is left unfinished, and the occurrence proves to be nothing but a repetition of the preceding one: 'And when it was noon.... The hours came and dragged on and on, drying out and withering away with great sorrow.'[75]

In this ambience of non-ending dreariness and gloomy anticipation, yearnings for the past are merely yearnings for an earlier version of the present. The narrator longs for 'those beautiful days of action', but when he begins to recall them, they turn out to be characterised by the same boredom, inaction and protracted anticipation that occur in the story.[76] As expectations for the future and yearnings for the past prove to be futile attempts to avoid the dreary present, the military action, too, loses its causality and purposefulness. When this happens, the entire grand causal structure, the same one that had organised journalistic and other writings of the time, seems to have disintegrated. However, as in the other cases, the causal dynamic structure is not altogether absent in the story, but is there in order to be criticised. At first, the military operation is fully described in the style of journalistic reportage with verbs succeeding one another in a dynamic, rapid succession. In this case, however, this dynamic has lost its moral justification: 'load them … transfer them … blow it up … burn it … forbid it … mop it up'.

The causal chain of events in the present is not the only one that is broken down in the story, for the connection with the historical past is broken as well. Thus, allusions to the Israeli past no longer strengthen confidence in the Israeli action in 'Hirbet Hiza'a'. Instead, they highlight the injustice of the expulsion.

Upon the ruins of the new Israeli narratives, and with no alternatives available, the old Jewish narrative is fully reconstructed on all its levels and shows another, hitherto unknown face. The dimension of Jewish ahistorical time driven by metaphysical forces in bold upheavals between Destruction and Redemption, rejected so adamantly by the Israeli culture, comes to the surface and bursts out in 'Hirbet Hiza'a'. In this case it no longer symbolises an arbitrary clinging to catastrophes or an unreasoning reliance on divine power. Rather, it embodies the viewpoint of those upon whom history has indeed brought sudden cataclysms and who find no path other than adherence to hopes of metaphysical redemption. 'Hirbet Hiza'a' eschews the explanations, reasons and justification that underlie the Israeli view of time, restoring the reasons and justification of the Jewish narrative that the Israelis had spurned. Now, however, that justification belongs to the Arabs, not the Jews.

The Arab village is overtaken by a sudden cataclysm, expressed in the narrative as 'tidings of a sudden, crushing disaster that froze and remained as a kind of curse that does not cross wretched lips'. This disaster is driven by a force that, from the Arab standpoint, cannot be repulsed – a god-like force, embodied in the figure of the Israeli, that seals the fate of the village by something like 'a hand that scribbled, arbitrarily, "no harvest"'.[77] The Israeli, who had spurned the metaphysical perception of the Jewish exile, now ironically proves to be the agent through whom these very perceptions are reinvigorated. After investing great efforts to take their fate into their own hands, and not to rely on divine powers, the Israelis have themselves become a superior and monstrous force.

In view of the arbitrariness of the forces abusing them, the magnitude of the disaster, and their own impotence in facing them, all the victims can do now is to await redemption in the form of a vengeful god who will appear and announce that the 'first sparks of redemption'[78] will emanate from the ruins. The protagonist-narrator attempts to reveal this destruction-to-redemption progression in both of his roles. As the protagonist, he strives for it explicitly, expecting – and hoping – that the exiles will mount an uprising. As the narrator, he attempts to construct such a progression by shifting within the continuum of the text from silent tears and desolate voices to a roar and a shattering scream.[79] He also does this when he shifts his description from the crippled and aged Arab villagers on the verge of death, to the mothers and children in whose faces he discerns hatred and rebelliousness.

The time continuum that consolidates the Israeli's place in history has thus lost its validity. The action that was meant to consummate his rights has lost its rationale and its purpose. After contemplating the disintegrated Israeli time which leads from nowhere to nowhere, the narrator prefers the Arab view of time, which is now based on the Jewish narrative's adherence to hopes of redemption. Thus the narrative rejected by the journalistic texts appears in literary ones where it both engages and undermines the dominant national narratives.

CONCLUSION

Amid a string of defeats – the unsuccessful battles for Latrun, the surrender of the Old City of Jerusalem, the evacuation of Kibbutz Yad Mordechai and the encirclement of Negba by Egyptian armour – the Hebrew press described the War of Independence as a progression leading slowly but surely to victory. At a time when Israel stood alone against the invading forces of five Arab countries with no assurance of help from the West, the press described the war as part of the European nations' front against a weakened and isolated East. In a war that claimed the lives of one per cent of the country's population and ten per cent of its youth, the writings hardly mention fatalities or death. The journalistic reports abstained from describing these facts of the War of Independence; instead they invoked culturally conventional narratives to articulate the consciousness of Israeli society. This consciousness played a decisive role in furthering the war effort, bolstering Israeli morale and leading to victory.

Even as the war raged, however, the Israeli-Jewish culture began to re-examine the price of this victory. After the war ended, this introspection increased and the voices that had been suppressed – voices of the Jewish heritage, of the Arab and of a universal humanism – were heard again. These voices, too, are integral parts of the Israeli culture, and the dialogue between them and the dominant voices is a factor that shapes the face of this culture in times of both peace and war. Israel's tempestuous history admittedly imposed – and imposes – certain dictates on the nation's consciousness, but how this consciousness responds to those dictates is determined by open, unfettered dialogue. This dialogue has not ceased, and it continues to affirm the Jewish maxim that although everything is predestined, man has his own free will.

NOTES

1. For the Orthodox-Jewish narrative, see G. Greenberg, 1988. A thorough description of the dichotomy of the Hebrew and the Jewish narratives appears in I. Even-Zohar, 1981, and in B. Harshav, 1988.
2. Most of the dailies at that time were party newspapers: *Al Ha-mishmar* was the newspaper of the Socialist Party Mapam; *Davar*, of the social democrat party, Mapai, then in power; *Ma'ariv* was a private evening newspaper; *Ha-boqer* was the newspaper of the liberal General Zionist Party; and *Ha-mashqif* was the newspaper of the right, the Revisionist Party.
3. M. Tzanin, 1948. The number of Germans who participated in the war alongside the Arabs was minimal. Articles of this type tend to exaggerate their number in order to fall in line with the narrative of an isolated people surrounded by enemies.
4. N. Arbel, 1981. B. Morris, 1987, maintains that Israel clearly had military superiority from the onset of the War of Independence. The dry facts, such as the high proportion of casualties and the large number of battles that ended in Israeli defeat, negate Morris's contention.
5. R. Azariah, 1948(a), 1948(b); A. Goldstein, 1948.
6. In *Al Ha-mishmar* the forces for progress are mainly those of socialism, which the Israeli nation joins in its struggle. In other newspapers these forces are the Allies. The terms by which the East is described here are taken from a well-known western stock repertoire used to describe the Orient. See also E. Said, 1979.
7. No name provided, 'The Syrians Exploited the Cease-Fire Twice', *Ma'ariv*, 21 July 1948.
8. G. Tzifroni, 1948(c).
9. Ibid.
10. See also Even-Zohar, 1981; M. Perry, 1986; R. Alter, 1977; G. Morahg, 1982; G. Ramras-Rauch, 1989. For the image of the Orient in western civilisation, see Said, 1979.
11. Yehoshua, 1948; Y. Yambour, 1948(a); Y. Aryeh, 1948; Yambour, 1948(b); respectively.
12. Yehoshua, 1948; S. Kaplan, 1948; respectively.
13. A. Gelblum, 1948. The description concerns the Eztion Bloc settlements, which were attacked by the Arab Legion and local farm villagers.

14. Over Orach (A passer-by), 1948.
15. Y. Hagederati, 1948(a); A. Goldstein, 1948.
16. Hagedareti, 1948(a).
17. No name provided, 'How the Way to the Old City Was Opened', *Davar*, 23 May 1948; Yambour 1948(a); Tzifroni, 1948(a); respectively.
18. Even-Zohar, 1981.
19. Y. Mastboim, 1948; Hagederati, 1948(b).
20. E. Carlibach, 1948.
21. P. Daromi, 1948.
22. Carlibach, 1948.
23. M. Talmi, 1948.
24. K. S. G. Amihai, 1948.
25. No name provided, 'Gebelia and Tel Arish Are Empty', *Al Hamish Mar*, 10 May 1948.
26. Hagedareti, 1948(a).
27. Talmi, 1948.
28. Special reporter, 1948; Z. Kremer, 1948.
29. Kremer, 1948.
30. Azariah, 1948(a).
31. Compare mainly with the article by A. Elon, 1948, but also with Azariah, 1948(a); D. Zaslavsky, 1948; A. Baruch, 1948.
32. Goldstein, 1948, concerning the fighting on the road to Sha'ar Hagai.
33. Special reporter, 1948.
34. Yambour, 1948(b).
35. Yehoshua, 1948.
36. Y. Bar-Yosef, 1948, describing the battle for Negba.
37. E. Oren, 1948.
38. S. N., 1948.
39. D. Gil'adi, 1948; Y. Yemini, 1948; No name provided, 'The Squad is Back and Gathering Forces', *Ma'ariv*, 15 July 1948; A. Shimshoni, 1948; No name provided, 'The Squad is Back', *Ma'ariv*, 15 July 1948; respectively.
40. Tzifroni, 1948(a).
41. Tzifroni, 1948(b).
42. Ibid.
43. On the *belles-lettres* of the War of Independence, see G. Shaked, 1971; R. Kritz, 1985.
44. Y. Mossinsohn, 'Blue Jeep', 1960; H. Guri, 1975.
45. See M. Shamir, 1967.
46. A. Kovner, 1953: 99.
47. D. Miron, 1988. Also in Miron, 1992.
48. Guri, 1975: 146.
49. See also Shaked, 1971.
50. For an analysis of literary texts, see my book, 1983.
51. N. Shaham, 1949.
52. Miron, 1988.
53. Miron, 1992.
54. S. Yizhar, 1949. For an analysis of this story, see Shaked, 1971; A. Sha'anan, 1976; R. Alter, 1977; A. Oz, unpublished.
55. A disputation with the literature of its time similar to that argued by this story is reviewed in my book, 1983 and is partially re-explored in Chapter 6.
56. See Yizhar, 1949: 44, 56, 92, 109, 134, 138, respectively.
57. Ibid., 106.
58. Hagedarati, 1948(a).
59. Yizhar, 1949: 58.

60. Ibid., 105.
61. Ibid., 78, 80.
62. Ibid., 126.
63. See 'The Prisoner', ibid., 97.
64. Ibid., 73, 198, 225, 283, 97, respectively.
65. Ibid., 45.
66. Hagederati, 1948(a).
67. Yizhar, 1949: 55, 56.
68. Ibid., 107.
69. Ibid., 110.
70. Much has been written about the Jewish history presented in this story. This chapter discusses the matter only with respect to the stereotype of the Arab as 'a Jew'.
71. Yizhar, 1949: 55, 71, respectively.
72. Ibid., 100, 101, 105, 69, respectively.
73. Bialik's poem echoes throughout the story. The opening scene in the vegetable field recalls the vegetable garden in 'In the City of Death'. The tone in which the description guides the onlooking narrator ('Don't spit in disgust, and avert your gaze, and flee the scene', Yizhar, 1949: 73) is the tone guiding the observer of the city in Bialik's poem. The call to Bialik's speaker ('Grit your teeth and melt away') reverberates in the behaviour of the narrator (who 'grits his teeth and clenches his fists'), and in that of the Arabs ('who grit their teeth in the silence', ibid., 107). The hate building up in the heart of Bialik's narrator like 'a snake in his pit' now surfaces as a 'viper in the heart' of the Arab child (ibid., 107). This is also discussed by A. Oz, unpublished.
74. Yizhar, 1949: 107, 86, 80, 109, respectively.
75. Ibid., 47.
76. Ibid., 47.
77. Ibid., 56, 95, 69, 98, respectively.
78. Ibid., 56, 95, respectively.
79. Ibid., 95, 107, 74, 110, respectively.

3

SONS OF LIGHT AND SONS OF DARKNESS: Speeches of Menachem Begin, 1981

In 1978 a peace agreement between Israel and Egypt was signed. Menachem Begin, then prime minister of Israel, promised that 'the land would have 40 years of rest'. But Israel did not 'have rest', either before the peace agreement or after. Between 1948 and 1988 Israel went through six wars, each of which had the effect of accelerating changes in the nation's collective consciousness and in the balance between its political forces. Each war also affected the hierarchy of its narratives, especially the two which dominated the Israeli scene in the 1980s. One of these narratives treated Jewish history as a metaphysical progression leading the Chosen People from Destruction to Redemption, and drove an irreparable wedge between Israel and the rest of the world. The other sought to reposition Israel within a broad, egalitarian human community and saw Israel's destiny as linked to that of the nations of Europe.

While neither of these narratives was new, the balance between them had shifted over the preceding decades. The narrative expounding a Jewish–gentile dichotomy had been, as described above, an integral facet of Orthodox-Jewish thought. It was categorically rejected by the new Zionist culture that took shape as its antithesis, and was expressed by the narrative of the new Israeli-Jews who took action to determine their fate and mould their history with their own hands. The latter narrative fashioned the image of Israeli society as the absolute negation of a passive, isolated Jewish entity that relied on divine forces to lift it from the cataclysm of Destruction to the halcyon drama of Redemption.

The earlier Orthodox-Jewish narrative had indeed been shunted to the periphery, but it had not vanished completely. It found its place in many corners of Israel's culture, including that of the political right, where it was embellished with such ostensibly contradictory concepts as dramatic victories, Greater Israel (consisting of what is now Israel, the West Bank and the Gaza Strip), trust in military might and faith in the strength of a powerful leader. Several momentous events contributed to this melding together of Jewish and rightist narratives and their penetration into mainstream Israeli society – the Eichmann trial, which generated renewed discussion of the Holocaust; the Six Day War, which awakened religious sentiments; the conquest and occupation of the West Bank, which constituted fulfilment of the ideology of a 'Greater Land of Israel'; the feeling of being an isolated nation, during the Six Day War and again, six years later, during the Yom Kippur War (which found Israel unprepared when attacked by the Egyptian and Syrian armies); and the weakening of Mapai and other Labor front parties and a waning of their ideological tenacity. In addition, many members of the lower-middle class deserted the Labor front, and towards the middle of the 1970s their identification with the right-wing Likud Party[1] reached a critical point. The Likud was able to instill in this sector of the population feelings of strength and national pride and a sense of belonging to the Israeli culture and society, and to restore a traditional Jewish orientation in place of the crumbling socialist-Zionist ideology of the Labor Party.

The new hybrid rightist-Jewish narrative spread into mainstream Israeli society especially strongly after the Six Day War (1967), when the right began to make deep inroads in both political and public affairs. After the Likud gained power in 1977 it became even more dominant, and was overtly expressed in Menachem Begin's speeches. In 1981, after four years as prime minister, Begin embarked on a forceful, re-election campaign. He made ardent speeches in town squares all over the country in which, swept away by the fervour of the vast crowds of lower-middle-class Israelis, he thunderously articulated the old-new rightist-Jewish narrative. As in other texts analysed in this book, the narrative is revealed much less in its content than in the structure of the speeches. This structure viewed the world as a great wasteland peopled by only two protagonists – 'we' and 'they' – who play out the final scene of the familiar drama in which the isolated few triumph over the mighty many. The struggle this time is not for a triumph of will, faith or resourcefulness, but for a massive military victory. In the course of this battle, not only do we-the-few defeat they-the-many but we destroy them and take their place.

Although the few-versus-many basis of the narrative is maintained, it is presented in a form so altered that it has acquired a completely different meaning. The confrontation is now presented as a contest between Israel and the rest of the world, one that can be resolved only through destruction or redemption. In this structure, as in the previous one, the local political opponent is completely identified with the enemy, and the Likud, the main party of the right, becomes the embodiment of the state of Israel. For the destruction of the enemy/opponent to be decisive, a sharp dichotomy between the two forces must be created, and to this end use is made of such clear and simple opposites as light and darkness, oblivion and immortality, sublime heights and abysmal depths:

> The [Iraqi] nuclear reactor collapsed, fell, is no more. Will be no more! The children of Israel will live. Will build homes. And the people of Israel will live in the Land of Israel forever, and none shall make it afraid. … You will tell us that in the Land of Israel it is forbidden to go to a place where Arabs reside? This is not our land? We are not allowed to set up Eilon Moreh above Nablus? Yes, Eilon Moreh can be seen from Nablus, high up on the mountain, a mighty mountain, a beacon by day and by night. (speech in Malchei Yisrael Square in Tel Aviv)

There are settlements on the plains and in the valleys as well, but Begin's specific reference to one on a high mountain is very symbolic: the higher the mountain, the greater the fall from it. And the more brightly the mountain is illuminated, the darker the eclipse that would be brought about by the rival Alignment Party (composed of Mapai and several smaller Labor front parties), which wants to give up that mountain. Zionism always likened its undertaking to a difficult mountain ascent, but only now has one of the aims of that ascent been to topple the opponent into the abyss below.

Beyond these absolute opposites an amazingly simple but dramatic story is constructed. Its purpose is to expand the concept of 'we' and 'us', and to diminish 'they' and 'them'. At the beginning of the speech, 'we' are only a small square in Lod, Tel Aviv or Netanya, filled with a random gathering of people burdened with problems and at odds with one another and with themselves. As the speech goes on the square expands to become a vast and mighty nation with women and children, soldiers, tanks and pilots, and cities and settlements. By the end of Begin's speech, 'we' are no longer the crowd in a small square but the army, the nation, the settlements, Jerusalem and the state; 'we' are the whole world. What began as a small, tentative gathering of local supporters, is transformed in the course of one speech into the many and the mighty. Along the way, 'we' have either confiscated the material and ideological property of 'them' and accredited it to 'us' (for example, the kibbutz idea, originally created by the Labor movement and presented in some of Begin's speeches as a collective national endeavour), or 'we' have banished 'them' from our midst (for example, Begin's rancorous attacks in which he heaped calumny on the kibbutz settlements). However, for the small audience in the town square to become so great it must consolidate its ranks, and this is accomplished when 'we' are opposed by a large and threatening body of 'them'. It is not at all important whether 'they' are opponents from within or enemies from without. In Begin's speech in Lod 'they' are variously the Alignment, terrorists, Iraqis and the Americans. By the end of his speech, these opponents have all joined hands to work against 'us'.

This is the basic structure of Begin's rhetoric, and on it he constructs variations. Each is another tale of how 'we' were few and weak, how the many and mighty 'they' contrived to destroy us, and how, at the last moment, 'our' soldiers sallied forth and dealt them a mighty blow. In such stories, the Holocaust and Jewish children, after being passed through a process of 'pathetisation', are major components. They become a feature in the private story of each person in the square. A person who was insignificant becomes, here in this square, a great and mighty identity – a first-person plural. Here, for example, are two variations from an election speech in Lod:

> We have built the Land of Israel along its length and breadth. On the mountain of Samaria there is a great light. It will never be extinguished. This is the Land of Israel, our land, our homeland, homeland of our fathers and our children. What does the Alignment want? It wants to hand over that high mountain, Samaria and Judea, to Arafat. And Arafat would install Katyushas [Soviet-made rocket-missiles], and Ramle and Lod would be in the range of those Katyushas. What does the Alignment think? What does it want? That Katyushas should fall here?

> Under the Alignment governments, the terrorists, the murderers, would come. They would kill every man, woman and child. As in Ma'alot, Nahariya, Misgav-Am, on the coastal road.[2] And then our fighting men would go out against them

> and strike at them. That was retaliation. But what do we gain from retaliation? It is not possible to avenge the blood of a small boy, of a small girl whose brains the terrorist-murderers cut up in the presence of her father and then murdered the father. We have changed the method. We no longer wait for them to come to us, to our homes, our cities, our settlements, our kibbutzim. No! The Israel Defence Forces go to their bases and hit them there. And the IDF knows how to strike! Once from the land, once from the sea, once from the air! That is how we have protected our people, our children, our women.

In these passages it is easy to see the absolute dichotomies between children and the Holocaust on the one hand and heroism and vengeance on the other. These pairs of opposites made it possible for the crowd in the square to wear two identities simultaneously – that of the downtrodden, the victim, the innocent child, and that of the avenging soldier. Now that children and the Holocaust have been evoked, only the sword can bridge between 'us' and 'them'. In speeches of this sort, Begin's syntax places the Alignment, terrorists and murderers on one side where they all share the common third-person plural 'they' or 'them', while 'our' fighting men are on the other side. Furthermore, when the atrocities perpetrated by the enemy are so terrible, the Alignment is perforce tainted by and charged with them.

The speech reaches its peak when Israel's pilots appear on the scene: 'And now I ask of you, of the whole nation, after the destruction of the Iraqi nuclear reactor, to give thanks to our Father in Heaven for having given us our pilots' (ibid.). At this point the applause and the call 'Be-gin! Be-gin!' reach new thunderous heights, followed by the chant 'Begin, King of Israel'. For at this moment the crowd is totally consolidated. It has attained the sense of being a great nation, and Begin, standing at its head, embodies this new identity.

Needless to say, charging the Alignment with treason fits well into such a schematic structure. The story is repeated: the enemy threatens our little children with annihilation (danger – the crowd tenses); our marvellous pilots head for battle (heroism – stormy applause). Then comes the Alignment, making common cause with those who condemn us:

> And what did the people of the Alignment say the next day? [boos and howls of rage] They announced that there was no danger from the reactor. And what they said was translated –

> that very day … into tens of languages. They sent their message to the whole world. They took a stand against the nation in Israel. Against the government of Israel. Against the interests of Israel. And they collaborated with outsiders seeking to harm us. (ibid.)

This story, in which 'we' the few and weak took our destiny into our own hands and triumphed over 'them' the many and mighty is the matrix that shapes Begin's view of the world. Thus, in Israel's relations with the entire world Begin tends to see only 'us' (pre-Holocaust Jews, downtrodden and outcast victims who strove to change their identity and became a strong power) and 'them' (Arabs, Nazis, or any others who threaten to destroy us). Some subjects have to be completely distorted in order to fit into this matrix. The kibbutzim and other settlements become nothing but an instrument for defying the Katyusha rockets, and peace is nothing but an instrument in Israel's strife with the Syrians and Iraqis: 'We have a score to settle with the Syrians, and we will settle it. But if it were not for the peace treaty with Egypt, today we would have had to mobilise almost all the reserves' (ibid.).

Relations between 'we' and 'they' are marked not only by hatred but by a certain kind of cynical humour. To bring this about 'they' becomes the plural 'you', and this 'you' functions as the silent partners in a dialogue in which 'we' show 'them' how strong 'we' are, and then rub their noses in it:

> I'll ask Habib [Philip Habib, an American mediator sent to the Middle East]: 'Will the [Syrian] missiles move [away] or won't they? Will you move them or will you not? If you won't move them, then we'll move them!' (ibid.)

The enemy in Begin's speeches, whether within or without, must be wiped out. In the world inhabited by the speaker and his audience there is room for none other than the collective 'we' that has become a 'great and numerous people'. It is thus clear why, in this world, space and time are 'our' eternal domain. In this way, Begin fine-tunes and sharpens a message voiced in previous years not only on the political right but also in modern Hebrew literature:[3]

> This land is our land, the land of our fathers from ancient times and the land of our children from generation to

> generation and to the end of all generations. And that is why we have built it, the Land of Israel, across the length and breadth, and will continue to build it – more buildings, more people, more Jews in the thousands and tens of thousands. And they will settle in Judea and Samaria, on the Golan Heights, in the Gaza Strip, and everywhere else. (speech in Malchei Yisrael Square in Tel Aviv)

'We' and 'they' did not originate in Begin's speeches. For years the elite of the left, the Labor movement, had constituted the 'we' of the country: 'we' were the pioneer settlers and builders of the land, and the ones who had established the state, manned the top government and military positions, and determined the society's character and its culture. The people listening to Begin in the town squares did not always possess a strong sense of belonging. After arriving in the country in the mass immigration of the early 1950s that followed Israel's establishment, they failed to assimilate the existing national identity or to fashion one of their own. Begin was acutely aware of the depth of their accumulated bitterness. When addressing these people, he gave them a framework to join, a first-person-plural 'we' that had formerly belonged only to the others. He expanded and inflated this new identity and endowed it with everything that had belonged to 'them', including even the kibbutz settlements, and transmuted it into a fierce giant. Once the historical Labor movement had lost its place in the centre of the political arena and room was made for other forces, the new order was not satisfied with just replacing it, but sought to subsume its components as well. Thus, Begin adopted the sense of power of the collective 'we'. At this time, however, it was not a power tempered by the need to integrate the rival parties and establish relations between Israel and the other nations. It was the raw power that sharpened the polarities between 'we' and 'they'.

Begin was not the originator of this type of rhetoric, and the struggle for the appropriation of national symbols, imageries and myths did not begin with his speeches but, rather, at the dawn of Zionism. As the reader will recall, each of the two large movements, Labor and Revisionism, had regarded itself as a handful of isolated, misunderstood 'few', forced to fulfil their beliefs and dreams in a bitter struggle with the hostile, threatening 'many' that was composed of the rival political parties and of foreign enemies. But despite their antagonisms both parties tended to use the same ideological narrative and to emphasise the points that united them rather than those that set them apart. The different atmosphere of these early years is very evident in speeches by the leaders of the two parties – David Ben-Gurion, chairman of the Labor movement, and Ze'ev (Vladimir) Jabotinsky, leader of the Revisionist right. The two fought vigorously, yet despite the bitterness and ferocity of their mutual aspersions, they both acknowledged the traditional tolerance for the right of one's opponents to express their beliefs. Although this tradition was in strong conflict with ideological zeal and intolerance, it was the core around which their speeches were structured.

Both Ben-Gurion and Jabotinsky subscribed, in the early years of modern pre-Israeli Jewish life in Palestine, to the narrative of the few against the many, an expression of a 'we-versus-they' worldview. However, both took care to remind their listeners that within its confines the world was still large enough to accommodate opposing views. Jabotinsky expressed his view in the term *hadar*, a majesty of sorts, of 'princely manners towards young and old, man and woman, Jew and gentile, friend and enemy'.[4] Their mutual recognition and respect allowed Jabotinsky and Ben-Gurion to keep their conflict within the domain of persuasion rather than of coercion or usurpation. Jabotinsky acknowledged the rights of the 'leftist movements'[5] and Ben-Gurion acknowledged the rights of the Revisionist youth:

> There are Jewish youth in the Diaspora who are being educated by the Revisionists. These teenagers immigrate to Palestine and want to work. What are you going to do about it? Bring them into the Histadrut?[6] Or say: 'You're fascists, we won't sit together with you?'

Two years later, he said:

> We have no reason to view the party's youth activities ungenerously or with envy – even if these activities are directed specifically against us. Our number-one enemy is stagnation in Zionist activity, disintegration of the movement, impotence. But we have nothing to fear from positive Zionist activity – even if it is not always to our liking.[7]

Even when Ben-Gurion or Jabotinsky denied their opponent's right to debate, this was not done to crush the latter but to prove that he was inconsistent with his own principles. Each tried to establish that his opponent was actually closer to 'our' positions than to his own. In order to do this, attempts were made to present the inconsistencies of the opponent's logic, to belittle his power, or to prove that 'our' merits were of far greater importance:

> We ... know how to esteem, to value the builders.... They have all done much for the movement for the redemption of [the Land of] Israel. But those who struggle between Tel-Hai and the gallows [that is, the Revisionists] are preferable to the rest of the children of Israel.[8]

The relative tolerance of those years also informed the attitude of both leaders towards the Arabs. Over and above all differences of views, both leaders acknowledged the existence of the Arab people, and maintained that the existence of 'our identity' did not entail the total negation of the existence of 'their identity'. Thus, Jabotinsky said,

> It is obvious that the Arab younger generation loves its homeland. Can there be any doubt that here, too, are pure young Arabs dreaming beautiful national dreams?... Let us assume that the justice of our cause outweighs theirs. But theirs still exists.[9]

While in Ben-Gurion's words:

> About a million Arabs live on both sides of the Jordan. They haven't been there since yesterday or the day before. They have a clear right to live on this land, to develop on it and to enjoy national independence, just as the Jewish people has a clear right to return to its homeland, make the desert bloom, and by the sweat of its brow, and with its money and resourcefulness, establish a society and a culture that will guarantee its autonomous national existence.... In working our land we know that we have to honour the rights of its present inhabitants; and if our first encounter with our neighbours was tragic, that was not our fault. Neither, perhaps, was it our neighbours' fault.[10]

In Ben-Gurion's and Jabotinsky's time the Jewish-Israeli national saga was strongly linked to universal truths, transforming it into a global human story. Both leaders were steeped in the humanistic tradition, although Ben-Gurion's was derived from his background in a small European Jewish community and Jabotinsky's from the liberal values of nineteenth-century western culture. Both of these traditions were founded on humanism, universalism and tolerance. Not only were the two leaders suffused with these values, but so too were their followers. Thus, each was able to conduct a dialogue in the name of those values with their own audiences or with their rival's followers.

To expand and universalise the national narrative, Jabotinsky enlarges his frame of reference ranged from nineteenth-century literature to classical and European folklore and mythology.[11] His worldview embraced such broad expanses of time and place that he had no need to censure his detractors; on the contrary, he spread his cultural wings over his followers and his opponents alike. To achieve a similar result, Ben-Gurion took an opposite course. He focused on the individual believer in Zionism and demanded that each search 'within himself, not outside himself [for the] Archimedian point'.[12] Ben-Gurion's basic assumption was that an individual searching within his own soul was no less universal than the culture he had built. The tradition of self-examination and personal example is deeply rooted in Jewish culture, and its legacy was an integral element in Zionist ideology.

The universalistic approach of the two leaders stemmed from their humanistic positions – their recognition of the oneness of all mankind and the individuality of each of its members. Jabotinsky put it in this way:

> [I am] a product of the nineteenth century. The view then prevailing in the world was that everyone, even a person who is evil and dirty, would be good and intelligent if given the proper education. That is my view.... I would rather die than accept the view that my son and the other's son are not equals, that my son and my shoemaker are not equals.[13]

Begin was a disciple of Jabotinsky, but he was not the only one. Jabotinsky's earliest disciples were members of a fringe group of young Palestinian Jewish Revisionists who set up a far-right organisation that called itself Brith Ha-biryonim, literally 'The Alliance of the Toughs'. It is in their speeches, and not in those of Jabotinsky, that one may find the origins of Begin's rhetorical style. His main source of inspiration insofar as style is concerned was Abba Ahimeir, a leading figure in Brith Ha-biryonim. Abba Ahimeir was the product of a climate altogether different from that of his mentor Jabotinsky. He was active in Palestine in the first decades of the century amidst confrontations between the right and the left. These were bitter conflicts, and with resources very scarce in the *Yishuv*, the battle for jobs and immigration certificates was fought with special vigour. The Jewish Agency[14] denied immigration certificates and the *Histadrut* labour exchanges withheld job opportunities from rightist Revisionist activists, who retaliated by breaking strikes and bringing Jewish Revisionist immigrants into Palestine clandestinely. In the world that descended from the lofty heights of pure Zionist ideology to the labour exchanges, a different tone was employed, one infused with violence and hatred. It amplified the force of the clash, which in turn further fuelled the verbal brutality.

In the landscape of Ahimeir's birthplace, as in that of his rivals, the rift between 'we' and 'they' grew wider. Here one can recognise the first signs of the dreams of the downtrodden minority, who would no longer live in a world free of oppression but in one where they reigned supreme, oppressing others when necessary. In Ahimeir's world one can find the two familiar 'we' and 'they' protagonists, who are separated by an unbridgeable chasm. To underscore this rift, Ahimeir used figurative antinomies – bright light and deep darkness, great heights and bottomless abysses, giants and midgets, humans and beasts, the sacred and the profane. While these could be found in the speeches and leaflets of both parties, Ahimeir juxtaposes them with greater forcefulness:

> The Hebron authorities are maliciously and systematically stealing our sacred patrimony, the Land of Zion, and are returning this Land, which is crying out for redemption, to the wild creatures of the desert, to the mosquitoes, to malaria, to the water buffalo.
>
> Here Wolfsohn[15] tried to continue in Herzl's giant steps, but then came the midgets, who had already fought Herzl in his lifetime, and began to engage in 'practicalities' – like the afforestation of the rocky ground of Ben-Shemen and Hulda, or efforts of the settlement-near-Lake Kinneret sort [that is, communal agricultural settlements]. Zionism was busy with all kinds of small-fry stuff.
>
> Oh, but that the stench of putrefaction in this town would fade away and that in its place patriotism would begin to emanate, the fragrance of motherland, a bit of sunlight and the scent of fertile fields.[16]

Mosquitoes are not mentioned merely by chance. They were part of a whole menagerie of animal epithets meant to diminish the antagonist by means of imagery or comparison, a device used later during the War of Independence to denigrate the Arab adversary. Ahimeir uses images and comparisons related to food and eating for a similar purpose, that of calling the leaders of the left a 'gang of satiated politicians' and, elsewhere, 'vapid vegetarians' (consistency not being a necessary trait). Adjectives and labels are also used by Ahimeir for emphasising his opponents' turpitude. Unlike Ben-Gurion and Jabotinsky, who often labelled a specific action of the other a crime or a murder, Ahimeir does not define any specific acts, but uses epithets such as 'liquidators of Zionism', 'old fools' and 'harem statesmen'.[17] The invective is inherent in the noun or in the adjective and as such does not require proof.

It may be that there were no substantial differences between the views of Ahimeir and Jabotinsky on the nature of agricultural settlement in Palestine, the relation between Herzl's political Zionism and the practical Zionism of the Labor movement or Britain's Middle East policy. The difference between the two lies not in the essence of their common worldview, but in its structure: Jabotinsky respects his opponents and tries to win them over; Ahimeir does not even acknowledge his opponents' existence and makes no attempt to convince them. It is enough for him to position his party, himself and his views on the side of the giants – nay the gods – and to range on the other side their absolute opposites – defilement, disease, blackness, bestiality, decay, dwarfishness. After turning the dichotomy of 'we' and 'they' into confrontations between God's word and blasphemy and between holiness and bestiality there are no grounds for persuasion or even communication – only for extirpation.

In the conflict between 'them' and 'us', Zionism is the counterpoint of justice, reason and democracy, and the strong link between the two sets of values is severed:

> Zionism is a goal in itself. All means for bringing it about are fine in our eyes.... Other ideals concern us only to the extent that they help us recognise the enemy's weakness or strength. We are duty-bound to reject the fight against any ideal other than Zionism, whatever it may be.... The golden calf and the cherubim above the holy ark cannot exist in the same place.[18]
>
> Until now the Zionism that 'liquidates' has silenced the Zionist conscience with notions of 'justice', and now it silences it with the notion of 'science'.... This is no place for meetings,

> discussions, votes, chairmen. Here there is room only for commanders and soldiers.... We are interested in quality, not quantity.[19]

In this world, there is no place for others; all space is 'ours', a theme that would reappear later in Begin's speeches. A variation of the narrative that pitted culture against the desert served to expound this perception:

> This land is a battlefield between the desert and the Garden of Eden.... The sirocco, blight and choleric diseases come from the desert, at the height of spring, when the plant is most delicate. Similarly, from time to time a desiccating human wind sweeps down on the springtime of our movement: savages come out of the desert and lay waste this land.[20]

Once the opposites have been set forth and the opponents eliminated, Ahimeir's presentation of the dramatic story of the few against the many becomes very simple: we, the few, are Zionist pioneers (*halutzim*); the many are just 'a herd'. We are the 'standard-bearers' of the militaristic Zionism of the heroes of Tel-Hai; the others are 'a pack of vapid vegetarians'. The struggle between us and them was decided long ago when 'Zionism was wiped out'; Herzl's doctrine was forgotten until 'Jabotinsky came along and revived it'. Today Brith Ha-biryonim are the guardians of the flag, the anthem and the idea of Hatiqvah (literally, 'the hope', and the title of Israel's national anthem).[21] The 'few' who were Brith Ha-biryonim had now turned themselves into the many.

The Zionist movement had traversed a great distance between Ben-Gurion and Jabotinsky to the Begin era. However, the gap between speech and action had already appeared in the early days, for when these two, Ben-Gurion and Jabotinsky, descended from the Olympian heights of pure intellect to fight the bare-fisted struggle for power, their tone, style of speech and behaviour changed. And as the clash became stormier, more violent and increasingly confrontational, so too did the intensity of their rhetoric. The workers movement of the left had the hegemony in the *Yishuv* and, later, in the state; it was able to relegate its opponents completely to the periphery and to present its narrative and identity as a national one. Some 40 years later, Begin's speeches became potent weapons in the right's 'usurpation' of this same national identity.

In the years preceding Begin's ascension to power, as a result of social and political changes and of the 'internal' power struggle between the right and the left, the humanistic character of the few-versus-many narrative underwent a series of gradual changes. While this was very prominent regarding the parties of the right, it occurred in the Labor Party too, as reflected in progressive changes in Ben-Gurion's speeches. While the few were formerly the isolated and scorned pioneers who by the force of their will settled the land and forged a bond with it, now they are beleaguered soldiers who by their courage and tenacity overcame powerful enemies and broadened the land. At this stage, in some of Ben-Gurion's speeches Israel's past and present enemies – British, Nazis and Arabs – are equated. And whereas the end-of-days vision had formerly been one in which people came from all over to admire the Zionist work of settlement, now it is of nations coming to admire Israel's conquests. The same language is used to portray both visions; the heroes alone have changed.

In the 1930s Ben-Gurion praised 'the dazzling sight that also amazes other peoples, the sight of a people rising up from its former decline ... to a life of daily heroism and hard work'.[22] In 1956, however, after the Sinai campaign, Ben-Gurion doubted

> that there is now an army more lauded in world public opinion than the Israel Defence Forces.... The leaders of cultured and primitive peoples have asked themselves: how has this small nation withstood, for more than ten years, enemies that outnumber it several times over?... What is the explanation for this remarkable puzzle?... Many of them came to Israel to witness the concrete manifestations of this supremacy and came away astonished.[23]

The end-of-days vision is the same in both instances. However, while in the 1930s the heroes were Zionist pioneers and their heroism was the conquest of the soil, in 1956 the heroes are Israeli soldiers and their heroism is military conquest.

These changes had occurred gradually. The first signs appeared as early as 1951 in Mapai placards in which former expressions such as 'building', 'creation', 'the conquest of labour' and 'self-defence' decreased and were replaced by formerly popular Revisionist slogans such as 'Jewish statism', 'basis for military liberation', 'establishment of a real Jewish power' and 'creation of Jewish space'. While in the 1930s the Revisionists had softened the tone of their ideological positions in order to bring them more in line with the Mapai-controlled national consensus, after the War of Independence Mapai's positions moved closer to those of the right, its style and tone changing along with this drift. A 1949 Mapai election poster, for example, is even based on a poem about anonymous soldiers written by Ya'ir Stern, the leader of the Stern Gang (an extremist underground right-wing organisation). Thus the poster reads: 'To you, anonymous soldier … to you, soldier who bore the vision of the State of Israel as you went out to meet the enemy on dark nights…', a rather obvious paraphrasing of the poem's 'anonymous soldiers … without uniforms … who in the scarlet days of pogroms and bloodletting / and in the dark nights of despair…'.

Mapai placards in 1951 credited the Israeli army with fulfilling national missions that a very different kind of elite – pioneers, farmers and public servants – had been charged with before:

> [The army is the] source of the spirit and strength to carry out brave pioneering objectives of conquest and settlement … the all-powerful instrument for realising the Ingathering of the Exiles [and the] workshop for the teaching of the Hebrew language.

Similarly, the powerful leader Ben-Gurion acquired a role that had previously been filled by the entire populace. In the War of Independence, the victory was attributed to the bravery and steadfastness of the entire population. Shortly after the Sinai campaign in 1956, an election leaflet attributes victory to the power of the leader, and the nation's obedience to him:

> At that time, you were able to feel an invisible hand, slowly winding a noose around your necks. But fear did not overcome you. Vigilant and calm, you raised your eyes to the nation's leadership. You knew – everyone knew – that only an experienced and capable leadership – and it alone – would be able to extricate us from the new peril.… Your certainty was founded on a solid basis, for, after all, it was this same leadership that was able to guide a small unarmed and undefended Jewish community through the long, brutal and bloody War of Independence, to the establishment of a fully autonomous state.

The changes in the images of the army and the nation's leader were paralleled by changes in the images of opponents within the country and enemies without. Thus the way was paved for the strengthening of the combined Orthodox-Jewish–rightist narrative. The ideology that had in the past characterised the political right took hold in increasingly larger segments of the population, and with it the strength of the right also swelled.

NOTES

1. The Likud was a merger of the right-wing Herut and the Liberal Party.
2. Sites of four well-remembered Palestinian terrorist attacks in which many Israelis were killed.
3. For example, the 1930s literature of the periphery. See Chapter 1.
4. Z. Jabotinsky, 1948(a): 368. Some of the articles quoted here were gathered, in several volumes, years after they were written. The dates relate to the years in which each collection was published.
5. Jabotinsky, 1943: 16.
6. See Chapter 1, n. 20.
7. D. Ben-Gurion, 1933: 222–3; Ben-Gurion, 1935: 274.
8. Jabotinsky, 1943: 19; Jabotinsky, 1948(a): 318; Ben-Gurion, 1933: 163; Jabotinsky, 1943: 16; Ben-Gurion, 1933: 193, 162; Jabotinsky, in H. Ben-Yeruham, 1976: 1000, respectively.
9. Jabotinsky, 1947: 297.
10. Ben-Gurion, 1935: 224.
11. See, for example, Jabotinsky, in Ben-Yeruham, 1976: 525–8.
12. Ben-Gurion, 1935: 229.
13. Jabotinsky, 1947: 153.
14. The Jewish Agency is the organisation through which Jews of the Diaspora helped the *Yishuv* and the state of Israel. It was also responsible for the allocation of immigration certificates.
15. President of the World Zionist Organisation from 1905 to 1911.
16. A. Ahimeir, 1972: 28; Ahimeir, 1933; Ahimeir, 1966: 12, respectively.
17. Ahimeir, 1933; Ahimeir, 1972: 125; Ahimeir, 1933; Ahimeir, 1966: 127, respectively.
18. Ahimeir, 1966: 49.
19. Ahimeir, 1972: 187.
20. Ahimeir, 1929.
21. Ahimeir, 1972: 42; Ahimeir, 1972: 89; Ahimeir, 1966: 25; Ahimeir, 1966: 88; Ahimeir, 1972: 78, respectively.
22. Ben-Gurion, 1935: 35.
23. Ben-Gurion, 1959: 356–7.

4

THE VOICE OF THE PEOPLE: Election Propaganda, 1977–1984

INTRODUCTION

The combination of the Orthodox-Jewish and the rightist narratives became increasingly rooted in Israeli society during the 1970s and 1980s. By tracing the changes in the parties' propaganda for the elections of 1977, 1981 and 1984, different elements of this development can be observed. The tone of the propaganda in these three election campaigns, as in earlier ones and in other political struggles, was not determined only, or even mainly, by the ideologies of the contending parties. It depended, rather, on the nature and demands of the electorate, and on the models that dominated the Israeli political system and society in general.[1] As in other cases, the parties sought to strengthen their positions by using popular or prestigious texts from *belles-lettres*, theatre, television, and so on, to communicate their messages to their voters.[2]

Two main traits characterised the electorate during these years – an on-going shift to the political right, and a rapid transition to a modern and prosperous consumer society. The shift to the right manifested itself in the 1977 elections, which resulted in the Likud[3] becoming the ruling party after 30 years of Mapai-Labor hegemony. The transition to a consumer society, which had intensified after the 1967 war, was strengthened even more by the Likud's encouragement of consumerism in all strata of society, but especially in the middle and lower classes. It is generally accepted that the political discourse in these three elections was addressed mainly to members of the lower-middle class (which, as described in Chapter 3, was composed mostly of Mizrahis, or Sepharadis, that is Jews who had immigrated from Arab countries in the 1950s) and to the country's young adults. An indication of this is, the general style of the election posters and slogans, which were adapted specifically to the material and psychological needs of these two sectors. Surveys had indicated that in addition to economic security, these needs included a feeling of belonging and a basis for national pride. Before the Yom Kippur War

(1973), these needs had been satisfied by the ideology and goals of the Mapai Party and, later, by the Alignment.[4] In 1977 this role fell to the Likud.[5]

In the elections of 1981, when it was already known that the vote of the lower-middle class had tipped the scale in favour of the Likud in 1977, this group was wooed by all the political parties.[6] In the 1984 elections, after questionnaires and surveys indicated that this sector was now disillusioned with the Likud's rule and therefore constituted most of the decisive floating vote, this courtship became even more ardent. That the views of this sector are more rightist than those of the general Israeli population (which was in any case shifting towards the right during these years) was generally recognised. This explains why the Alignment came out with some of the rightist policies of the Likud in its pronouncements, and carefully avoided enunciating its own positions. It also sheds light on the Alignment's adoption of a populist style, a Likud stand-by, and the abandonment of any attempt to breathe new life into the time-worn narratives of Mapai and the historical Labor movement.

The analysis of these three election campaigns is based on party advertisements that appeared in the two largest Israeli newspapers, *Ma'ariv* and *Yedioth Ahronoth*, during the month preceding each of the elections. These were paid announcements formulated by public relations specialists on the basis of surveys that established the populace's general mood.[7] This analysis will illuminate Israeli society's development into a consumer society along with its shift to the political right. It will specifically deal with the way in which the new models initiated by the Likud after its electoral victory in 1977, especially the rightist-Jewish narrative, were embraced by other parties and, first and foremost, by the Alignment.

THE IMAGE OF THE LEADER

The head of the Likud, Menachem Begin, had for years borne the label of a 'fascist leader', one who whips up the emotions of his supporters by dramatic proclamations of nationalistic slogans. The 'fascist' label placed him at an electoral disadvantage and was one of the many factors that blocked his way to political rule. In 1973, however, the traumatic Yom Kippur War presented his party with an opportunity to depict him as an alternative to the leaders of the Labor Party, whose prestige had been severely undermined, most recently by their 'blunder' of not recognising the imminent attack that marked the onset of the Yom Kippur War.[8] This was effected by replacing the 'fascist' label with that of 'populist' which, at least in Israeli society, was not identified with fascism. The strategy adopted was to present Begin as a fatherly figure who attends to the people's needs and expresses their deepest aspirations, and is also humble and modest:

> An honest, incorruptible statesman … a lover of the Land and its People, deeply attached to them, a great believer in Zionism, a man of great experience.… A man who pursues a humble, quiet way of life, the only leader for whom the people's well-being, as opposed to his own, is important, whose real interest is the people's good and not his own. (Likud advertisement, 1973)

This presentation was devised to depict Begin as the exact opposite of the leaders of the Alignment, some of whom were deeply involved in corruption scandals and power struggles at that time. The depiction of his concern for the masses resembled the concern of a benign father for his children. This type of presentation encourages sectors of society that prefer not to think or act on their own, and to place their trust in a father-leader who would do both for them:

> We want to sleep in peace and know that up there, at the head of the Israeli Government, stands a man who knows how to navigate, who can stand firm in difficult situations, who can diffuse an atmosphere of faith, productivity and achievement. (ibid.)

The image of protective father became more and more pronounced in the course of the 1977 and 1981 campaigns. In 1984 it was used to promote Yitzhak Shamir, Begin's successor as head of the Likud and the government: 'The people of Israel as a whole are very important to him. The life of each citizen [and] the future of each child are close to his heart' (Likud advertisement, 1984).

In the 1977 and 1981 elections the Alignment, still unaware of the effectiveness of this father-figure image, continued to rely on the earlier imagery of Zionist pioneers and trail-blazing leaders, markedly shaped along the lines of the heroes of westerns. The weaker the status of these images became, the harder the Alignment tried to strengthen them by turning them into a myth. For example, in election campaigns in the country's early years Ben-Gurion's spiritual and ideological stature was emphasised by presenting him as being viewed admiringly even by enemies and rivals, and not only by those who loved him. Labor Party Chairman Shimon Peres was presented in a similar way in the 1977 elections – but from the point of view of world leaders: 'strong, decisive, able to overcome difficulties and make daring decisions. A determined man with the make-up of a leader. A man who has done much to save Israel.'

In 1981, Abba Eban, the foreign minister in the Alignment government, was described by quotes from world personalities such as the USA's Secretary of State Henry Kissinger (during Nixon's presidency), who had 'never met anyone who can match his expressive abilities'. James Reston (of the *New York Times*) said that, after listening to a debate between Abba Eban and Russian Prime Minister Alexei Kosygin, it was 'easy to understand why the Russians objected to freedom of speech', and that Eban had demolished Kosygin's claim just like the IDF (Israel Defence Forces) had demolished the Arab tanks in the desert. The repetition of the military simile used by Reston was not without design. Its purpose was to ground Eban's authority on that of the army and its officers. Such an association in both this specific case, and in others, however, was too far removed from reality to be effective as neither Shimon Peres nor Abba Eban, prominent Alignment leaders, had had military careers.

The most pathetic attempt to base a leader's crumbling authority on a by-gone myth was the presentation of Haim Bar-Lev (one of the Alignment leaders and a former Israeli army chief of staff) as a hero – a combination of biblical warrior and Hollywood cowboy who arrives just in time to prevent disaster, carries out a 'mission impossible' and saves the day. As in the example regarding Ben-Gurion, the role of others in achieving victory is replaced by the action of this single omnipotent figure. Such descriptions had been widely used after the Sinai campaign (1957) and the Six Day War (1967). Now they were used again in order to counter the new image of the Likud leader:

> The Six Day War. The Egyptians blockade Eilat. The long wait begins. The government rushes Haim Bar Lev home from Paris and appoints him Deputy Chief of Staff. When the war comes, Haim Bar Lev carries out his famous motto, 'Quickly, powerfully, and elegantly.' / The Yom Kippur War. The northern front. Bad news from all fronts. The government dispatches Haim Bar Lev, Minister of Industry

> and Trade, to the north. The ex-Chief of Staff stabilises the Golan front and restores IDF confidence as the Syrians are pushed back. / The Yom Kippur War. The southern front. The situation in the south is still critical. Haim Bar Lev is appointed commander of the front. The IDF recovers and goes on to a glorious victory. (Labor advertisement, 1981)

The use of an on-going or real-time present tense was the accepted norm for the documentary literature of Israel's wars and battles, and for radio and television reportage. The use of this grammatical tense in building up the image of a leader served to ensure that that leader is with us – now. It signified that he can be sent at any time to any dangerous front line and will succeed in attaining a permanent victory. In addition, this leader is master not only of time, but of space, an airborne superman who crosses seas and continents to bring victory. Time and space, which were dominated in the old narratives by the Jewish nation-people, are now reigned over by its leaders.

However, this glorification also strengthened the images of the Alignment's leaders as aloof and arrogant, and made it easy to undermine them, for it was viewed in the same light as the patronising attitude towards the lower, largely Sepharadi, classes that the leaders of the left had expressed in the early years of Israel's independence. By 1977, it had turned a large proportion of these classes against Labor. The use of the imagery of the earlier leaders, which did not appeal to the broad public, increased the gap between it and the Alignment leadership, a gap which the Likud was quick to decry and exploit. By 1984 the Alignment had abandoned the leader images of the past and, like the other parties, had adopted the father-image used by the Likud.

The 1984 elections were held while the Lebanon War was still going on. The campaign was carried out in a period of political uncertainty and economic insecurity that caused intense anxiety in all sectors of the society. The image of an omnipotent father-leader who could assuage the nation's anxieties appeared in the campaigns of all the parties, irrespective of their position on the political spectrum. It was especially prominent in the campaign publicity of small neophyte parties such as Yahad (led by Ezer Weizman, who would, ten years later, become the president of Israel) and Ometz (led by Yig'al Hurwitz, who, following the elections, joined Begin's government and became its finance minister). Both parties were composed mostly of break-aways from the Likud. An Ometz advertisement that appeared frequently was: 'Yig'al Hurwitz is the man who can rekindle the light of the crumbling economy / … / because Hurwitz *yig'al* [Hebrew for 'will redeem'] the economy.' An advertisement for Yahad portrayed party leader Ezer Weizmann as a comforting father speaking to the frightened citizens:

> I know you're scared. / I know how frightened you get every time the phone rings. / I know how anxious you get every time people rush to the banks. / You're scared and you're right. / But the minute you've decided to vote Yahad you can stop being scared. / There will be some people in the next government who feel just like you do. (Yahad advertisement, 1984)

The figure presented in the earlier campaigns was that of a leader who marched at the head of the camp and urged the people to follow. The new image was composed of two very different and mutually dependent components – a messianic figure promising salvation through miracles, and a loving father comforting his children and lulling them to sleep.[9] The two parts of the image come together in the anticipation of redemption that characterises the rightist-Jewish 'apocalyptic' narrative. The Zionist society of the 1920s and 1930s viewed this apocalyptic narrative, with its passivity and faith in a predestined redemption, as a negative feature of Diaspora Judaism and struggled against it. The messages of the election campaigns of the 1980s returned this narrative to a central position, endowing the leader with the role of father-messiah.

ATTITUDES TOWARDS TIME

In the campaign of 1984 the past and the future virtually disappeared from all the election propaganda; the present was the time focused on. Moreover, this was not an ordinary 'simple-present' tense, but rather a dramatic on-going moment in which the dream of a miracle and redemption is repeatedly recounted. The anticipation of imminent miraculous redemption had been propagated by the Likud in previous elections; in the political and economic uncertainty of 1984 it appeared in the advertisements of all the parties.

The disintegration of the past actually began after the Likud came to power. By 1981, after four years at the helm, the Likud was more certain of its strength and very aware of its broadened electorate, which included many of the lower-middle-class voters who had deserted the Alignment. With considerable confidence the Likud now proceeded to reconstruct the history of the state of Israel. The country's achievements prior to 1977 were thus attributed to the right (especially to Herut, the central party within the Likud), while its failures were blamed on Mapai. This involved a revision of events such as the creation and establishment of Israel, the Sinai campaign, the Six Day War and the unification of Jerusalem. Herut's decisive role in all these was emphasised by means of a formulation that presented Begin as the agent of action, although this was not the case as neither Herut nor Begin was then in power. The accounts of his actions, therefore, actually describe his passive, or sometimes active, non-interference in the events:

> You [Begin] are responsible for the prevention of civil war in Israel, during the darkest hour of oppression from without and hatred from within. / You are responsible for the reinforcement of Israel's democracy, as head of the responsible, democratic, parliamentary opposition for 29 years. / You are responsible for the national unity of the Sinai campaign period. / You are responsible, as one of its first initiators, for the formation of a National Unity Government on the eve of the Six Day War. (Likud advertisement, 1981)

Thus, the establishment of the state, winning the two wars mentioned and, in addition, preserving the nation's democracy and unity were credited to Begin and the Herut Party. To Labor was left the responsibility for the failures – the poor handling of the new-immigrant 'transit' camps in the 1950s, monopolisation of resources, favouritism and damaging the very fabric of the state through sectarianism and class distinctions. All these were injustices to which the immigrants of the 1950s, especially the Sepharadi Jews, were highly sensitive, for they still remembered them vividly and considered them unredressed grievances. The pre-state period, with which this sector of the populace was unfamiliar, virtually disappeared from the Likud's election posters and advertisements.

In the 1981 election campaign, the Alignment faced difficulties in finding a suitable approach. Most of the issues with which it could have attacked the Likud and strengthened its own position could not be used without provoking adverse reactions. It avoided taking credit for the establishment and early development of the state as these were too closely associated with memories of injustices and hardships suffered by many of the Sepharadi Jews, with whom the Alignment wished to renew a dialogue after their defection to the Likud in the 1977 election. Military victories under Mapai leadership were untenable, for the memory of its 'blunder' in the 1973 Yom Kippur War was still too fresh in the public's mind. It also had to withhold criticism of the Likud's foreign policy, which seemed to comprise one success after another (the peace treaty with Egypt in 1978 and the bombing of Iraq's nuclear reactor in 1981) and was unlikely to be accepted. It even found it hard to attack the Likud government's economic policy (which had led to galloping inflation), since it encouraged the availability of consumer goods and was therefore received with great enthusiasm. Furthermore, in fear of losing touch with a public that was leaning more and more to the right, Labor also refrained from enunciating its views on social, defence, and settlement issues in clear-cut terms. With all these paths barred, the Alignment was left with no choice but to repeat its earlier line of propaganda. It continued to invoke the achievements of the original Labor movement, while calling for a return to the social democratic and humanistic ideals of the past: 'This is a struggle for the very essence and future of a democratic, Jewish, enlightened and cultured State of Israel – the fulfilment of an age-old dream and a rebirth achieved by the Zionist movement and the Jewish people of today' (Labor advertisement, 1981).

But this rhetoric had lost its vigour. In the past it had expressed adherence to humanistic ideals within the Zionist ideology. In 1981, however, there were fateful issues in need of urgent attention on the national agenda – such as the Likud's foreign policy, and its programme of massive settlement in the West Bank and Gaza – which this rhetoric failed to address. On the contrary, it transmitted a message completely different from the one it had conveyed in the past – evasion of the real and pressing problems and escape to the safety of abstractions and clichés unrelated to current reality. In any case, any effectiveness this rhetoric may once have had was mitigated by the fact that a great part of the electorate of the 1980s, consisting largely of young adults and the now 'absorbed' new immigrants of the 1950s, had not been part of the historical Labor movement's Zionist endeavour.

This may be one of the reasons for the disappearance of 'the past' in the 1984 campaign. Labor realised it was pointless, and perhaps even counterproductive, to mention it. The Likud no longer needed it because it had succeeded in turning the past into a continuous present as it were: Labor's favouritism, monopolisation, bureaucracy and corruption were successfully portrayed as on-going iniquities that must still be fought. Thus, although the Likud had now been in power for seven years, the Labor regime was successfully depicted as one that still had to be toppled:

> The Alignment is in power. The Alignment controlled and still controls the *Histadrut* and *Hevrat Ha-ovdim* [the Histadrut-owned holding company]. / The Alignment controls television, the radio, the press. / A sensible citizen won't let a single party control all the country's power potential and the government as well. (Likud advertisement, 1984)

The obliteration of the past was surely the result of the parties' struggle for power. It succeeded in casting aspersions on the past and presenting change, the future and a new page as the 'only hope'. However, as the campaign progressed, the future, too, faded away. The advertisements mention the present and 'tomorrow', that is, only the very immediate future: 'The third power will make them keep – tomorrow – the promises they're making today' (Yahad advertisement, 1984). This gradual disappearance of a natural time scale was the result not only of party struggles and the domination of the Likud narrative, but also of the prevailing atmosphere of anxiety, which the parties actively fomented. In such an atmosphere the past seems irrelevant and the future vague and frightening. The public wanted to know what the morrow would bring, and the poll-conscious parties' reply was that the moment the right choice is made, the public will be free of its fears. Even though this is the forecast for the near future, the time of reference here is not real but rather a legendary time of miracles that will turn reality into the 'happily-ever-after' with a magic wand, and 'Then you'll wake up smiling' (Yahad advertisement, 1984).

Thus, in the parties' encounter with the needs and dictates of the campaign and the populace, the Alignment and the other parties accepted the notion of time as an everlasting present that had been introduced by the Likud in 1981. This perception merged with the old Orthodox-Jewish narrative that the right had previously appropriated, the one which perceives history as an eternal repetition of destruction and redemption driven by metaphysical rather than human forces.

THE STYLISTIC PLANE

The adoption of the Likud election propaganda was accompanied by a gradual shift in style to one used in the press, advertising and television. The Likud was the first to do this, in the election campaign of 1977, aiming its dialogue at the consumer-public, the younger sector and the lower-middle class. The Alignment, however, remained loyal to the relatively elitist literary style of its previous years, and continued its dialogue with the intelligentsia and with the cultural elite, as can be seen in the language it used in its election propaganda. The right had no previous literary tradition to which it would remain faithful, and succeeded in speaking to the lower and middle classes in their own language. In the election campaign of 1981 the Alignment abandoned its 'archaic' style and adopted the new media-speak. The rest of the parties were not long in following.

Sentence Structure

In 1984 an assertive and clipped sentence structure borrowed from news flashes, headlines and advertisements, that had appeared occasionally in previous campaigns, was extensively employed. It was used, among other reasons, to counteract the need to take real action and to present every act or step as a kind of instant miracle:

> We'll leave Lebanon. / We'll tax the government, not the citizens. / National funds will stop backing banks and start backing high-tech industries. / Income tax will go down. / The Labour Federation will participate in a social contract. / Overseas investments will be doubled. / Then you'll wake up smiling. (Yahad advertisement, 1984)

This Yahad advertisement predicts a seven-stage miracle: six swift steps must be taken, in the style of a military operation, and then it will be possible to awaken to a new and wonderful world.

The election propaganda of 1984 did not deal with values and beliefs, nor did it call for any national action; it did, rather, carry the assurance of the promised miracle. And since these announcements were formulated by public relations specialists and were aimed at an audience of passive consumers, the promised miracle was expressed in the language used for describing the acquisition of visible and tangible goods: 'The minute you decide to vote Yahad you'll be acquiring strength' (Yahad advertisement, 1984); 'If you vote Shinui [Hebrew for 'change' and the name of a centre party], you'll be getting the Alignment with changes' (Shinui advertisement, 1984); and 'In the next government you'll have Weizman' (Yahad advertisement, 1984); Weizman won't lead or guide you, nor will he urge you to follow him;

you'll simply 'have him', in the way that you have money in a safe or food in the refrigerator.

The appeal to an easily alarmed, irrational public of passive consumers resulted in a dialogue based on emotions rather than reason. The sentence 'You must have the Alignment' transmitted an almost physical sensation to the voter and differed radically from the 1981 call for positive action: 'This time you have to vote.' The appeal to the voters' emotions is clearly seen in advertisements that use visual materials. Pictures were selected to arouse fear (pressing crowds, lonely boat on great sea) or instill sensations of calm and security (flourishing agriculture, surfboard-rider on waves), and photographs of children were used to arouse feelings of beauty, hope, pleasure and warmth, or to point out a need for protection.

Sometimes 'scenic' language similar to that used in promoting tourism is employed: 'If you love the smell of tilled earth after the rain / If you love smiling oranges and gloriously blooming greenhouses / Vote Alignment.' In other words, vote Alignment and the miracle will suddenly occur and the country will turn into a picture postcard, a place to be travelled through and looked at – not a place that needs to be developed or worked at. This is a style directed towards passive consumers expecting, like a tourist visiting a foreign country, to be showered with pleasures and goods.

The content, tone and sentence structures of the advertisements thus promised an economic miracle. But this miracle was deeply intertwined with fears of disaster and downfall on the one hand, and with an even greater promise on the other – that of redemption.

Identity of the Speaker

Emulating the television-documentary style, party advertisements in the newspapers used the voter-in-the-street format to convey their messages. These messages were therefore neither doctrines issued by the party leadership nor statements based on official party positions. They were *vox populi* – the voice of the public. They called on citizens to succumb and follow, to merge with it and become 'Emet too' (*Emet* is the acronym that designates the Alignment, and is also the Hebrew word for 'truth'), or, on the other side of the political spectrum, to become part of 'the national camp' (Likud advertisement).

As early as the elections of 1959, a citizen from the rank-and-file appeared to present his or her problems and opinions, but before 1977 this occurred only occasionally. Even then such speakers, especially in

Alignment advertisements, were obviously not ordinary interlocutors, but carefully selected 'models'. The voice of the people became a more critical force in the Likud announcements, especially in 1977. Although the Likud was still unaware of the electoral strength of the young and lower-middle-class voters, and thus did not address them directly, it marked its openness to them by inviting them, at rallies and other public events, to express themselves, in their own language, about their own difficulties.

Thus, rather than a party spokesman, it is a voice from the rank-and-file that acclaims the leader: 'We want Menachem Begin' (Likud advertisement, 1981). And, in the same vein, the vernacular is usually preferred for laudatory descriptions: 'The camera is not for him, and he is not hooked up to a microphone' (Likud advertisement, 1981). The Likud's advertisements, more than those of the Alignment, employed popular genres such as comic strips, magazine polls, quizzes and sketches. The Alignment also attempted to make use of this popular style, but its long tradition of dialogue with a literate, rational public augured a clumsy result. For example, the advertisement that begins 'Shimon, we're counting on you' was designed to convey a warm, intimate relationship with the Alignment leader Shimon Peres through its use of familiarities. This style of speech, however, was remote from the current jargon, and the phrase itself was typical of an exclusive clique of old buddies who had shared the experiences of the War of Independence. Such a tone was bound to alienate any segment of the public that did not identify with this exclusive group.

In 1981 Labor was still not aware that the voice of the people, in and of itself, could be used as a message. By 1984 all the parties were using it. They either presented it as a voice speaking in the first person or in embedded speech:

> You know better than anyone else what a sick economy means. You're the one who has to make do with a shrinking salary as you anxiously watch prices rising. The economic situation at home and at work is tough, really tough. Loved ones go to the army and you wait in fear. The future is unclear, unstable, and maybe even insecure. (Yahad advertisement, 1984)

In this text (which uses the Hebrew feminine 'you') the speaker is a fatherly figure who reads the mind and heart of an average woman and expresses her anxieties. To do this he adopts her own language. The result emphasises the identification of the authoritative speaker with the bewildered and troubled woman. However, the speaker does not offer any guidance or suggestions. Consequently, the very act of identification with, and acceptance of, her fears constitutes the central message of the advertisement.

The voice-of-the-people format was used mostly in radio and television spots. Ordinary citizens interviewed for election propaganda in the media tended to imitate the language used by party leaders at political rallies. In these spots, the imitation of Likud leaders was much more natural than that of Alignment leaders. Supporters speaking on the Alignment's televised propaganda repeated terms such as 'the morass of Lebanon' or 'a war of choice', copied from the oratory of that party's elite. Coming from the mouths of ordinary citizens this jargon seemed artificial and overly sophisticated. However, when speakers for the Likud imitated Begin's oratory style the result was convincing, because Begin himself, in his speeches, used the language of the rank-and-file. Sometimes, however, even supporters of the Alignment used the style of the Likud:

> It's high time the population living in public housing punished the Likud and sent them back to the opposition. The people shouldn't let them get away with their arrogance and their complacency. Let them sit in the opposition for a while; it won't hurt 'em. (a televised interview promoting Labor)

It is ironic that the formulation in this spot is an almost verbatim repetition of Begin's frequent exhortations accusing Labor of arrogance and suggesting that its leaders be punished by being 'sent to the opposition'. Clearly a citizen using Begin's language reveals that his empathy is with him even if the views he is voicing are anti-Likud.

The forced, overly sophisticated style of the Alignment was especially evident in televised interviews with Labor leaders, where there were obvious attempts on the part of ordinary people to imitate an educated style of speech. In the course of a televised question-and-answer evening with Shimon Peres, a young girl says, in flawless Hebrew: 'My name is Claire and I live in Kfar Saba. If, with the people's help, the Alignment attains power, will you help the elderly?' While the well-being of the elderly is undoubtedly not Claire's most burning interest, even if it were she would probably not express it this way. The question itself, and the wording, had obviously been dictated from above. Peres's answer testifies to this: 'Thank you, Claire. I see that you're a wonderful little girl and that you keep one of the ten commandments, "Honour thy father and thy mother".' Both question and answer seem to have been prepared by a party copywriter.

The right could more easily adopt the style, tone, and values of the middle and lower classes because it did not have a strong tradition of dialogue with the literate or intellectual elite. When the Alignment realised how difficult it would be to fight the Likud for the votes of this sector of the electorate, it hired the popular *Ha-gashash Ha-hiver* entertainment group for its television campaign. This trio had enjoyed great success on the stage, radio and television for many years, and there was widespread use and imitation of the idioms it coined and its jokes, style and punch-lines. While it was an integral part of the Israeli folk culture, this group's popularity was also due to the extent to which it expressed the style and atmosphere typical of the lower-middle classes, while directing its barbs at the distant, alien culture of the elite. This trio's skits had given society's lower strata a notable degree of self-respect at the expense of the upper classes. When the trio was hired by the Alignment, some of their well-known skits were redesigned for the election campaign and were adapted to identify the Alignment with the lower classes and their culture and the Likud with the upper classes, and to focus its humorous but biting attacks on the Likud. One sketch, for example, mocks Likud leaders pretending to enjoy spicy oriental dishes (in order to ingratiate potential Sepharadi voters). In the original skit, of which this was a take-off, the group mocked bourgeois good manners, while in the election skit, it mocks the forced good manners of the Likud leaders. The fun and humour that overturn the social hierarchy, lowering the high and elevating the low, are not used here for social commentary, but to ridicule the Likud.

Employing this popular entertainment trio in its election campaign enabled the Alignment to establish contact with the lower-middle class through models with which this public was familiar. In doing this, the Alignment participated in the gradual transformation of Israel's formerly highly literate electioneering style to a popular one. This was but one of the many processes which led the entire political system gradually to adopt the elements of the Likud's election propaganda.

The analysis of the changes in the texts and style of Israel's election propaganda thus sheds light on the entire range of changes in the nation's master narratives. These changes include the transition from the figure of a leader who guides the nation to that of a leader who expresses the citizens' fears and desires; the transition from the perception of time as leading from past goals to their accomplishment in the future to time perceived as miraculous and legendary; and, finally, the transition from the dynamism and action of the entire nation and its leaders to a passive nation's fear of destruction and its hopes for a miraculous redemption.

NOTES

1. The hegemonic models are, in this case, those of the leading party. According to these models, the other forces in the field shape their stands by either revolt or identification. See P. Bourdieu, 1980.
2. See I. Even-Zohar, 1990, who analyses this phenomenon of the system's adoption of models according to its needs.
3. See Chapter 3, n.1.
4. The Alignment was a merger between Mapai and another leftist party, Ahdut Ha'avoda (The Unity of Labour).
5. See S. Weiss, 1981. On the ideology of the Likud, see Y. Shavit, 1986, 1987.
6. Weiss, 1981.
7. Since all party election advertisements were published simultaneously in all the major newspapers, their names are not specified. The advertisements were designed and formulated by public relations professionals in consultation – and often in vehement argumentation – with party representatives. This usually resulted in a product that was a compromise between the two sides. Some of the televised compaign spots will be analysed for comparison.
8. The simultaneous Egyptian and Syrian attacks on the unprepared Israeli forces in Sinai and on the Golan Heights respectively resulted in an initial set-back and a very large number of Israeli casualties, although the war itself ended in an Israeli victory.
9. The messages delivered by the election propaganda were not necessarily in line with the party's ideology. In the 1984 elections Yig'al Hurwitz called for real concessions in order to rescue the country from its economic crisis. The fact that he, too, found it necesssary to use the messianic image is indicative of his awareness of the voters' needs.

5

A PEOPLE THAT DWELLS APART: Newspaper Coverage of the Lebanon War, 1982

INTRODUCTION

On 3 June 1982 Israel's ambassador to Great Britain, Sh'lomo Argov, was seriously injured by Palestinian terrorists. On the following two days Israeli planes bombed targets in Lebanon, leading to reprisal Katyusha rocket attacks on the northern town of Kiriyat Sh'monah. This, in turn, led to the Israeli invasion of Lebanon, in the course of which the Israeli army reached Beirut and put it under siege. Israel's war in Lebanon, the first assessed by the public as one initiated by Israel and not forced upon it, aroused vehement debate within the country. There was a considerable lack of consensus with regard to several of its goals, such as the destruction of the infrastructure of the Palestine Liberation Organisation (PLO), then strongly based in Lebanon, and the establishment of a new political order in Lebanon. However, during the very first weeks of the war, when neither its real objectives nor the extent of the casualties were known to the general public, the military action was generally regarded as a defensive operation and had broad collective support. Yet even then the government's policy was strongly opposed by various anti-war groups. The polemics for and against this war assumed the form of a struggle between two narratives that had dominated Israeli society before the war itself – the rightist narrative which was merged with the Jewish orthodox one and had recently become a dominant element in the Israeli culture, and the humanistic-universal narrative that had always been embedded in the Zionist ideology.

These two narratives, although mutually antagonistic, were forced into a complex, though also symbiotic, relationship. The rightist-Jewish narrative could not ignore the widely accepted humanistic one, and the humanistic narrative had to contend with the growing strength of the rightist-Jewish one. A similar struggle between these narratives had taken place earlier in the polemics surrounding the Six Day War, but it was more prominent in the controversy surrounding the Lebanon War. This chapter will attempt to explore the struggle between the two narratives during the first three months of the war, through reportage and interviews published in the four main daily Israeli newspapers (*Ha'aretz*, *Davar*, *Yedioth Aharonoth* and *Ma'ariv*) and one magazine (*Ba-mahane*). On both sides of the polemical barricade there were not only journalists, but prominent authors. Expressing the rightist-Jewish narrative were Aharon Megged and Haim Guri, the latter a well-known poet whose works are taught in schools and recited in important public ceremonies. Both of them were associated with the generation that had fought in the War of Independence. The humanistic narrative was expressed by younger writers such as Amos Oz and A. B. Yehoshua, two of the most prominent writers of the succeeding generation who started writing in the 1960s. They were joined by others such as Amos Kenan and Adam Baruch. Another author of the War of Independence generation, S. Yizhar, who had always deviated from the accepted norms of the time, wrote some reportage during the Lebanon War. In his attacks on the old-new narrative that dominated the Lebanon War, Yizhar was actually continuing in the path he had pioneered in the 1930s and continued in the War of Independence, when he expressed the accepted narratives of the time, but criticised and parodied them at the same time.[1]

Opposition to the Lebanon War was especially strong in the poetry of the time, with authors such as Natan Zach, Dalia Rabikovich and Meir Viseltir among the most dominant, along with other less recognised names. Hundreds of poems critical of the war were published in the daily newspapers, and some in anthologies, most notably one compiled by two scholars of literature, Hanan Hever and Moshe Ron (1983).

Somewhat later this opposition also found expression in the cinema, in films such as 'Cherry Seasons' and 'Ricochets'. This chapter, however, will deal only with the more immediate expressions of this opposition that appeared in reportage during the first three months of the war. The anti-war newspaper writings of A. B. Yehoshua and Amos Oz will not be analysed as they were opinion columns and not reportage.

ISRAEL VERSUS THE WORLD

The rightist-Jewish narrative was not explicitly articulated in the press. On the contrary, a humanistic, egalitarian ethos is clearly reflected in most of these newspaper articles. The polemic struggle between the two elements can be discerned only by analysing the relationship between the texts and the subtexts within the articles. Although articles that support the rightist-Jewish narrative are explicit in their adherence to humanism, this latter attitude loses some of its validity when it is organised within the deep structure of the rightist-Jewish narrative. In this structure, proof of the Israeli humanist ethos is not necessarily derived from the facts, actions, and empirical evidence that confirm its own humanistic behaviour, but rather from the inhumanity and contempt for human life displayed by 'others'. These 'others' are all the nations of the world, treated as one great, abstract generality that serves as a basis for defining Israeli uniqueness. An example is provided in the journalist Yair Amikam's interview with two soldiers. One of them says:

> Look, people are sitting here, in Lebanon, and talking with you about how the civilian is more important to us, in the army, than the soldier. It's simply unbelievable. Did anyone in the United States consider how many civilians would be killed when they decided to drop atom bombs on Hiroshima and Nagasaki? In the invasion of Normandy did anyone think about the women and children? … My headline for the whole operation is 'The IDF [Israel Defence Force], Army of Peace'.[2]

The 'others' in this example are not real; they exist only as the abstract opposites of ethical, humane Israeli-ness. Their existence is mentioned frequently to serve as an off-stage foil, consisting of anything and anyone that is 'other', and whose purpose is to underscore everything that the Israeli is not:

> The shouting of victors was not seen here; it's not an account of 'Glory, Glory Hallelujah'. This isn't Vietnam or Cambodia. The IDF is a special army; you probably won't find soldiers like the IDF's in any other army in the world.[3]

In all such cases the 'others' serve as a distant echo of non-Jews, who glorify their heroes, exult in their victories, or act with cruel inhumanity to the vanquished. Within such a structure the positive qualities of the Israelis are defined in terms of the negative qualities of others, and facts are powerless to affirm or contradict them. It is the structure of contrast, rather than facts, that establishes their existence. Thus, the speaker establishes the superior qualities of the Israelis on the basis of the moral inferiority of the others: 'In any other country the man would have been shot. Here, no one dared open fire.' This done, he feels free to suggest a revision of the facts and adds 'over-caution, in my opinion'.[4]

In all these instances, it is not the enemy that is negated; that is a natural phenomenon in wartime. The entity being negated is the entire world, that is, anyone who is not Jewish, not Israeli. This 'entire world' had been considered a moral partner in Israel's struggle to achieve victory in the War of Independence. Following the Six Day War, and especially after the Yom Kippur War, it appears with increasing frequency as an abstract and total adversary. The first signs of this can be detected in the press of the Six Day War. Most of the articles written in this war are replete with praise for the 'Israeli uniqueness' and stress the gap between those defined as the Chosen People and those defined as the Rest of the World. Thus, Haim Guri declares in *Yedioth Aharonoth*: 'The most justified war ever ... no other nation and no other people in the history of the world has ever fought one like it ... a special privilege that does not fall to every country.' The journalist Yig'al Lev, writing in *Ma'ariv*, is even more definitive:

> It is apparent that the Jews will never succeed in being an army of conquest in the same way that we have seen other armies.... We who are fighting here are teaching the world a new lesson in how to be conquerors.... Soldiers who give a kid water to drink, a company commander who looks for the mother of a crying child.... These simple and natural boys are showing the world how the Jewish fighter behaves when he conquers a land.[5]

In these and many other articles written during the Six Day War, the Chosen People are described as a model for all of the nations of the world. In doing this they follow a well-known formula used during and immediately after the War of Independence. In the course of time this formula underwent a transformation, the result of which was that the contrast between Israel and 'the others' intensified. This is exemplified by Menachem Begin's speeches, although the basis for rejecting 'the others' in these speeches was a mythic dichotomy of light and darkness. In the press accounts analysed here, the basis is the Israeli humanist ethos.

ISRAEL VERSUS THE ARAB WORLD

Within this monolithic world front of all 'the others', invoked as a means of defining the positive Israeli qualities, the direct adversaries were the Palestinian Arabs. The style and terminology used in Israel's previous wars to negate Arabs were also utilised in the Lebanon War. However, in this war Lebanese citizens were the victims of military actions that were not aimed directly against them. Thus, the Lebanese people posed the greatest threat to the humanist components within this narrative. The writers and their interlocutors all recognised and expressed the pain and sorrow they felt about the injustice of what was inflicted on them. Despite this, they unconsciously and indirectly identified the Lebanese with the rest of the world, thus placing them in the same negative category as 'the others'. Lebanon loses its identity as a nation by being described as 'a land of tribes, factions and splinters, of ethnic groups and clans, where all wage war against all' and 'devour one another'; and where 'the only common denominator is avarice'.[6]

This characterisation of Lebanon as a non-nation is constructed almost as a negative of the Israeli image. The articles attribute to the Lebanese some of the traits of pre-Israeli Jews: they do not fight, they are passive, they do not struggle for independence or national honour – traits that had also been ascribed to Arabs during the War of Independence. One of the soldiers says: 'I felt sorry for them. To me a people that doesn't fight for its independence and its honour is not fit to be a people.'[7] The Lebanese are presented as a nonentity not only on a national level but also on an individual level when the devastation of Lebanon is depicted as a game, a picture or an exercise in pure aesthetics. In an almost offhand manner the terror they are undergoing is blunted and converted into a mere show, something on display. A journalist sweeping through Lebanon discovers temporary refugee camps that look like 'lots of people having a picnic in the forest or on the beach'. Hungry children are described as at play: 'The soldiers toss sweets or pieces of bread at them, and the children leap into the air as if playing basketball.' Shattered towns are depicted as 'sets for a surrealistic disaster movie' and wounded children are 'like propaganda posters of the crudest kind'. The reporter takes a stroll to find out whether 'the Paris of the Middle East is really burning', and discovers that 'for the time being at least, it isn't'.[8]

The entire country is described in aesthetic terms, like tour guides prattling excitedly about the scenery and ignoring the living people in its midst. Furthermore, the journalists display a fascination for the villas, the Mercedes-Benz automobiles, the private swimming pools and an overall similarity to Switzerland or Beverly Hills. This enthusiasm ultimately causes the reader to ignore the specific political-historical facts of the war and its bloody reality. It presents the country as pure entertainment exclusively at the disposal of the hedonistic tourist, a picture postcard fashioned by an experienced artist. It is therefore filled with tourist attractions rather than daily life, with aesthetic sights rather than a real and complex existence. This mode of description, borrowed from the genre of travelogues,[9] is combined with other diversions that de-legitimise the existence of the Lebanese people.

In all these cases, the national and humanistic Israeli essence constitutes the supreme truth. It is contrasted with the non-existence of 'the others', who are depicted as being a mere game or theatre, a negative phantom. The fact that most of the articles are silent with regard to the viewpoints of all others, not just those of Israel's adversaries, only serves to make those others even more unreal.

Thus, on this Lebanese battlefield a kind of rear-guard action was carried out, one meant to safeguard the combination of two narratives – the humanistic one and the one that separates Israel from the rest of the world. But in this action the humanistic ethic was deprived of one of its central principles – the universal equality of human beings – and was mobilised for a struggle to prove that Israelis are superior to other peoples, a claim that by definition is alien to that same lauded ethic. The tension between these two approaches had already existed in the past and had been revealed in articles that were written during the War of Independence. In the Lebanon War it became a central and dominant issue.

DEMONSTRATING ISRAEL'S HUMANNESS: SPEECH VERSUS ACTION

The role played by humanist components in this narrative can also be detected in analyses of Israeli soldiers' conversations, which reveal guilt about the violation of humanist values as a result of the war. Such conversations, very common during and after previous wars, expressed the confusion of young Israelis who had been nurtured on humanist values but did not adhere to them during the war.[10] This sensitivity to human values, however, like other expressions of the humanist ethic during the Lebanon War, is contrasted with actions that refute it. When choosing between words and actions, the soldiers choose actions: 'But along with the misgivings and the confusion ... if called [the Israeli soldier] will go, even to Lebanon, even to a combat unit.' The soldiers' deliberations and moral qualms, that seem to be divorced from their acts, are actually closely connected to them. They license these acts and provide an apology for their commission: 'We're not bloodthirsty – just the opposite.' In this way the soldiers establish their position for the humanistic ethic within the bounds of which they express the other view reflected in their actions: 'But if it's war, we didn't volunteer for combat units [in order] to stay at the rear. If it's war, then we want to be at the front.'[11]

The tension between words and actions is even more pronounced when it concerns the journalists rather than the soldiers being interviewed. Thus Aharon Bachar, a leading journalist for the newspaper *Yedioth Aharonoth*, first describes his own compunctions: 'Whether I'm right or wrong, for or against, I'm lost and confused,' and Haim Guri, upon viewing the bombed city of Beirut, adds:

> Suddenly ... from my place at the sidelines, I grasped the horror [of the bombing of Beirut]. The disaster made my blood run cold.... Yes, there is such a moment of fear and regret in the very midst of a thrust forward – as if it wasn't us, as if it was someone else there in that city.[12]

Such words express the writers' confusion through the perspective of their humanist values. Their confusion is resolved when they choose to identify with the soldiers: 'I'm here because all these people are here, even if they're confused and unsure and tense.... This war began in controversy. I want to be with the men, to share their fate.' The conclusions drawn from the writers' deliberations are decisive: 'So when dawn came we decided to make it to our forces as fast as we could, to be with them.' The wish to be part of 'our forces' is also implied in the journalists' adoption of military slang, in the uniforms they donned, and in descriptions of their own movements in combat terms: 'We speed through Tyre and bivouac on the outskirts of Sidon.'[13]

The triumph of action over words is clearly revealed when the writer draws an explicit comparison between the army's dynamic, active deeds and the 'futile' talk that characterises the home front. Such comparisons express the writers' scorn for the 'passive babblers' and 'bleeding hearts' who engage in moral musings without understanding the real war. Aharon Bachar, in Sidon with the paratroopers who attacked the forward positions, asks:

> But who am I to tell Tel Aviv what goes on in Sidon?... I don't envy them, especially the know-it-all journalists ... because in this war they're obsolete.... When we went into Beirut they sat in Tel Aviv and told us what we were seeing and feeling.... It was funny to be in Beirut and hear them arguing heatedly for or against taking Damour. When we were in Damour they argued about taking Tyre and Sidon.... The journalists and politicians are all ready for the Yom Kippur War [nine years earlier]. This time they're not going to be taken by surprise.[14]

METAPHYSICAL STRUCTURE OF TIME: BETWEEN DESTRUCTION AND REDEMPTION

The new narrative, a combination of the rightist and the Jewish orthodox ones, is also manifested in the shaping of the time dimensions in the articles. The causal historical time continuum that dominated the writing of the past (for example, the journalism of the War of Independence) is replaced in the journalistic reports of the Lebanon War by two significant antipodal concepts: destruction and redemption. Thus the nation's past is presented as the collective trauma of previous wars, pogroms and the Holocaust, while its future is portrayed as absolute redemption. The only memories acknowledged in most of these articles are those of devastation and disaster. They see the past as pure shame, a trauma that can be healed only by absolute redemption, which would 'wipe out the shame of the Yom Kippur War once and for all'.[15] The frustrations of past military actions such as the 1956 Sinai campaign, and the 1978 Operation Litani[16] would thus be nullified, and the flagrant arrogance that followed the Six Day War and the shame for the blunder of the country's leadership in the Yom Kippur War would be erased from memory.

In contrast to devastation, the dramatic moment of conquest is depicted as a quasi-religious moment, a miracle accompanied by lightning and voices, darkness and storms, the burning bush and the appearance of an angel:

> [First] the longer-than-expected flicker in the mist and a stop short at the edge of West Beirut. Then there is darkness. [The storm breaks and the people hear the voices.] And suddenly we were in the eye of the storm.... We couldn't see the hits, only their sounds kept reaching us. Finally the quaking earth opens up.[17]

This type of description had appeared frequently in the Six Day War and was developed in subsequent hostilities. A description by Aharon Megged in *La-merhav* during the Six Day War is an example of this type:

> This war stopped the sun in its orbit. It seemed that all the powers above were taking part in it. If war was being waged in the skies, then it was not the air force alone that was fighting; and if all the armies of the land, then it was not the Israeli army alone. The events that rapidly succeeded one another did not seem like signs and portents ... the entire space was filled with biblical verses, biblical prophesies, psalms, kabbalistic [that is, occultic] homilies, mystic symbols.[18]

This dramatic perception of time was developed in the years that followed, and in the Lebanon War was expressed in a plot structure that propelled its heroes in sudden turnabouts between two points only – death and rebirth. Thus the historical poles of destruction and redemption were paralleled in the individual life and death of each soldier. Accordingly, and irrespective of their actual sequence, the events tend to be ordered by the plot so that descriptions of fear, injury and death always appear just before those of moments of triumph, of hardships overcome, of healing and rebirth. Depictions of death accompany descriptions of misgivings, fear and wounds; depictions of life are scattered throughout those of triumph and perseverance. The entire structure of the article turns into an upheaval leading from death to rebirth.

Such tales of rebirth dictate the organisation of parts or even whole articles. In an interview by the reporter Avi Valentine for the daily *Ha'aretz*, Dr Hezi, a physician treating war casualties, is harrowed by the deaths of nineteen-year-olds. The text, however, rather than belabouring this point, jumps quickly to the miracles of modern medicine, which 'functioned remarkably well' and brought the wounded back to life. Other parts of the same article move from soldiers' indecision and fear to their complying bravely with orders and setting out for battle. The article as a whole begins with the dead and wounded and ends with victory, the power of medicine and survival. Similarly, another article begins by describing the funeral of a soldier, advances to an account of the squad's loss and burial of nine of its men, and ends with a glorification of the brigade and its strength and ability to overcome obstacles by virtue of the profound camaraderie. This enables it 'to resurrect itself from the ashes'.[19]

Such perseverance is sometimes described as a revelation, thus enhancing its religious aura. A soldier named Haim Avitzur fears that the war is pointless: 'All these dead, and for what?' Nevertheless, he continues fighting and, at the article's end, reaches an ancient synagogue with the biblical verse 'I have set the Lord always before me' inscribed over the doorway. 'At that moment', we are told, 'the loose ends came together for Haim Avitzur, with the growing sense that, after all, it hadn't all been in vain.'[20]

In many cases, these sharp and dramatic movements in time are accompanied by similar jumps in space, such as a sudden leap taking the IDF to the outskirts of Beirut from the distant village of Alei. Giant leaps of this type are depicted as almost divine triumphs over time, sharply illuminating the rebirth of the Israeli soldier who rises, phoenix-like, from the midst of defeat and loss. In various interviews, soldiers repeatedly stress the miraculous nature of this movement: 'The IDF outflanked the enemy in 24 hours. We started at Kibbutz Misgav Am and now we're outside Beirut. Who would have thought this possible a week ago?'[21]

METAPHYSICAL FORCES

In the case of the treatment of time, there is a seemingly inextricable contradiction between the rightist and Orthodox-Jewish elements of the narrative: total faith in the Israeli army's ability to control events is inconsistent with reliance on metaphysical forces that propel events forward in a miraculous, precipitous fashion. This contradiction is resolved, however, when the army itself is portrayed as a divine force. A portrayal of this type, too, is not new and had been especially pervasive in the press reports of the Six Day War. The reporter Gavriel

Tzifroni, writing in *Ma'ariv*, described the IDF's entry into East Jerusalem in 1967 thus:

> Yesterday the messiah arrived in Jerusalem – tired, grey, and riding on the back of a tank. He led a column of armoured vehicles forward as Arab mortars showered shells upon them.... The messiah was wearing an army uniform this time. An IDF soldier, a Jewish warrior.... I saw him. And so did many others.[22]

In the Lebanon War this form was consolidated and incorporated into the perception of history as driven by metaphysical forces, the most prominent of these being the army commanding officer. Against the background of babbling on the home front and the vacillations of enlisted men, this officer shows his presence here in a silence that bespeaks a towering truth. Hesitations and uncertainties are juxtaposed against an unuttered truth, one that assumes a mystical, religious dimension – the same dimension imparted to the political leader in the election advertisements in 1984.

The military commanders are strong-but-silent types whose rare utterances seem to embody secret knowledge: 'I play with ideas of what I would say to [the soldiers] if I were in [the officer's] place and I can't come up with a single idea', says Aharon Bachar. Then, after hearing the officer speak with his men, he admits that he 'stood among the soldiers and ... silently saluted this commander.... Blessed is the army whose commanders are like him.'[23]

The ultimate status of the commander is not usually revealed immediately to the ordinary civilian (despite the numerous decipherable signs supplied). Consequently, it does not inspire adoration at first: 'I have to admit that although I didn't doubt any of what he said, I thought a good deal of it was a pilot's fortitude. Only later did I realise how right he had been.'[24] In another article an officer's terse prediction is accepted as prophetic foresight, although not at once:

> 'The war,' the commander dictated, 'is inevitable.' 'I don't understand,' replied the secretary as she interrupted her note-taking. 'The war', the commander repeated, 'is inevitable.' And the soldiers, like the secretary, nodded their heads in unison.

This commander, using the charismatic light of truth rather than mere words, convinces the non-believers: 'I believed Colonel A ... because of the way he presented this description.' Indeed, the moment belief in the officer has been established, the journalist, like any good believer, can sense his presence: 'Although I hadn't seen Colonel A, I knew he was at the air force base commanding our planes.' He controls operations like a distant and invisible god whose pounding heart powers all life:

> The nerve centre of Operation Peace for the Galilee[25] is in a stone house surrounded by pines. Around it are similar buildings, creating a pastoral, rural atmosphere.... [The exterior seems quite ordinary but] Inside, in the war room ... beats the pulse of the battles being fought elsewhere.[26]

It is to such a unique, all-powerful commander that one would naturally turn when in need, as he knows his soldiers through and through and understands them:

> Only one man can control the dallying and cut through the dead wood. That man is Raful [IDF Chief of Staff Rafael Eitan]. That's because Raful is a real soldier, maybe the best-loved soldier in the whole army. He's an insider and he can look straight into the heart of his people.[27]

In their effort to bestow a mantle of sanctity upon the entire army, the writers sometimes use the expressions of admiration and awe they heard from Jewish inhabitants of Lebanon. Aharon Bachar, for example, selects an old Jew to describe the Israeli army:

> And then he cried out: 'Hear O Israel' – and embraced those boys; he took some coins and candy out of his pockets to give to them and clung, with trembling hands, to the armoured vehicles. As the iron chariots rumbled into the city, his voice was lost in the uproar. The old Jew, about 80 years old, stood and trembled at the roadside as the long column passed by and he surely must have had the same thoughts that came to the ancient prophet: 'My father, my father, the chariot of Israel and the horsemen thereof.'[28]

Although Bachar's declared positions were identified with the Israeli left, this report is no different from those of writers of the political centre or right. The inaugural flight of the Lavi (an Israeli-developed war plane), for example, was described quite similarly by Ge'ula Cohen, a leader of the extreme right-wing party Hat'hia:

> With the same love and the same clinging attachment [with which] my father embraced and consecrated the Scroll of the Law – from which, he believed, all of the life and life spirit of this nation were derived – so … those who dreamt, designed and built the Lavi, embraced and loved and clung to it.[29]

On their surface level the articles written about the Lebanon War express belief in the dynamic force of the Israeli army. But beyond the words, the old faith in metaphysical forces that led Jewish history from destruction to redemption can readily be glimpsed. The rightist and Orthodox-Jewish elements have been combined in these texts to form a new plot, a new narrative.

CRACKS IN THE STRUCTURE

As the war in Lebanon dragged on, the writers began to express doubts regarding its course and ultimate goals. These doubts did not undermine the narrative or the plot on which it was based, and can be perceived only in the facts left out, forgotten or contradicted. An analysis of letters written from the battlefield (and published in the daily newspaper *Ma'ariv*) serves as an example.[30] The first pieces are tightly organised, leading from fears and difficulties to resolution and victory. The writer of the letter even includes fictitious victories by mentioning battles he knows of only by hearsay: 'The Beaufort [Castle] has been taken', 'Tyre is surrounded', 'They're pushing on towards Beirut.' The structure, leading so confidently from hardships to triumph, from death to rebirth, does not allow contemplation of anything that might damage its message – such as the dead and wounded. These are mentioned in passing in the middle of the plot, before the account of conquest and victory, or at the end of each piece in the form of a postscript: 'I forgot: our forces have suffered six wounded so far', or 'Oh, and another thing, one of our pilots was taken prisoner, and at this point, that's what counts.' Also, 'By the way, a terrorist unit hit a vehicle with rocket-propelled-grenade fire around noon and one of the soldiers was wounded.'[31]

The fighting in Lebanon continued for much longer than expected and the well-formed plot began to lose its momentum, its central axis breaking up into isolated scenes. At this stage, the dead and wounded move from postscript to centre, or from mid-plot to the end. Many articles now end with reports of death, even when these did not occur during the course of the incident described. In order to do this, the writer has to digress from the time and space of the events. Articles like these seem to be structured along familiar lines, describing heroic life-saving medical procedures on the field of battle, but ending with the dark truth of the death of the wounded soldier. In one case, for example, two tanks were hit in battle and one of the soldiers was injured. In a heroic rescue effort the wounded soldier was evacuated from the firing line. Thus, the rescue succeeded; the soldier was evacuated. Only in the very last lines is this happy end betrayed when the reader is informed that 'the armoured troop carrier evacuating the soldier was hit by a missile and the injured soldier was killed'. Another report describes a complicated and dangerous tracheotomy, performed by a field surgeon under fire. At the end of the write-up, however, the officer saved by this life-saving procedure is reported to have died in the helicopter *en route* to the hospital.[32]

THE HUMANIST NARRATIVE

The texts written in the style of the rightist-Jewish narrative, which had filled the newspapers during the first three months of the war, were attacked and already impugned in the war's first stages by articles drawing on humanistic and universal ideas. As the war continued in its fitful course and the magnitude of the casualties incurred and the suffering inflicted on civilians were revealed, articles of this type increased, becoming part of a political, literary and journalistic attack on the government's policy. This attack is articulated in many cases as one against the rightist-Jewish narrative. The articles written in the humanistic mode attempt to describe the horrors of the war as viewed by the Arab, a viewpoint totally different from the one used to portray them in the earlier articles written in the rightist-Jewish mode: 'If anyone comes back from Lebanon and says "It's not so bad", don't believe them', Yizhar writes. And his own riposte to this is:

> Not that bad as opposed to what? As opposed to complete and utter devastation.... How would they describe that devastation and in what words, if it by chance befell their city, their neighbourhood ... if their own houses had collapsed and were smoking in ruin?[33]

The view expressed here sees the Arab as a person, a real being, and not a game or a theatrical play. Picturesque descriptions and aesthetic attitudes are attacked by such pieces. Yizhar's report from Lebanon exemplifies this kind of writing: 'No, not landscapes and picturesque villages, not mountains and cedars. There are no landscapes in Lebanon, there is only suffering.... Whoever sees landscapes in Lebanon today shows cruelty and insensitivity.'[34]

Writers such as Yizhar attempted to undermine the aesthetic mode of description by either avoiding such descriptions altogether or by parodying them. The article from which the above excerpt was taken was entitled 'Postcards from Lebanon', but it contained no descriptions whatsoever. Its writer traversed Israeli-occupied Lebanon admonishing and warning rather than describing. The writer and journalist Adam Baruch breaks with accepted models when he begins with a description of wonderful landscapes, thus arousing expectations of standard picturesque commentary. This is broken when the article veers abruptly to painful statements:

> From the gorgeous verandah of the restaurant one can see the boys at play.... There, on the verandah overlooking the divine, green, lush, thrilling landscape ... you hear of a brigade commander who [because he has refused to participate in the invasion of Beirut] has asked to be relieved of his post.... The blue lake stretches out before you as you look through the window.... Whoever was killed there later, was killed on his own.[35]

The humanistic journalism tried to expand the Israeli identity to include a broad universality, and strove to sense the existence, suffering and agony of others. Such efforts, however, were not always successful. While they did present life and the individual as ultimate values rather than as symbols that serve a specific national cause, they presented them in such sweeping generalisations that the underlying existence of Palestinians and Lebanese as individuals or as nations was blurred:[36]

> At any given moment, somewhere in the world, there are people suddenly and fearfully packing belongings and hustling children into whatever they have at hand, abandoning their homes and setting out in whatever direction.... The moves are always bigger than any individual, the strategies are greater than any whole life and death ... and from a general standpoint

> all this is always just people subject to disaster ... and all that was formerly divided into beliefs and opinions, religions and ethnic groups, justifying or incriminating evidence – is now ground together.[37]

When the people who are suffering are not specified, the distinction between conqueror and conquered, and between victor and vanquished, is lost: 'Woe to the conquerors and woe to the conquered. Woe to us all.'[38]

In a few cases the articles attempt to lend the Arab something specific by comparing him to the Jew: 'A nation outside the nations – absorbed nowhere, wanted nowhere, the lepers of the world.'[39] But this attempt still leaves the Arab as an abstract entity, one that was previously lost in the universal generalisation and is lost again within the Jewish identity. As they seek out the 'other' – the Palestinian or the Lebanese – the writers succeed only in finding themselves – an Israeli identity that construes universal humanism in its own shape and image.

The futility of these attempts at universality may explain the desperate tenor of the humanistic writings. They criticise the rightist-Jewish narrative, but have nothing to offer in its place. Their existentialist view of time attests to this; the articles reject sudden vacillations between apocalyptic destruction and divinely predestined redemption: 'There is nothing human about a corpse, and nothing national about a corpse, and the only thing death can contribute to life is a stench.'[40] They reject, too, the gradual, slow continuum of time fashioned by the narratives of the past. Theirs is the existential time first prevalent in modern Hebrew literature and later adopted by journalistic discourse. From afar it seems like an endless cycle of strife and death, with entire dynasties of fathers, sons and grandsons lost in wars. A closer look will bring into focus the underlying single fleeting moment – not of redemption, which lies at the heart of the rightist-Jewish texts, but that moment in which the writer-observer sees neither antecedent reasons nor future purpose: all that had transpired before was a past foreign to the Israeli (for example, the Crusader past in which the Beaufort Castle was built, hundreds of years before its conquest by the Israeli forces), and what will come after is seen through Arab eyes.[41] Therefore, time does not bring consolation, and death and suffering do not lead to redemption or to rebirth.

Modern Hebrew literature has viewed time in this existential manner for years. A classic example is A. B. Yehoshua's 1962 novel

'Facing the Forests'. It is also seen in this way in newspaper articles written during the 1973 Yom Kippur War. This view of time perceives neither a linear continuum from the historical past to the national future nor a dramatic vacillation between destruction and redemption. It is a time of one who is hurled into this world and is unable to find in it any refuge in national miracles.

While criticising the metaphysical structure of time, the writers also undermine the plots designed to reflect it. Instead of brilliant leaps from death to victory, from the village of Alei to Beirut, the plots waver aimlessly between opposite poles, dwelling on marginal details or disintegrating into unconnected scenes. The breakdown of plot occurs when the writers pause over marginal, seemingly meaningless scenes in the manner of existentialist literature, often zooming in on purely physical objects such as steamrollers, irrigation pipes, a pulley and cans of food, or on such mundane acts as buying fresh-baked bread in a local bakery, or catching sight of some flea-infested soldiers urinating or stretching.[42] The war is thus presented in discrete pictures, with neither explanations nor connections. Whatever was formerly steeped in meaning has now disappeared; whatever was marginal and unworthy of attention now emerges at centre stage. Accordingly, the heroes here are not the fighters of the previous articles but rather sleeping soldiers, misfits, the dead. The sharp break of the dramatic movement in time is accompanied by a break in confidence in the possibility of dominating space. The writer's viewpoint is now limited to his own immediate vicinity. In it he sees only himself and his own movements, and these are always confined to a single spot even when they look like thrusts forward. From this spot the writer beholds a vision of an all-encompassing humanity – longed-for but unattainable.

CONCLUSION

The views expressed in the rightist-Jewish press reports in the first three months of the war in Lebanon were far from those articulated in the speeches of Begin that were discussed in Chapter 3. The reports contained neither explicit and unequivocal formulations concerning the superiority of the People of Israel over other peoples nor exhortations about faith in God's will. On the contrary: they affirmed the writers' liberal-humanistic values. The structure within which the themes and the events are organised, however, belied these proclamations and attested to the existence of an underlying narrative whose origins are in the ideologies of the right and of Orthodox Judaism. At the centre of this narrative is the idea of the Jewish people being 'a people that dwells apart'. The articles discussed in this chapter testify to the fact that the rightist-Jewish narrative was not limited during this period of time to a marginal segment of Israeli society, but was accepted by its Zionist liberal centre as well.

From the onset of the Lebanon War, and especially as it drew to its end, the rightist-Jewish narrative was attacked in an increasingly large number of articles in the newspapers, in poems and songs, and in the cinema and television. These texts were only partially successful in articulating an identity that did not see Israel as severed from the world and in elucidating a history that does not rise and fall 'in blood and in fire'. The search for such an identity and history is dealt with in the next chapter.

NOTES

1. And see Chapters 1 and 2.
2. Y. Amikam, 1982; see also A. Valentine, 1982(a) and (b). The Israeli attitude towards other nations is examined here and in the following chapters on the basis of Foucault's analysis of the process by which a society banishes values, ways of thinking and types of behaviour by turning some people into 'others'. See Foucault, 1972. These theories are more fully discussed in Chapter 7.
3. Y. Litani, 1982; M. Michelson, 1982; G. Lior, 1982, respectively.
4. Amikam, 1982.
5. The excerpts quoted here were taken from Hadari-Remedge, 1982.
6. H. Guri, 1982; Y. Bar-Yosef, 1982; Guri, 1982, respectively.
7. Amikam, 1982.
8. Litani, 1982; T. Segev, 1982; Y. Ben-Ner, 1982; U. Dayan, 1982, respectively.
9. As described in Barthes, 1982. As explained in Chapter 3, the Israeli existence was described in the same manner in the election campaign of 1984, although it served different functions in it.
10. See, for example, Siah Lohamim, 'Soldiers Talk about the Six-Day War', a well-known collection of impressions and deliberations of IDF soldiers compiled after the Six Day War.
11. M. Meiron, 1982.
12. A. Bachar, 1982; Guri, 1982.
13. Guri, 1982; Dayan, 1982.
14. Bachar, 1982. The Israeli-versus-Jew dichotomy, though not dominant in these years, can be detected here in the opposition between the active, dymanic soldier and the passive, 'spiritual' civilian.
15. Y. Erez, 1982(a).
16. The Sinai campaign was terminated when Israel was constrained by international pressure to relinquish the Sinai Desert it had conquered; Operation Litani in Lebanon was cut short before its objective of disabling the harassing militias was completed.

17. Guri, 1982; E. Haber, 1982.
18. The excerpt is from Hadari-Remedge, 1982.
19. Valentine, 1982(a) and (b); Erez, 1982(e); Bachar, 1982, respectively.
20. Y. Walter, 1982.
21. Erez, 1982(a).
22. Hadari-Remedge, 1982.
23. Bachar, 1982.
24. Erez, 1982(c).
25. The official Israeli name for the Lebanon War.
26. Haber, 1982; Erez, 1982(c); Erez, 1982(b), respectively.
27. Bachar, 1982.
28. Ibid.
29. G. Cohen, 1986.
30. A. Rahav, 1982.
31. Ibid.
32. See D. Miron, 1992.
33. Y. Smilansky, 1982.
34. Ibid.
35. A. Baruch, 1982(b).
36. The concept of humaneness used by these writers is a particularistic one that embraces only the parochial identity of the speakers and their surroundings. See J. Lyotard, in A. Benjamin, 1989. Chapter 7 provides a thorough analysis of this subject and elucidates the theoretical background of the discussion.
37. Smilansky, 1982.
38. A. Kenan, 1982.
39. Smilansky, 1982.
40. Kenan, 1982.
41. Ibid.
42. Baruch, 1982(a), 1982(b).

6

A DIFFERENT PERCEPTION OF SPACE: Israeli Literature and Cinema in the 1980s

INTRODUCTION

Ariel (Arik) Sharon, who was the Israeli defence minister in the Lebanon War, declared in an interview that he valued the welfare of the Jews above any other consideration: 'Anything that strengthens the Jewish stance,' he said, 'anything that strengthens Judaism is important. This is the doctrine to which we must adhere, from which no one may deviate.'[1] In response to these remarks, film director Rafi Bukai created, in the film *Avanti Popolo* (1986), one of the most stunning scenes in the history of Israeli cinema. In this scene, two Egyptian soldiers, fleeing homeward at the end of the Six Day War, encounter a group of Israeli soldiers. The Arabs, exhausted and half-dead from thirst, ask the Israelis for some water and get a burst of gunfire in response. Then one of them, an actor in civilian life, declaims Shylock's speech:

> I am a Jew. Hath not a Jew eyes? Hath not a Jew hands, organs, dimensions, senses, affections, passions? Fed with the same food, hurt with the same weapons, subject to the same diseases, healed by the same means, warmed and cooled by the same winter and summer as a Christian is? If you prick us, do we not bleed? If you tickle us, do we not laugh? If you poison us, do we not die?

The speech elicits laughter among the Israeli soldiers. One of them claims that the Arab has 'mixed up his roles'. But the ice between the two camps melts quickly and what follows are several scenes of Israeli–Arab fraternity.

The whole idea of creating an Arab Shylock, Rafi Bukai says, came to him when he read an article on Arik Sharon as Israel's 'Man of the

Year': 'I was stunned by his incapacity to perceive the other side, his inability to understand that there are other people who deserve to exist with dignity in this world.'[2] Israel sent the film *Avanti Popolo* to the Oscar competition for foreign films. In so doing, it provoked a public outcry. The 'Council for Films and Plays' that had decided to present this film was dissolved and replaced with a council whose members were rightists. Sharon took this opportunity to express regret in parliament that Israeli films 'are short of motives that evoke Jewish pride, [and contain] elements that hold Israel up to contempt'.[3]

Avanti Popolo is but one work within a large corpus of films, books and plays in the 1980s that deal with Jewish–Arab relations and constitute a counter-narrative to the quasi-official narratives of their time. In doing this they were actually following a tradition of *belles-lettres* and the arts that, throughout the years of the *Yishuv* and the state of Israel, and especially those following the Six Day War, negated the prevailing narratives. These works cannot be understood without recognising the on-going dispute with the image of the Arab that surfaced in the rightist-Jewish narrative, in Begin's speeches, in election advertisements and in the journalistic reports of the Lebanon War. Against the formless, dehumanised Arab depicted in the rightist-Jewish narrative, these works portray an Arab who seems to be more real than the Israeli. In reaction to viewpoints that single out nationalistic markers as the only ones by which to identify and with which to negate the 'other', these works strip their heroes of all national labels or reverse their roles: Israelis look and behave like Arabs, and vice versa.

Throughout its history the Jewish-Israeli society used the Arab in order to define its own identity. This is why, in so many of the texts discussed in this book, the key to the identity, desires and fears of this society was held by the Arab. The Arab, perceived as alien vis-à-vis Israeli Jewish society, was the one who defined this society and thereby forced it, in the words of Foucault, 'to seek itself in an entity alien to it'.[4] The discussion over the portrayal of the Arab thus concerned the very definition of the Israeli identity, its history, its purposes, and its place in the world.[5] Each of the arts argues in this dispute in its own poetic language, and in keeping with its history, repertoire of models, constraints and possibilities. Major literary works in the 1980s used post-modernistic models and de-constructivist perspectives in attempts to dismantle all national and human identities, and with them all binary oppositions (for example, past and present, reality and legend). They attempted to build a new basis for the definition of both the individual and the national entity. The cinema of the 1980s, while adhering to modernist models, reversed the Jewish and Arab national identities that had continued to exist within the parameters of the old definitions.[6] Rather than dismantle the dichotomies that distinguish between Israeli and Arab, it switched them. And then, upon the now-reversed identities, it constructed, again and again, a bridge that unites Israelis and Arabs on a shared human basis. Although the results were often the same, in many cases – because the cinema left the basic dichotomy in place – the bridge that brought Jews and Arabs together seemed to have been built according to a Jewish blueprint. It was, for this very reason, a 'Jewish bridge'. In these instances (as in the story 'Hirbet Hiza'a' and in the 'humanistic' reports from Lebanon), the 'Arab' is still the bearer of a Jewish heritage.[7] He reminds the Israelis of their ethical and national origins, he looks like a Jew, and in his history he embodies the suffering, dreams and yearnings of the Jews. Even though he thereby breaks the Jewish national insularity, the Arab fails to become an autonomous entity and remains a tool in the Israeli's quest for identity: he continues to bear the meaning that the Israelis assign to him.[8]

THE IDENTITY OF 'THE ISRAELI' AND 'THE OTHER'

Taken at face value, the film 'Fictitious Marriage', made in 1988 by Haim Buzaglo, prefers the Palestinian Arab identity to the Israeli one. Its Israeli protagonist, an unpretentious schoolteacher, has no identity of his own, but is perceived differently by the people with whom he interrelates. He has spent all his life as a meticulous teacher, and his wife and friends perceive him in this way. During a stint of reserve duty in the territories, where he must oversee and control a rebellious Palestinian population in the midst of an uprising, his identity begins to waver and he decides to flee it. He tells his wife and children that he is going to America. At the last moment, however, he returns to Tel Aviv from the airport and takes a room in a cheap hotel where the owner mistakes him for a wealthy Israeli-American. Thus he assumes a new identity – that of a *yored*, an Israeli expatriate. One day, however, he accidentally joins a group of Palestinian building workers who mistake him for one of them. He thus acquires a Palestinian alter-identity and sticks to it.

In fact, however, the film fails to describe such an alternative identity. Instead, it shapes it as a caricature of an Israeli one familiar from earlier Israeli films. The Palestinian workmen entertain themselves by furtively observing a Jewish woman through her window and issuing a torrent of jokes on what they see. In so doing they establish a milieu of male camaraderie that contains elements of an erotic relationship. Such male bonding is frequently portrayed in the Israeli cinema: the men all spout ridicule, relate to women and display their machismo in a similar way. This time, however, the group is composed of Palestinians, not Israelis.

Even in the more serious moments of the film the Palestinian Arab is merely an Israeli in disguise. In these moments he reminds the viewer of something the Israeli identity has long since forgotten – the simplicity and connection with landscape and nature that are signified by the Palestinian Arab's hometown of Gaza – scenery and a lifestyle far removed from that of Americanised Tel Aviv. Compared with the Israelis, who dream about a trip to America, the Palestinian personifies the original values of Zionism: 'I can't join you,' he tells an Israeli woman in his broken Hebrew, 'I can't leave our homeland.'

This phenomenon can be detected in *Avanti Popolo*, though in a much more sophisticated manner. Here, the Egyptian is the main protagonist, and the most heroic event in Israeli history – the Six Day War – is depicted through his eyes and in his own voice and language, Arabic. However, when he reveals himself to be a professional actor, not just an Egyptian soldier, he clothes himself not only in the traits of a human being but in those of a Jew – as manifested by the Shylock speech.[9]

Both of these films thus attempt to break through the boundaries of the Israeli national identity: in one the Israeli no longer wants to be Israeli; in the other Israel's great epic of the Six Day War is shattered when seen through Arab eyes. They try to allow the voices suppressed by the Israeli collective to be heard, but invariably fail to do so. The voices still lack a reality of their own, and no alternative identity lies beyond the one that was shattered. In much the same way no alternative identity lies beyond the one shattered in literature. The central literature of the 1980s, however, searches for the unattainable voice of 'the other' by destroying all identities, all dichotomies, all barriers. A. B. Yehoshua's novel 'Mr Mani' is a salient example of this strategy.

The facts revealed to the reader in the fifth chapter of 'Mr Mani' are as follows. The old Rabbi Haddaya brings Dona Flora from Jerusalem to Constantinople in order to marry her off to Abraham Mani, whom he regards as a surrogate son. After she turns down the match, he marries her himself. The marriage succeeds because Rabbi Haddaya is away from home most of the time. Abraham Mani, inseparably attached to his rabbi but stirred by dreams of marrying Dona Flora, brings the couple a gift, or a gift-sacrifice – his own son – whom he entrusts to their care. Thus Mani's son becomes the son of the person who is his own father-figure and of the woman whom he himself dreams of marrying. Dona Flora pampers Mani's son as she would her own, but also lets him play the role of her husband by placing him in her bed, in the place of her missing husband. In the end, when the youngster reaches adulthood, she marries him off to her niece, who resembles her in every way, and the young couple move to Jerusalem. Thus Abraham Mani's son marries a mirror image of the person who has, in disguise as it were, filled the roles of both his mother and his wife. Arriving in Jerusalem for a visit, the father discovers that his son's marriage has not been consummated and that the couple have no marital relations. He tries to force them to bear him an heir, but the son is killed before he can succeed. The father usurps the son's role, sleeping with his daughter-in-law and siring his own grandson. No role, no identity is left intact within this family thicket: the son is not a son; his father is not his father; the wife is not a wife; the mother is not a mother. Each transcends his or her defined role and gropes about in search of other roles. In the course of these quests, everything is possible, anything goes, anyone can be everyone.

The family level of the plot corresponds to the national plane. When the father reaches Jerusalem and locates his son, he finds that the latter has become the prisoner of an *idée fixe*: he is convinced that the Muslim residents of the country are, in fact, Jews who have lost track of their roots – 'who still don't know that they're Jews' – and that it is his duty to show them what they have forgotten. To this end he leaves his home and his wife, steps through the boundaries of the Jewish community, and spends most of his time in the Christian and Muslim quarters of the city. In his wanderings, he is supported by the British consul in Jerusalem, who believes that the Jews are Christians destined to return to Christianity. He therefore regards them not as flesh-and-blood people but as 'literary heroes, who stepped out of the Old Testament and are fated to enter the New Testament in the End of Days; all we must do in the meantime is make sure they don't enter another book by mistake'. In the end, the direction in which the son is heading is not altogether clear. Is he indeed attempting to remind the Muslims that they are in fact Jews? Or is it the other way around: is he trying to forget that he himself is a Jew? 'Instead of discovering Jews who forgot they are Jews, he will himself become something like that in the meantime, a master copy of sorts.' The two processes actually express a single desire, one 'that knows no satisfaction, that always seeks to mix with people and fight what it regards as insularity or self-segregation'. Eventually, when the son approaches the 'others' to remind them of their Jewishness, he assimilates into their community and remains with them until he is killed by an Arab mob.

Thus, while shattering the family identities, the story leads to the collapse of the national identities as well. The father, the son, the wife and the mother, who transcend the boundaries of their roles, are a mere microcosm of a world in which all frameworks are shattered. Jews are not Jews, Christians are not Christians, and Muslims are not Muslims. All come together in one great universe. This universe, however, is but a dream and a fantasy, and the son who dreams and fantasises it is ultimately sacrificed on its altar.

Both cinema and literature therefore contend with the same difficulty of breaking down the insularity of Israeli society, of letting it include the personality of the 'other', and thus challenge the dominant rightist-Jewish narrative. One may gauge the difference between the two ways of contending with this difficulty by analysing two corresponding works, one belonging to each art form – David Grossman's novel 'The Smile of the Lamb', and Shimon Dotan's film based on it. The novel places a Palestinian Arab at centre stage and endows him with a role that was previously given only to the Jewish hero – that of the main protagonist. This protagonist drives the plot and serves as an authoritative voice within it, and is also, apparently, the focus of values within the book. As a matter of fact, he is but a figment of the Jewish imagination, not a real human being. He is a creature of nature, inhabiting an innocent world of legend and fantasy, a new metamorphosis of the combined noble savage and biblical Jew who had served the Israeli as an exemplar in texts of previous years. The novel, however, extricates itself from the old imagery and progresses beyond the conventional exchange of roles. Rather than merely replacing a Jew's voice with that of an Arab, it dismantles the entire chorus. Every voice in the novel sings to itself, irrespective of others. The absolute authority of the Israeli culture is shattered and replaced not by an alternative authority but rather by non-authority, a regime without masters.[10] In this game, the right of every individual to recognition and dignity is upheld, but there is a profound hidden wonder about the very possibility of proposing any kind of authoritative counter-truth against the truth that was shattered. Truth itself crumbles into fragments that defy assessment and judgment.[11]

The novel 'The Smile of the Lamb' is built in the form of a series of monologues that elucidate events from the viewpoints of four protagonists – three Israelis (Uri, Katzman and Shosh), and one Palestinian (Hilmi). Hilmi is not only the narrator in his monologues, he is also the major addressee of the monologues of Uri, who is his friend; he is a guiding voice, so to speak, for the Israeli, and the one who propels the major events in the story. Old Hilmi had spent his life advocating passive resistance to the Israeli occupation; however, after his adopted son is killed in a clash with IDF soldiers he takes his friend Uri hostage and presents one demand in exchange for his release – within 24 hours, the Israeli army must retreat from all the territories it occupied in 1967.

The novel 'The Smile of the Lamb' gives the Arab protagonist more than the central role; it also endows him with an independent set of values that are neither derived from nor connected with the Israeli milieu. It is not the occupation itself that distresses Hilmi, as it distresses the 'leftists' in the novel, but rather the insult and the indignity that it creates. The physical injury is less important to him than the indignity caused to an elderly Arab man when an Israeli woman soldier orders him to show her his papers. What crushes the Arabs into the ground, he says, is the Israelis' contempt, not necessarily their rifles. Uri, the Israeli hero, is unable to comprehend these matters, his good intentions notwithstanding.

The independence granted to the Arab values subverts the possibility of combining Hilmi and the Israeli into one pair of dichotomies. The novel does not offer a common criterion by which their two worlds may be judged. The Israelis judge the conflict in terms of power, the Arabs in terms of honour. Nothing connects these two sets of concepts, whether by way of contradiction or of similarity. Each exists independently of the other, contained completely within its own culture. Thus the work attempts to break the stereotype of the Arab as the noble savage and to invest him with an independent existence, one that belongs to him and is neither derived from nor in the service of the Jewish world. The dichotomy of Jew and Arab is further fractured when each of its domains is itself fragmented into contrasting pairs. Each of these contrasts then fragments again and again, until a stage is reached at which there is no point in dichotomising the heroes of the novel into clashing collectives. At this point each hero must be contemplated in terms of his own uniqueness.

True, Hilmi is a Palestinian. His style, his folk tales, his values are all fuelled by the Palestinian reality around him. But he is crazy. He lives in a cave some distance away from the village, is shunned by the villagers, and suffers from their contempt and abuse. Hilmi, however, is not the only deranged character in the novel. The novel is populated by outsiders, or 'others', who are either Jewish Holocaust survivors wounded in body and spirit and unable to integrate into Israeli society, or, like the Sepharadi protagonist Uri, are outsiders in Ashkenazi society. Like Hilmi, Uri too lives in a world of daydreams, and he, too, is ostracised by those around him.

Thus the relationships between Uri and Hilmi, and between them and other dreamers and outsiders in the novel, shatter the Arab–Israeli dichotomy and replace it with one of individual outsiders versus the collective. This new dichotomy too, however, is fractured because the novel judges similar actions erratically and differently. The flight from reality is presented successively as a lie, a manifestation of a sublimely profound truth, the fulfilment of untenable, absolute values, and as a destructive act. Even the grouping of people who live within the collective is not fully valid, for those who try to elude the collective actually belong to it; and those who choose to seek refuge in the collective also try to extricate themselves from it. Consequently, there is no way to organise and judge the themes within a single pair of oppositions that might define the contrast between the collective and the outsiders, or between the Israelis and the Arabs.

Thus, if the Palestinian Arab is not an Arab but an outsider in Palestinian society, and if the Israeli becomes demented and makes common cause with the outcasts of both Palestinian and Israeli societies, then it is no longer meaningful to distinguish between groups, between collectives, between nations. Every individual must be contemplated as an individual – outside the collective, outside the group, outside the labels. And even then that individual remains complex, inexplicable, incomprehensible.

The willingness of the novel to host a rich plurality of beliefs and viewpoints does express a humanistic tolerance towards everything that is strange and 'other', not only the Arab but also those whom mainstream Israeli culture had ignored – the Sepharadi, the lunatic, the Holocaust-survivor Jew, the dreamer and the stranger. Thus, 'The Smile of the Lamb' does take a stance in the dispute with the narrative that would purge Israeli society of outsiders and 'others'. However, it also expresses a sense of despair, one that is shared by other authors. Like various books, films, newspaper articles and other texts of the time, it finds it hard to offer a realistic stance by whose means one may extricate oneself from the impossible political situation that befouls the characters' existence in the fictional reality of the novel – and not there alone.

The film 'The Smile of the Lamb' strives in its own way to breach the lines that demarcate the collective identities of all the characters. Despite this, however, these lines are not breached in the film: the Israeli-Jewish and Arab-Palestinian identities struggle with each other, switch positions, exchange melodies and languages – but remain, nevertheless, posited against each other in a state of firm dichotomy. As in Yizhar's story 'Hirbet Hiza'a', the Arab world in the film 'The Smile of the Lamb' is the source of the Israeli's yearnings. Thus, when all is said and done, this Arab world is not given its own, independent contours; instead, it serves to define the Israeli identity. The locations in which the Jewish protagonists of the film move about are closed, dark, narrow spaces, either raucous and bustling or alien and estranged. They are contrasted with the open spaces of the fields in which the Arab moves about, and with the bold, contrasting colours of the landscape in which he lives.

The struggle between the Jewish-Israeli and the Arab-Palestinian cultures also surfaces in the film in the way time is measured. The flow of day succeeds unobtrusively into night in the Arab scenery, as against the precise counting of hours and minutes in the Israeli one: 'Everything straightens out within 24 hours', Katzman promises, or 'The ultimatum will expire at 04:00 hours', as another officer explains. Arab time is also historical time. The Israeli protagonists' parents are not mentioned in the film, nor do they have children. Hilmi, by contrast, has two parents and two children (even if only in fantasy), and the film depicts his past by means of flashbacks. The sterility of the Israeli world is thus contrasted with the fertility of the Arab world; it is associated with the closed spaces, the alien voices and the precise counting of time as attributes of a tired, senescent culture. Yizhar depicted this dichotomy in much the same way.

Not only are the Israeli and the Arab worlds contrasted with each other; they are transposed. At first, Uri and Hilmi switch positions, alternating between the foreground and the background of the picture. Later on, Uri, who has been active and energetic, becomes lethargic, while Hilmi brims with vigour and motion. In the meantime the two characters also exchange garments: Uri takes off his army uniform and puts on Hilmi's hat and robe. Now he, like Hilmi, blends into the landscape instead of relentlessly scampering about within it.

The novel 'The Smile of the Lamb' shatters the categories in which the Israeli and Palestinian societies are separated. The film uses these categories but modifies and reverses the value judgments they make: Arab time, space and sounds are the ones the film prefers. The main Israeli protagonist forfeits his primacy to the Arab hero; the Israeli and the Arab exchange positions and clothing. Such switches were very common in the cinema of the 1980s. They were aimed at challenging the conventional wisdom of the rightist-Jewish narrative, that of the supremacy of Israeli culture over Arab culture, and strove instead to set both within a broad universal framework where human markers transcend national ones. In fact, however, such a broad universal façade is not created here, or in other works, because even though the Jewish identity has lost its traits, the Arab culture shaped in its place lacks defining traits of its own.

Thus, if the Jewish voice is faint and false, the Arab voice is, for all practical purposes, not heard at all. It is articulated in silences or by adopting the Israeli voices. All the rest – the beauty of the Arab's fields, his natural landscapes, his history – are nothing but the Israeli Zionist dream projected onto the Palestinian Arab, a dream in which the Israeli immerses himself in the country's indigenous landscapes, colours, history, and pace of time. The novel 'The Smile of the Lamb' reduces this dream to its constituent parts and, by so doing, shatters the Arab stereotype. The film leaves this stereotype intact.

Under such conditions the possibility of genuine cultural exchange and true dialogue is ruled out. Since this is the situation, the shattering of rightist perceptions and the creation of a broad humanistic platform in which the identity and dignity of each national group are upheld is also impossible. The tragic dimension portrayed in the Israeli cinema of the 1980s, and of the humanist narrative as a whole, is the direct result of this impasse: the human world envisaged by them seems to be unobtainable.[12]

CONCLUSION

The *belles-lettres* and the cinema of the 1980s both carry forward the same ideological dispute with the rightist-Jewish narrative. The main writers and directors in both these systems were affiliated with the left wing of Israeli politics, and this is expressed in their works. However, each of these art forms conducts the dispute in its own distinctive language, which in turn generates differences in their basic common ideology. The two art forms communicate from the standpoint of different evolutionary stages, different economic constraints, different statuses in the culture and different relationships with their respective audiences. Israeli *belles-lettres* of the 1980s used western, post-modernist models, and through them created a rich collage of loosely interrelated fragments. The post-modernist models are consolidated in the literary system of this period because the community of scholars and critics propels them towards the centre and also towards the reader. The nature of this process was dictated by a combination of the entrenched status of literature and its institutions and the popularity of its texts.

The Israeli political cinema of the 1980s took shape in a system that had neither traditional repertoires nor canons, and thus lacked a consistent history in the course of which models of the centre and the periphery could reverse their positions. This cinema also did not enjoy the prestige and popularity of literature. Non-entrenched systems, such as this one, usually tend to rely on other systems as their sources for change and rejuvenation. However, they usually simplify their models or adopt old ones which have already coalesced into other systems. In this particular case, old models from literature and journalism were used. These models were already intimately familiar to the elite audience and could therefore endow the cinema with the prestige and popularity that it needed so desperately in view of its unconsolidated status in the culture.

The models are different, the language is different and, consequently, the ideology is different. Nonetheless, both the *belles-lettres* and the cinema articulated the same malaise, an anguish that stemmed from their common realisation that, at the present stage of Israeli history, it seemed almost impossible to break out of the narrow boundaries of the Israeli identity. In this sense they were merely different voices waging the same disputation with the dominant rightist-Jewish narrative of Israeli society. They conveyed not only the possibilities and constraints of their individual systems, but also a critical attitude that they shared with other forms of communication. Together they expressed the distress of those seeking to break away from the ethnocentric and parochial Jewish history. All these texts stumbled as they sought a way through this labyrinth. They tried to break clear of its limitations and to invest Israeli culture with everything it had rejected – Diaspora Jews, Sepharadi Jews, Christians, Muslims. In an act of despair they clung to the impossible possibility of expressing a different Israeliness within a different humanity. In that specific historical moment, they could set it only in a dream.

NOTES

1. The daily newspaper *Hadashot*.
2. A. Rotem, 1986.
3. M. Basok, 1989.
4. M. Foucault, 1972; see also E. Said, 1979. The image of the Arab in previous years was discussed in Chapters 1, 2 and 5.
5. See Y. Feldman, 1989.
6. To use Derrida's terms, the literature attempts to touch the area that lies between the binary oppositions and beyond our field of knowledge (J. Derrida, 1967; see also E. Tavor-Bannet, 1989). In doing this it attempts to break old literary models as well, including modernist ones (see H. Kronfeld, in press). A few examples of the literary post-modernist writings are O. Kastel-Bloom, 'Hostile Surroundings', 1989; I. Levi, 'Letters of Sun, Letters of Moon', 1991; D. Grossman, 'See Under: Love', 1986, 'The Smile of the Lamb', 1983; A. B. Yehoshua, 'Mr Mani', 1990.
7. Forty years previously, Yizhar's short story 'Hirbet Hiza'a' stunned Israeli society by describing the Arab as the authentic bearer of the Israeli and Jewish heritage and values. Now, 40 years later, this did not seem sufficient.
8. The centre of strength and meaning, in Lyotard's terms, is still Israeli. Every imposition of meaning (J. Lyotard, 1983) is a form of rule over others – 'a colonialism of logic'. The problem is not one of the Arab's point of view not being reported, as E. Shohat (1989) asserts, but of dependency on Jewish definitions and meaning.
9. See A. Shamas, 1990.
10. This is the vision of ruination of the western ethno-centricity of the white man, who regards his consciousness as universal and his postures as omnipotent. See Derrida, 1967; Lyotard, 1983; H. White, 1978.
11. This attempt to transcend the framework of defined values is yet another embodiment of the ideas of post-modernist philosophers. Among other things, it is an attempt to shatter the binary oppositions which, in Lacan's words, 'programme human beings according to others' programmes' (J. Lacan, 1966).
12. In Lyotard's terms, everything alien to Israeli culture is nevertheless organised within its frameworks (Lyotard, in Benjamin, 1989). This culture has not yet found a way to acknowledge 'the other' within and without it, to preserve his other-ness, and to respect him for being different and distinct (Derrida, 1967). Consequently, this culture has not generated a broad concept of humanism that would embrace all the grammatical 'persons' – first, second and third (Lyotard, 1983).

7

A DIFFERENT PERCEPTION OF TIME: Israeli Literature and Cinema, 1960–1990

ANGUISH AND FEARS

Outwardly it appeared that the Yom Kippur War (1973) had rocked the Israeli consciousness and quashed the feelings of strength, confidence and invincibility that the 'new Israeli' had acquired after the country's swift victory in the Six Day War (1967). In reality, this feeling of confidence had been fragile and unstable even before then, as can be perceived in a number of central literary works written before the two wars and in the short period of time between them.

Some of the writings of this type attempted to examine what lay beneath the national confidence – a sense of isolation, fears of devastation, and painful hopes for redemption. Thus they dealt with the destruction-to-redemption perception of time during the years when the rightist-Jewish narrative was not the central one, criticising the way in which the old Jewish fears of a world 'that is all against us' were turned into national aggressiveness and also the way in which Israeli society turned war and destruction into the means of achieving exaltation and national redemption. Yitzhak Ben-Ner's story 'After the Rain' (1977), for example, which was published in the daily *Ha-aretz*,[1] is a description of Tel Aviv after it has been destroyed. It is a lawless city where roaming street gangs rule, while solitary frightened people wander through the streets because they fear to stay at home, for there, too, danger lurks. All hope for a sudden miracle – the discovery of oil in the desert, a diplomatic breakthrough with China – anything to end the nightmare and to 'bathe them in a light of happiness'. In Amos Kenan's 'Holocaust 2' (1975), written in part before but completed after the Yom Kippur War, the survivors of a Tel Aviv devastated in an apocalyptic war that encompasses the whole world live in an immense refugee camp in an unspecified tropical region. The sky cannot be seen in this camp, and there is neither day nor night there, and no birds or trees or nature. There is, in this place, no past and no future. A. B. Yehoshua's novel 'The Lover' (1977), on the other hand, is not about destruction, but deals with war and death. Its protagonist is a young Israeli garage owner who has lost his capacity to function in a normal human way: Arabs do his work for him and others go to war for him; he needs someone to love his wife for him, someone to dream for him and someone to hope for him. The real dreams in the story are those of an Arab boy who works in his garage. The last example, Amos Oz's 'The Hill of Evil Counsel' (1976), also does not contain a terrifying apocalyptic vision, but portrays the disintegration of a family in Jerusalem before the country's statehood in 1948. While this is ostensibly an account of the family's breakdown, it is also an analogy of the shattering of dreams about Israeli independence and statehood even before these began to be realised.

However, even before the Yom Kippur War, Israeli *belles-lettres* dealt with the fears, even in his own homeland, of the persecuted Jew. In different works, various causes for these fears are proposed: destruction and disaster must inevitably be repeated (Aaron Apelfeld, 'Smoke', 1962); past and future in Israel belong not to the Jew but to the Arab (A. B. Yehoshua, 'Facing the Forests', 1968);[2] or, again, 'this evil land' with its inhabitants, the jackals and the Arabs, is hostile to the Jews (Amos Oz, 'The Hill of Evil Counsel', 1976). The protagonists of each of these stories overcome these fears through violence and warfare.

Oz's story 'Late Love' (in 'Unto Death', 1971) is about an eccentric and forsaken old man who wanders from kibbutz to kibbutz to warn the Jews living there of the Russian menace. He thinks Israel is weak and unstable, a sort of cardboard decoration set up on shaky ground and surrounded by hostile forces – the enemies of the past as well as those of the present – all threatening to destroy it:

> One heavy Russian snowfall, I say, could wipe Tel Aviv completely off the face of the earth. And my heart contracts at the thought. We are fragile, all this is so impermanent. They will appear suddenly out of the ground. Or out of the blue sky.

The fears of this old Jew are a parodied version of fears that appeared in newspaper articles, Hebrew songs, political speeches and other texts in the Israeli culture. His response to them is also a parody of these texts: he dreams he will fight and take vengeance, and on all of Israel's enemies, past and present, together; he fantasises that he will lead the

Israeli army of the Six Day War to the forests of Poland, where he will cut down with gunfire all who stand in his way:

> … long Nazi convoys, trenches, bleak fortifications. A hurricane of destruction is unleashed on Poland and no force in the world can stop it. An armoured Jewish maelstrom sweeps across the Slavic landscape, devastating forests and fields, thundering on and on and on. … hundreds of furious Jewish tanks crossing the length and breadth of Poland, brutally trampling our murderers underfoot. … With furious wrath they hound all the bands of butchers of the Jews – Poles, Lithuanians, Ukrainians. In a single panting rush. Without a break. Without looking back to see what is burned and what is crushed. Eastward. The vast fields of snow are torn to shreds. A mighty whip-blow over the length and breadth of all the cursed Slavic lands.[3]

War as a way to escape and to overcome fears and resolve distress appears again in a later work, Yehoshua's 'The Lover'.[4] This novel opens with a description of the Yom Kippur War and the disappearance, during the fighting, of 'the lover' of the book's title. At this point, there is a long flashback in which the reader is told how the story's main protagonist, Adam, a garage owner, turned a visiting Israeli who had returned to see his dying grandmother, into his wife Assia's lover. The novel returns to a second description of the war, this time in the form of a monologue by an Arab lad who works in Adam's garage, and then goes on to describe the search for the lover, who has disappeared during the fighting. When the description reaches the point where he is found the war is described a third time, as an eyewitness account in the form of a monologue by the lover. He describes his call-up to the army, being sent to a battlefield in the Sinai Desert, and how he fled from it.

There are thus three different descriptions of the Yom Kippur War, which occurred only once. The war opens the story and thus is presented as the cause of everything that takes place in it. The story also ends with the war, so that the lasting impression when the reading is over is of a war which seems to repeat itself again and again. It thus appears to be long and endless, 'as if the war that has ended is still decomposing and seething, and from its putrefying remains a new war is already sprouting'.

The interface between descriptions of war and of love (between the

Arab lad and Adam and Assia's daughter) and between war and rebirth (the lover's grandmother recovers during the war) turn the war from a repetitive objective reality into an ideal, into a means leading to renewal. This phenomenon reappears in the novel in several other ways: accidents, death and war bring prosperity and renewal to the protagonists in Assia's dreams; the death of Adam and Assia's son restores the bonds between the boy's grandfather and the family and friends who had alienated themselves from him, and this leads indirectly to the renewed prosperity of Adam's garage; the lover's disappearance leads to additional prosperity, because the night-time searches for him enable Adam to make a lot of money towing cars; and although the searches end with a fatal accident in which a couple and their child are killed, this too leads to even more prosperity, for as a result Adam conceives of the revolutionary idea of making one new car from two smashed-up ones, an invention that will bring profitable business to his garage.

In Oz's 'Late Love', the protagonist turns the fear of destruction and death in war into military reawakening and victorious conquest. The protagonist in A. B. Yehoshua's 'The Lover' turns war, destruction and death into a source of personal renewal and national redemption. These mixtures of fears and aggressions, and of destruction and redemption, have been analysed frequently in Israeli writing through the use of existentionalist models of alienation and despair (e.g. the works of Kafka, Camus, Sartre). These models were restructured and adapted to answer the new need to describe the Jewish-Israeli consciousness and, moreover, to criticise it. This mixture of existential and national themes is the underlying model in Kenan's 'Holocaust 2', in which the setting of a refugee camp, after the destruction of Israel, is described in both existential and Israeli-political terms. There is, for example, a daily execution in the camp, but since no one knows who the next victim will be, every day may be one's last. As the protagonist puts it, 'The truth is that I know that every minute is the last minute of my life. That's a strong physical feeling.'[5] The situation is defined in existential terms, but the explanation is a political one – national holocaust. There are no hopes in this camp, and memory, too, is confounded: the protagonist repeatedly tries to recall the beautiful Tel Aviv he knew, but his recollections give way to memories of death and destruction; he tries to remember the golden sands of its seashore, but instead recalls the Zealots' deaths on Masada; he wants to picture a camel caravan on that same shore, but remembers the day of mourning for the destruction of the Temple in Jerusalem (in AD 70) and the Spanish Inquisition and

Expulsion (in 1492). Where there is no hope, there is no memory, except that of death. The assumption is the familiar existential one, but in this story an Israeli-Jewish variant has been introduced: the fate and death of an individual symbolise the devastation and destruction of the nation.

In this novel not only time, but space as well, is expanded to points of destruction: dreams of far-away, exotic places become thoughts of distant Masada, and memories of pine forests, blue skies and snow-covered landscapes lead to visions of the transports to Nazi death camps. In the same way, the dreams of a realistic and miraculous redemption that fill this story turn into dreams of fear and destruction: two people dream of building a new world, a magician builds a golden city for children in a forest filled with dwarfs and fairies, princes and animals, and people build a kibbutz with ploughed fields and thick woods. However, these beautiful dreams turn into nightmares: the kibbutz slowly sinks into a quagmire, the two who dreamed of a new world become maimed, the magician's forest is surrounded by tanks, and the procession of fairies, children, princes and gnomes begins to march towards death. The dream of a miracle and redemption does not end in destruction but is itself turned into destruction. When the children, princes and animals ask the magician where they are going, he answers, 'We are going to a new country', and then:

> They all begin to rejoice, their mouths joined in clear and soft and delicate singing to the orchestra of the little gnomes. The bears growl, the lions roar, the crickets chirp, the dolphins and whales spout water to the blue skies, the enchanted birds of pure gold twitter and sing, and behind them the tanks are shooting, pounding, trampling the castles that descend from the air and the towers that slowly sink down, and the orchestra of little imps and the mouths and the princes and the lions and everything.[6]

The book thus constructs an existentialist world that is without time and space, and devoid of hope and dreams. The background of this existentialist world, however, and the explanation for it, are not rooted in the universal human situation, but in the specific Israeli context. Thus, Israeli *belles-lettres* examined Israeli and Jewish histories, disillusionment about dreams that were never realised, the relentless fear of holocaust and pogroms, and the ever-present reality of war that pursues the protagonists even to their place of refuge. The stories reveal the historical background of the rightist-Jewish narrative but also criticise it; they present a society that, having turned destruction itself into redemption, awaits catastrophe in order to turn its fears into the exhilaration of warfare.

In the literary works described above, and in others, catastrophes are not only a way out of national fears but also out of the guilt feelings of a bourgeois society. These works were written during the years in which Israeli society was rapidly acquiring the features of an affluent western consumer society, along with which it developed an increasingly bourgeois individualist ideology. This ideology was expressed in many texts, including election advertisements (analysed in Chapter 4). The literary works criticised these texts while exposing the ways in which they combined bourgeois ideology with the narrative of destruction and redemption. As they did this, they ironically redefined the war not only as a path to a national redemption but to a personal one – a redemption from an empty life of mundane vanities. This role was filled by the Yom Kippur War in 'The Lover', and by the Six Day War in Amos Oz's 'My Michael' (1968). In this last book, the war parallels the wild and violent orgies that the protagonist, Hannah, experiences in her dreams. The war, like her dreams, provides an escape from the petit-bourgeois life that she lives in her modest little apartment in an old Jerusalem neighbourhood. In this and in other works bourgeois life is intertwined with fears of disaster and holocaust. The individualistic bourgeois ideology epitomised by the protagonists is thus combined with the rightist-Jewish narrative, as in the sentences that open the fifth chapter of a later (1982) Oz work, 'A Perfect Peace':

> Many people travel every day from one place to another in order to buy, to sell, to change their place and their luck, to check the pulse of business, to check things out and see if there are any new possibilities ... middle-aged survivors [of the Holocaust] ... with the faces of men in a dream.

The apparent serenity on these people's faces does not express their real feelings:

> Refugees like these look at a modern office building but see a pile of ruins. A car drives by and they hear a bombardment. A melody on the radio, and their blood freezes in their veins. They gaze at a tree and see a fire.[7]

The nation's fears on the one hand and the vacuity of petit-bourgeois life on the other are what draw the protagonists to redeem their lives in catastrophe or destruction. To do this they resort to the army and war.

EN ROUTE TO AN IMPASSE

While dismantling the rightist-Jewish apocalyptic narrative that envisions abrupt movements between destruction and redemption, the literature of the 1960s and 1970s found it difficult to offer any other view of time. In these works, time goes nowhere. The protagonists move boldly and vigorously, but make no progress; they are always in motion, but never arrive; they lurch towards the past, but are jolted back to the present. The Israeli hero – who worked his fields in the literature of the 1930s and 1940s, conquered his homeland in the War of Independence, and trampled through Lebanon in the rightist-Jewish press reports of the Lebanon War – is consigned to impotence and aimless meandering towards unattainable goals. The protagonist of the main literature of the 1960s and 1970s reappears in the central Israeli cinema of the 1980s and in the humanist press during the Lebanon War. He will serve as the basis for discussion of the sense of impasse that beset Israeli culture in the 1980s.

The cinema of this decade, like the works of A. B. Yehoshua, Amos Oz and Yitshak Ben-Ner written in the 1960s and 1970s, reveals the tragic denouement of their plots at the very beginning. Their plots progress from death to death or end where they begin, in a circular path that returns to the point of departure. That beneath this structure lies the dispute with the rightist-Jewish narrative becomes clear in those cases where the 'circle' being trodden is a morass of interminable wars.

The film 'The Smile of the Lamb' (discussed in Chapter 6) is an unbroken progression from death to death, and from separations to endings. It begins, in an Arab village, with a lofty oration by the Israeli protagonist Uri to a sparse audience. Two voices accompany his speech – that of the narrator, who explains that this scene is in fact 'the beginning of the end' of the story, and that of the old Arab Hilmi, who has come down from his cave on the mountain shouting 'Tuta tuta halas't al-haduta' (It's all over). Thus, what is presented at the beginning of the film is its end. From this end, events lead into a lengthy series of additional endings – the death of Hilmi's son; the end of a donkey, shot by an Israeli soldier; the end of Uri's relationship with his wife Shosh; the end of the relationship between Shosh and Katzman, Uri's close friend and his officer in the army; and the end of Uri himself.

The transition from the miraculous leaps in time of the rightist-Jewish narrative to time standing still is connected with the change from wide open spaces to alienated restricted ones. In contrast with the rightist-Jewish dream of a Greater Israel in which there are no Arabs, Israeli *belles-lettres* portrayed time and again since Yizhar's story 'Hirbet Hiza'a', an Israel without Jews, a land populated only by Arabs and by wild animals. Israeli cinema of the 1980s reflects this pattern, using its own cinematic means. The events of these films are often acted out behind bars and metal balustrades, their protagonists are filmed through doorways, under lintels, crowded into cramped, claustrophobic apartments, between walls, surrounded by heavy, gloomy architecture (for example, in 'Himo, King of Jerusalem' and 'No'a at Seventeen'). Many of the shots in these films begin with close-ups, but even when the camera pulls away, the object remains 'imprisoned' between the walls of a jail or an apartment, hemmed in by people and objects, and unable to cover the entire space (for example, in 'Behind the Walls').[8]

The protagonists emerge from this suffocating density into a splendidly colourful landscape only for the purpose of war or manoeuvres ('One of Us', 'Mark of Cain') or at times of despair or death ('Queen of the Class', 'The Dreamers'). Then, and only then, do they gain sight of the horizon; then, and only then, does the camera embrace the space around them in its full length, breadth and depth. This space also comes into view, however, when the camera leaves the collective zone and ventures into Arab locations (an Arab village or fields in 'Green Fields', and the cities of Ramallah in 'A Very Narrow Bridge', Gaza in 'Fictitious Marriage' and Jaffa in 'Till the End of the Night'). In these cases, lovely romantic scenery unfolds, veiled in rain and mist ('A Very Narrow Bridge'), illuminated with sharp colours, the bold hues of yellow, green and brown of the countryside, or with the bluish-grey luminescence of night ('The Smile of the Lamb', 'A Very Narrow Bridge'). The colours are those of the land, but this is a strange land; it is an Arab land, not a Jewish one.

Even when a placid Israeli landscape is unfolded in these films – fields of a kibbutz or *moshav*, a beach, or the desert – it does not look as if it belongs to the Israeli protagonist. Israeli scenery either alternates with foreign American landscapes ('Fictitious Marriage') or is accompanied by foreign music ('The Smile of the Lamb'). The sea in these films is a place where people die and not a place where they live ('Till the End of the Night', 'Fellow Traveller'), and it signifies despair rather than hope ('Repeat Dive'). The high-angle long shots that display the full, splendid depth of this landscape are merely so much mockery; the protagonist who has died ('Fellow Traveller'), or has sunk into a dead-end life ('Repeat Dive'), can neither see nor enjoy them.

This is the landscape that is described again and again in the Israeli literature of the 1960s, the same dry and barren landscape of 'Three Days and a Child' and 'My Michael'. This is the same landscape that Shraga, the protagonist of Amos Oz's 'Late Love', watches from the window of his apartment:

> Eight o'clock. Tel Aviv is already boiling and steaming. As if the very buildings will soon evaporate in the heat. Before we built this city on this spot the sand dunes stretched right down to the beach. The desert touched the sea. In other words, we came here and forced these two furious elements asunder. As if we poked our heads into the jaws of the sea and the desert. There are moments on hot summer days when I have a sudden feeling that the jaws are trying to snap shut again. On us. The whole city suddenly seems to me almost unbelievably insubstantial. Even the trees we have planted along the edges of the pavements appear hardly to be joined to the ground. More like a stage set than a city. Nothing but a cardboard façade dividing the desert from the sea. One heavy Russian winter snowstorm, I say, could wipe Tel Aviv completely off the face of the earth. And my heart contracts at the thought. We are so fragile, all this is so impermanent.... The breath of the desert in our face. The hateful sun.[9]

FROM REALITY TO FANTASY AND DREAM

Some of the works erupt from the restricting borders of the Israeli reality into a world of fantasy, legend, literature, and art. There, in this imaginary world, they create the dream of a broad humanity with no borders or limits. The film *Avanti Popolo* is an example of this. The film begins with black-and-white semi-documentary footage of the Six Day War and ends with a closing caption explaining the fate of the protagonists after the end of the film, thereby bringing the events back to reality. Between these two real events, the plot takes off to points beyond – dream and fantasy, literature, poetry and theatre. There and only there, do the barriers between Israelis and Arabs fall.

The process is slow and gradual. At the beginning of the film the

Egyptian soldiers appear in Egyptian uniforms, clutching assault rifles. Later they hurl the rifles aside and shed their uniforms, thus 'going over' from the initial documentary reality of the war to a more human reality, the film's fictional reality. The protagonists of this reality are human beings, not Egyptian soldiers. The film 'promotes' them again when, with the help of a bottle of liquor, they cross over from the fictional world of the film into a higher world of fiction within fiction – one of poetry and song. The estrangement between the Israeli and the Arab soldiers dissipates after the Egyptian soldier has delivered the Shylock speech, and the relationship between them gains strength as they march across the sand-dunes, chanting in unison the song 'Avanti Popolo'. In this world of song and drama national borders are breached; the Egyptian and Israeli soldiers may now relate to one another on the human basis that they all share.

The photography and sound track of the film cross the same territory taken by the plot; they move from reality to the realm beyond, and back. From their own point of departure – semi-documentary footage and the tumult of war – they shift to the silence and bluish light of the desert, investing the terror-scapes of reality with the aesthetics of cinema. From the conflict between the Israeli and Arab groups, they switch to a long shot in which the soldiers' figures look like a painting of silhouettes melting together into the horizon, illuminated in an enchanted golden sunset. From the racket of the radio network they switch, at the end, to the shared song that brings the Israelis and the Arabs together.

The surrealistic cinematography is meant to achieve the same goal of turning reality into fiction. The war cinematography is shown to be pointless absurdity against the desert backdrop – a dead UN soldier with a parasol above him, a jeep lurching forward to the sound of military marches, a group of soldiers marching to the sound of a large chorus and, finally, the song 'Avanti Popolo', once used to encourage the masses to political action. All of these seem pointless in the stark setting of the desert, where there is neither a multitude nor political action. This pointlessness, however, is the very trait that lends these scenes their artistic, surrealistic quality – that of the purposeless beauty of art.

In this fashion, the cinematography is a partner in the process experienced by the actors – a process of self-elevation that transports them beyond the reality of death, anomie and war to the spheres of art, music and poetry, from which one may view the world in a new light. This light causes everything that separates the different national groups to fade and vanish, and the groups thus meld into a single new milieu. This new milieu, however, disintegrates the moment the characters return from fiction to reality.

NEW OPTIONS

In the late 1980s, as violent Palestinian resistance to the Israeli occupation, the *Intifada*, gathered momentum, and more and more Israelis became increasingly fatigued by the policies of the right, new ideological options began to surface in the country's politics, and in its culture. As before, the medium of *belles-lettres* was the first to examine these options in the course of its re-examination of both the nation's past and its present situation. Other texts, including the cinema, followed. To do so, some literary works used the same post-modernist models that served them as a way to break the Israeli-Jewish and Palestinian-Arab identities. By means of these models they portrayed Zionist history as a collection of images, quotations, posturings and possibilities, some of them fulfilled, others not. Thus they reduced this history to unconnected components and presented other, imaginary histories to replace it. They resurrected discarded postulates as new options for the past and the present together – an Arab–Jewish a-nationalism; a partitioning of the land between Jews and Arabs; a cosmopolitan co-existence based on co-operation; an 'indigenous movement' that wishes to detach itself from the Jewish heritage and integrate into the surrounding Middle East; and so on. Sometimes these were in the form of a fantasy or a dream, a reality unrealised in the present or in the past.

An example of this may be found in Yehoshua's novel 'Mr Mani' discussed in Chapter 6. The protagonist-speaker of Yehoshua's second chapter is Egon, a German soldier during the Second World War.[10] Like characters in other parts of the book, Egon dreams of a different national identity existing within a different history, one that glides peacefully on placid waters, and not on streams of blood and fire. Again like the other protagonists in this novel, Egon seeks this different history in the ancient past. While he is still mired in the bloody strife of present history, he finds a different history in dreams of the Minoan civilisation. Thus, in this chapter, two histories are engaged in a highly controversial debate that is exemplified by two narratives – the narrative that perceives history as a vicious circle of wars and defeats and eras of redemption, and a different narrative that allows for a progressional history of calm and peaceful times. The first narrative advocates racial and national closedness, while the second espouses a universal humanistic society.

The events in this chapter are constructed as irreversibly predestined. At the beginning of the chapter Egon is almost sacrificed on the altar of the Nazi Fuehrer's megalomanic dreams when, parachuting with the army in Crete, he is nearly killed. At the end of the chapter he learns that his grandmother is on her way with an order to have him transferred to the Russian front, where he will very likely be killed. Since preceding this chapter there is a description of Egon's brother's death, and after it that of his mother, Egon is surrounded by death in much the same way that the protagonsists in 'The Lover' are surrounded by war. He is thus blocked from any chance of 'getting out once and for all from this history, either forwards in time or backwards in it'.[11] The history that Egon is trying to escape is one of death and wars, and although it is the history of Germany, carefully drawn parallels are made between this chapter and others in the novel (especially the first) that deal with Jewish and Israeli history. In addition, parallels are also drawn between the events and protagonists of this chapter and those in other books by A. B. Yehoshua that deal with the Israeli reality.[12] In many of these the protagonists try to break the historical cycle in which they are caught up by finding a new beginning on which to construct a different history.[13]

On the first day of the German army's invasion of Crete, Egon meets a Jewish tourist guide named Mani. It is Mani who introduces him to the Minoan civilisation, and describes it to him as the antithesis of the modern western one; in it there are no gods and no wars, no sin or guilt, and it does not shut itself away from the rest of the world. Egon adopts Mani's description with enthusiasm and aspires to establish, on the basis of the Minoan civilisation, a non-national history of peace and brotherhood,[14] a different kind of future 'for European souls who are free of guilt and fear'.[15] Nevertheless, creating a different civilisation is impossible since (as in all Yehoshua's other books) it is accomplished through destruction: Egon believes that in order to re-establish the ideal civilisation as in ancient times, the existing one must be cleansed of Jews – and first of all of the tourist guide Mani. Thus the way out of present history and to (Egon's) human-universal redemption is through death and destruction. Such a path to redemption is thus a repetition of the very same cyclical history of violence that its proponent (Egon) claims to negate.

In addition, the possibility of breaking out of history is nullified because the Minoan civilisation was, in fact, very different from what – on the basis of Mr Mani's stories – Egon imagines it to have been. Most of the information about it, learned from Mr Mani, is questionable, as can be ascertained from historical sources. It was, apparently, far from the exemplificaton of history moving along 'on still waters' and was, rather, a tumultuous cycle of wars, deaths and downfalls.[16] The novel thus presents us with two parallel but contradictory histories – one that is constructed in the minds of the two protagonists and envisions a history of peace and tranquillity; and one based on informed knowledge that shows that such a history never took place. The similarities between the ancient Minoan history and modern history reveal that there is no other, 'different', history, a theme that appears in Yehoshua's other books. In his attempt to free himself of the 'rusty chain of history' made up of links of wars and death, Egon adds another rusty link to it by causing the death of another Jew in yet another act of Nazi violence.

However, unlike the denouement in Yehoshua's earlier stories, the failure here is not total, for Egon finally succeeds in breaking the cyclical predestined fate forced upon him. He tears up the order that his mother has brought and is thus not transferred to the Russian front to be sacrificed on the altar of Nazi ideology. In his place, the grandmother pays the price, for she is killed in a plane shot down by a British pilot. The cycle is thus completed and closed, but the choice is left to the protagonists, and this choice is one of the main facets of the book. This chapter of 'Mr Mani' thus shapes the familiar rightist-Jewish narrative, but also presents different ways to escape from it. The ways presented are at one and the same time realistic and fantastic, and they offer both possible and impossible historical options. It is these options that are dealt with in many literary works of the 1980s and 1990s.

NOTES

1. The story was published later in a collection of the writer's stories, 'After the Rain', Y. Ben-Ner, 1979. On Hebrew literature during this period see, mainly, G. Shaked, 1971, and also my book, 1983.
2. This story appeared in the literary periodical *Keshet* in 1962 and in several anthologies, among them A. B. Yehoshua, 'Nine Stories', 1972.
3. Appears in A. Oz, 'Unto Death', 1971: 72, 73.
4. For a complete analysis of this novel, see my book, 1983.
5. A. Kenan, 1975: 12.
6. Kenan, 1975: 138.
7. Oz, 1982: 119, 126.
8. N. Ben-Shaul, 1997.

9. Oz, 1971: 119.
10. Yehoshua, 1990. For a thorough analysis of this chapter, see my article, 1995.
11. Yehoshua, 1990: 99, 94, 107, respectively.
12. For details of this parallel, see my article, 1995.
13. The Arab village in Yehoshua's story 'Facing the Forests', for example, or the Bible in his 'Early Summer', 1970.
14. The phenomenon has been analysed by many critics. See, among others, D. Miron, 1995.
15. Yehoshua, 1990: 133.
16. For the historical sources on Crete, see M. Amit, 1984.

8

ROUTINE AND NORMALITY AS OBJECTS OF DESIRE:
The 1991 Gulf War and Its Aftermath

INTRODUCTION

President George Bush attempted to present the Gulf War to the American public by using a Second World War model that depicted the struggle of a coalition of democracies against a world-threatening tyrant. For this purpose he invoked a narrative, well known in the American popular culture, in which monstrous, wicked forces driven by malevolence attack the existing order and its leaders who, after struggling with grave doubts, are forced to go to its defence.[1] While this narrative succeeded in uniting the American people around its leaders during the war, it failed to survive it. Among other reasons, it clashed with the necessity of minimising the descriptions of the war's horrors in order to prevent identifying the conflict with Iraq with the Vietnam War. The Gulf War seen on American network television was clean, bloodless and corpse-free, more reminiscent of a video game than of a real battlefield. This made it difficult to sustain the Hitlerian characterisation of the enemy and to justify the war against him as a struggle against a monstrous and evil force.[2]

The attempt of the Israeli leadership to invoke old narratives in order to boost public morale during the Gulf War ended in a similar failure, and for comparable reasons. The Gulf War was the first in which Israel was involved but did not have an active role. Israeli forces took no part in the actual fighting or bombing, or even in decision-making at the command level. This passivity was in no way reflected in the political rhetoric of the leadership which, on the contrary, attempted to glorify the war and Israel's role in it. To do this, all the old narratives of previous wars were dredged up from the old repertoire, with particular use being made of the apocalyptic rightist-Jewish narrative.

The attempt to resurrect the old national narratives and link them with the rightist-Jewish narrative was doomed to failure from the outset because of the wide gap between the resolute bravery and heroism they praise and the absence of any bravery and heroism in this war. This gap was all too readily perceived by the public. Together with the leadership's noticeable inconsistency in its declamations, this helps explain the lack of credibility of the combined narratives. Israeli leaders' speeches to the public were filled with the pathos of the old narratives, but their briefings to the media played down the dangers of the war: in these briefings the pathos was toned down, and narratives that would magnify it were avoided.

While the war weakened the rightist-Jewish and national narratives, it contributed to the strengthening of others. Among these were a personal a-political narrative that had always existed in Israeli culture and the Labor movement narrative of the pre-independence period of the *Yishuv.* The latter had served in its own time, and again during the Gulf War, to describe and justify the policy of self-restraint in the face of enemy attack (*havlagah*). The two narratives began gathering strength anew in Israeli society after the Lebanon War in the early 1980s and with the onset of the *Intifada* at the end of the decade, events which deepened the public's fatigue with the never-ending state of belligerency. Public surveys carried out during these years indicated that the general public was shifting gradually to the left and, indeed, in the elections held in 1992 the Alignment emerged victorious. The Gulf War merely accelerated and underscored this process,[3] which was the exact opposite of the one that had taken place during and after the Six Day War. At that time, in the national euphoria that followed the successes of the war, the prevalent personal and Labor movement narratives, in the moderate, humanistic versions they had acquired during the tenure of Prime Minister Levi Eshkol were relegated to the sidelines and the rightist-Jewish narratives became dominant. This chapter uses speeches of the national leaders, propaganda films, wartime news commentaries, newspaper articles, films, and advertisements to attest to the struggle that took place between national and personal narratives during the Gulf War.

LEADERS' SPEECHES

Prime Minister Yitzhak Shamir's speech in the Knesset (parliament) on 4 February 1991 ended with the following: 'May the words of the

Torah in *Mishpatim* [the weekly reading from the Bible] be fulfilled: "And I shall expose the enemy's necks before you" – that is to say, the necks of the enemy in flight.' Not only does Shamir's speech as a whole return to the biblical text, it reconstructs a rich lexicon that the pre-state *Yishuv* had used whenever faced with a crisis. This lexicon combines the biblical style with that of rituals of Jewish festivals, and adds those of early-century journalism, underground and War of Independence pamphlets, and the speeches of Ben-Gurion, Jabotinsky, Begin, and many others. The narrative that is emphasised in this mixture is the one that depicts Jewish and Israeli history as a series of destruction/redemption crises and stresses the uniqueness of the Jewish people amongst all other nations and its isolation within them.

Yitzhak Shamir always filled his rhetoric with talk of 'times of crisis' and 'ordeal', effectively constructing a philosophy of history as a progression from crisis to crisis and depicting a society reborn through them. The Gulf War gave him a pretext to use this rhetoric more widely and openly, as in a speech in the Knesset on 27 February 1991:

> We are in the throes of a great era. These are days of trial and tribulation.... They have put us to a test the likes of which we have never experienced ... tests occasioned by this time of emergency.... The time of international reckoning ... has yet to come.

This is the language of the pre-independence Disturbances and of the War of Independence. Compare Shamir's statements with the headlines of wall posters in the period of the Disturbances:

> We are in the midst of difficult times. / We are in times of an historic ordeal, the likes of which we have not faced perhaps since the Destruction of the Second Temple. / These are times of trouble, famine and carnage for the nation.

Shamir uses this language as one pole in the absolute contrast of destruction and redemption. Thus, although these are times of trial and crisis, they are also

> days of inner exaltation and true unity within our midst, ability to stand together against the murderous, ruthless and amoral enemy. Facing his satanic missiles in our sealed rooms, all of us, men, women and children of all groups, feel the

> common pulse that pounds in our bodies, the determination to maintain our independent existence, and our love of homeland and country.

Thus, at this time of crisis, the 'uniqueness of the Jewish people' comes to light. Consequently, Shamir defines the war not only as a time of trial and tribulation but also as a 'glorious period' and a 'great moment in history', when the Jewish nation demonstrates its greatness, superiority, uniqueness and unity.

This reading of events is also characteristic of the speeches of other Israeli leaders, of the left and of the right, during the war. Consider, for example, remarks by opposition leader Shimon Peres on 23 January 1991:

> There's a way to withstand these dangers and to emerge from them intact.... We shall not yield to any measure of despair. We shall emerge from this trial as one of the victors, but we shall surely be strengthened in all senses of our existence and future, and when this tempest passes, the State of Israel will have new horizons.

This formulation is borrowed from the well-known war repertoire and had been put to particularly intensive use in the Six Day War. Similar proclamations were made, for example, in Knesset meetings in May and June of 1967:

> There are moments when the nation knows how to transcend circumstances and emphasise its unity. / We stand united in our wish to defend our country in these days of tension and readiness, these days of wonderful manifestations of endurance on the part of the entire populace. / These have been days of awesome splendour, days of exaltation of man and his spirit... / This nation, with its hidden reserves of strength, of which even its members are unaware, was prepared to suffer and to make sacrifices in order to ensure its independence.[4]

In Shamir's speech, the crisis, the cause of this exaltation, leads to redemption. Thus his speech promises that 'we shall look forward to days of renewed momentum in building and development, great days of prosperity, of ingathering of exiles, and of anticipation of total redemption'. In this case, Shamir invokes the rhetoric of Ben-Gurion who, for example, defined the War of Independence as 'a time of trial':

> We have reached a turning point more ramified perhaps than any we have ever experienced... / [The war] has not diminished us ... [it has] strengthened us, tempered our spirits, unified our camp. / [This war therefore leads to the final victory] of immigration, settlement, building and development, and the ingathering of exiles. / [This, in turn, is] a single vision that points in one direction – total redemption.[5]

The perception of the crisis revealed in Shamir's speech is shared by the Israeli right and left, and it emerged in the wars of the past as well as of the present. Shamir, however, casts it into a mould that characterises chiefly the right, one that took hold in Israeli culture in the 1970s and 1980s. He describes the Gulf War in terms of destruction and holocaust, and of struggle and vengeance in terms of redemption. This structure, in a more intensified form, dominated Begin's speeches and other texts of the right.[6] It dictated the description of the outcome of the war as one of eradication of the enemy – 'the demise of the tyrant'.

Using a standard format of Zionist rhetoric, Shamir depicts the war as one of 'the few against the many' and of the 'sons of light against the sons of darkness'. He thus envelops the Gulf conflict in the mantle of wars of the Jews' against the Greeks and Romans 2,000 years ago. To achieve this effect, the speech reverts to traditional childhood lore and invokes images culled from accounts of Passover, Hanukka and Purim. Thus, against 'the evil and tyrannical regime' of Saddam Hussein and his 'legions' (Hanukka), which aims to 'kill Jews and destroy their country' (Purim), stands 'every fair-minded, freedom-loving person in the entire world' who wishes 'to witness the eradication of tyranny' (Hanukka again). All these, together, ensure victory: the freedom fighters, Israel among them, know that 'The demise of the tyrant who is trying to rise up against us and destroy us [Passover] is nigh.'[7]

This rhetoric of the Jewish festivals was invoked during previous wars, especially the War of Independence, in which the Israeli fighters are described as freedom fighters: 'free men [who] volunteered to liberate the homeland once and for all from the yoke of aliens', 'tyrants [and] slave-masters' who 'rose up against us' to 'destroy us [in an] onslaught of malevolence and evil'.[8]

The Gulf War is described in the speech by Shamir as a direct continuation of the War of Independence ('The veterans [of 1948] remember the ordeals that the civilian population endured in the War of Independence'), of the 1956 Sinai campaign (the Iraqi dictator replaces the Egyptian tyrant, Nasser, of Ben-Gurion's rhetoric), and so on. Thus, all these earlier wars are channelled into the most recent conflict, which is again portrayed as one of freedom fighters struggling against a ruthless dictatorship. In describing the relationship between the Jewish people and its enemies Shamir again entwines widely accepted formulations with the rightist-Jewish narrative. The perception of the regional conflicts as struggles of a weak and isolated nation against a large and broad front of enemies was shared by all factions, in one way or another, during the periods of the *Yishuv* and of independent statehood. In the 1980s and 1990s the right nourished this view and carried it to its extreme, while the left sought ways of refuting it and replacing it with a narrative that had also been current in the period of the *Yishuv* and early independence, one which perceived the Jewish people as a member of the family of nations.

The gap between these two perceptions was clearly articulated during the Gulf War. Those affiliated with the Alignment and the left repeatedly confirmed the importance of Israeli participation in the European–American coalition. In the Knesset on 23 January 1991, Shimon Peres declared that 'President Bush has succeeded in forming a very impressive coalition. This is a confrontation between most of the Free World and Iraq. It is not an Israeli–Arab duel.' Those on the right, in contrast, attempted to minimise the value of this coalition. On the one hand, they appended the *Intifada* and the Lebanon War to the Gulf War, thereby broadening the belligerent anti-Israel front, and, on the other, they 'dismantled' the western coalition, linking its members to that front. In either case, they preserved the formula of an isolated nation facing a hostile front. Eliahu Ben-Elissar, for example, a member of the Likud and Israel's first ambassador to Egypt in the early 1980s, in addressing the Knesset on 23 January 1993, takes all the countries of the coalition to account:

> We shall not forgive those nations that helped Iraq arm itself.... The Iraqis are using both German and French technical know-how to improve the [Scud] missiles that the Soviet Union provided it with. Not only the Germans equipped Iraq with know-how in chemical [warfare]. The French and the Italians and the Swiss, and others, were also involved. When the time [of reckoning] comes ... we shall remember this.

The enemy, in this case, consists of the countries of the coalition that have been correlated with the Arabs: 'Nor shall we forgive the Palestinian Arabs.... We all know to whom the Mufti of Jerusalem ran in his time, and Arafat is [allied] with Saddam Hussein today.' In this strong and invincible array of enemies, even the Americans are included:

> When the day [of reckoning] comes, both the Americans and the British will have to remember the danger in which we exist.... They will have to remember it, and we shall also remind them of it. We will not be able to accept guarantees or assurances, but will continue to rely only on ourselves.

Although the parties of the far right expressed themselves in more extreme terms, their attitude was similar. In the same Knesset session referred to above, for example, Geula Cohen, a member of the extreme right-wing Tehiya Party, said:

> Kuwait was the PLO's number-one supporter. What does it mean to give in and to show consideration for this so-called sensitivity, which stems from the hatred of Israel of these Arab states and their identification with Saddam Hussein? Why don't they want us in the coalition? ... [It's] because they say, 'Now we're fighting Saddam Hussein. Afterwards, we'll be free to fight you.' The United States should not have acquiesced in the first place, by taking into account this type of sensitivity, which is based on hatred of Israel.... I'm not referring to the hypocritical nations of Europe, to Germany, which, it transpires, is not so different [from what it was], or France, whose Vichy regime, it transpires, is not so much a thing of the past.... [The US] cannot come to terms with, or surrender to the wish of, some of its partners to, in fact, destroy another state.

To preserve this perception of Israeli isolation and the view of history as one of recurring destruction, Shamir hardly refers to the true reason for the outbreak of the war, Iraq's takeover of Kuwait and its oil resources. Instead, he describes it as the continuation of baseless terror directed against the Jews:

> This war is very similar to the one that the terrorists are

> waging against us. The purpose is to murder, and to murder civilians in particular – any civilians.... This drawn-out terror has exposed to the hilt the intentions of the Iraqi dictator and all those who cheered him on – to kill Jews and destroy their state.'[9]

The perception of an isolated nation facing a hostile front necessitates reliance on the Israeli army, and on it alone. Therefore, to the very end of the Gulf War, the leaders never ceased promising an Israeli action, even when it was abundantly clear that no such action would take place: 'I haven't a shadow of a doubt', said Eliahu Ben-Elissar, 'that Israel will take action. It will act when it sees fit to act' (23 January 1991), and Shamir later promised:

> [This] war will not end without Israeli intervention. ... We have not changed our policy since the establishment of the state or before it. Israel has only one way to defend itself from attack. We safeguard our principle of action. We shall act in the most effective way, the way that inflicts the greatest harm on the enemy and distances the menace from us.[10]

The country's leadership renounced the Israeli army's principle of swift retaliation in deed, but not in word. Although this principle was strongly entrenched in Israeli thinking, the Alignment and the left were able to renounce it because their ideology allowed them to rely on the Allied coalition and to regard Israel as a partner in it. In the eyes of the right, however, such a partnership was inconceivable: isolated Israel could rely only on the IDF. Therefore, even when the government was constrained to relinquish the option of IDF action, it continued to laud such action in its rhetoric.

In the Gulf War, as in all Israel's other wars, the strength of the Israeli army is emphasised, and along with it the nation's unity and uniqueness (for example, 'the common pulse beating in our midst' and '[the ability] to withstand the murderous enemy together'). Shamir repeats a familiar locution, culled from Ben-Gurion's speeches:

> I ask myself, what power do we have? In fact, this honourable and orderly behaviour conveys a kind of power, the power of an isolated nation that is prepared to withstand all attacks, all injury, together.[11]

Compare this with Ben-Gurion's remarks:

> The leaders of cultured and primitive nations ask themselves what is the power of this small nation, that it can withstand enemies far greater than it for over ten years? … What is the answer to this wondrous riddle?[12]

Shamir's phrasing is indeed like Ben-Gurion's, but in his terminology relative terms such as 'small nation' and 'far greater' have been replaced with absolute terms. In Shamir's rhetoric, an isolated nation withstands all attacks, all injury, all enemies. Moreover, the type of relationship that Shamir constructs between himself and the people is reminiscent of that formed by Begin, not Ben-Gurion. It is the relationship between a caring father, 'for whom the good of the nation and the entire populace, not personal advantage, is what counts' (Likud election poster, 1977). Thus, when asked by an interviewer how he feels when the siren is sounded, Shamir replies: 'I think of the entire Nation of Israel, which is together, as one, in the same predicament, obedient and disciplined, uncomplaining, doing what it is called upon to do.' This is not merely laudatory approval; it is the praise of a father who is proud of his children:

> Despite the damage, we have reason to be proud of the way our public has accepted this attempt to kill it, to murder it. Men, women and children have acted in an exemplary manner despite the cruelty of this war.[13]

The image of the nation as 'honourable and orderly' was marred by a massive flight from Tel Aviv after several Scud missiles fell and caused damage and injuries. In this case, the sacrosanct Zionist ideal of standing firm and holding on to Israel and its soil at any price was called into question. In newspaper reports and in pronouncements by national leaders those abandoning the city were depicted as refugees and deserters, and Shlomo Lahat, the mayor of Tel Aviv, even likened the flight from Tel Aviv to abandonment of Israel or desertion of the frontline in a war. The gravity with which such an accusation was perceived explains why Shamir tended to not even mention it. When he praises the nation for its 'internal exaltation', 'endurance' and 'love of homeland and state', and its decision 'to be strong, overcome obstacles, and continue producing', he is repeating well-remembered formulations from the days of the Disturbances: 'we continued to overcome and to work and produce.... While courageously enduring and defending ourselves, we have not stopped building the country, nor has traffic on the roads ceased.' Shamir, however, makes no mention of the main imperative of these declamations: 'Not one settlement outpost has withdrawn or been abandoned.'

PROPAGANDA DOCUMENTARIES

A different manifestation of the narrative used by Prime Minister Shamir may be found in films, journalistic writing and propaganda meant to support government policies. An example of these is a documentary film produced by the Israel Broadcasting Authority shortly after the war, Yarin Kimor's *Nachash Tzefa* (Code Word Viper, interjected into radio and television broadcasts during the Gulf War to notify the operators to activate the air-raid sirens). The film has the form of a drama constructed through elements that appeared in the speeches of national leaders, especially those of Shamir. It portrays history as a series of crises and reversals, each of which contains the threat of destruction and the hope of resurrection. This takes place in the form of a power struggle between the forces of light and the forces of darkness, between an isolated but united nation and a broad hostile front. This struggle can end only with the elimination of the rival.

The film opens with a shot of dark skies ripped by explosions of light, and then cuts to a close-up of a broken doll, after which the camera pans slowly to the blood-covered face of a wounded girl. In the background is the menacing rumble of drums. The most distinct graphic indicators of destruction, terror and suffering are present – explosions, a broken doll, a wounded child and threatening sounds. From destruction and dread, the film switches suddenly to 'the joy of redemption' – a recent celebration in honour of the two-hundred-thousandth immigrant to reach Israel in 1990. Another switch, from the happiness associated with Jewish immigrants arriving in Israel to the horror of death and destruction, follows quickly as a shot of a bloodied, mangled corpse and agitated crowds in an Israeli street market are seen. The narrator declares: 'This is not the first bomb that's gone off in this place, which has already experienced much bloodshed amid its stalls of juicy fruits.' The film ends in a similar manner. It switches from the costumes and festivities of Purim, on the day the Gulf War ended, to death, as the narrator announces:

> The day the war ended was the festival of Purim. That very day, a Palestinian terrorist murdered a young Jewish man in Jerusalem. Joy on the one hand and pain on the other – this sums up the essence of life in Israel.

Terror and celebration, destruction and redemption are thus intertwined in both the opening and closing scenes of the film. In the course of the film, too, there are abrupt and unexpected transitions from one direction to the other. These are usually brought about by moving quickly from shots of tranquillity and routine, such as children at home, families, debates in the Knesset and singing choirs, to sirens and scenes of destruction that suddenly cut into them. This swift cutting from one situation to another, accompanied by sudden transitions from day to night, from light to darkness, or vice versa, heighten the dramatic effects. For example, a shot of children playing on a kibbutz lawn suddenly cuts to a night scene with flashing lights of police cars and ambulance sirens in the background. The voice-over states:

> That night, 23 January, Ramat Gan absorbed the most serious attack that occurred so far. The toll: one dead, 100 injured. Hundreds of houses were hit. Some were totally destroyed. Balconies collapsed. Windowpanes were shattered. Gas canisters exploded and added to the devastation. Rescue teams … are attempting to locate survivors amid the ruins.

The structure of the film as a series of sudden shifts between tranquillity and catastrophe is meant to intensify the dramatic effect. It also reveals the same perception of history – as a series of crises that informs Shamir's speeches. The film neither describes processes nor dwells on the stages leading to the missile barrage but depicts the Scud missiles as sudden disasters descending from Heaven. It describes the entire war in a similar vein, as one that erupted suddenly and inexplicably and ended, as the voice-over explains, 'as suddenly as it began'. A description of the developments that led up to the Gulf War might have made it seem less sudden, but would also have reduced the dramatic effect.

Although the war begins and ends suddenly, it is not perceived as a single crisis but rather as a link in a chain of similar calamities. Thus, while the film's primary theme is the Gulf War, it portrays the state of war in general as an on-going and endless situation, a perception brought out by both beginning and ending the film with the *Intifada.* In this way the Iraqis are equated with the Palestinians, and both are used interchangeably throughout: 'Television announcers and reporters describe the countdown in grave tones,' the voice track explains, 'but the military correspondent is still covering Fatah Day' (a shot of an Arab village follows, accompanied by threatening music). The air force 'scrambles into the Israeli skies', we are told elsewhere in the film, 'but back on the ground people are preparing for the menace at home'. Also, 'The inhabitants of the Territories [the Palestinians in the West Bank and Gaza] proclaim their support of Saddam Hussein.... The greater the Israelis' distress, the greater the rejoicing in the Territories' (shot of an Arab town, threatening music, an interview with a pro-war Palestinian). The war is expanded geographically as well – from Arab villages in the West Bank to south Lebanon, 'where life is following an emergency routine that has been going on for years – a terror routine', and from the mosques of Jerusalem to Scud-demolished buildings in Ramat Gan in greater Tel Aviv.

The Germans and the Nazis are appended to the Arab enemy. George Bush, in his speeches, frequently likened the Gulf War to the Second World War in order to equate the coalition's struggle against Saddam Hussein with that of the Allies against Hitler. Israeli leaders on both the left and the right frequently invoked this parallelism (especially in the Knesset debate on this subject on 23 January 1991). However, Kimor's film, like the speeches of some right-wing leaders, harnesses it to the imperative of expanding the enemy front Israel is facing by linking present and past. Thus, present-day Germany is equated with the Germany of the past: 'The fickleness of fate is amusing. The gas masks were distributed on the day Germany was reunified.... There are some people who have become used to taking the Final Solution of the Jewish Problem seriously.' Both these are linked with the malicious deeds of Saddam Hussein and his 'threats of destruction and secret weapons'. At certain moments, as in the leaders' speeches, even the Americans are portrayed as belonging to the enemy side: 'Concerning these pictures [of the destruction caused by the Scud missiles], General Schwarzkopf said that the thunderclaps in Georgia [USA] are stronger. His remarks provoked serious anger in Israel.' The need to adhere to a narrative that characterises Israel's wars as the struggles of 'a people that dwells alone' against a broad hostile front prompts the narrator to explain that the missile barrages are part of a never-ending onslaught that keeps Israel in perpetual isolation: 'When all is said and done, we prefer today's danger with all the nations to the danger of tomorrow alone.' The appropriate response to this onslaught is 'anger and lust for vengeance'.

The film cannot demonstrate the actual struggle, vengeance and retaliation, but it reconstructs them figuratively by editing, thus making sudden switches between the threats and actions of Saddam Hussein and the Iraqi army, and shots that symbolise the power and strength of the Israeli nation, army and leadership. These are shots of the Israeli flag, the Israeli army and Prime Minister Yitzhak Shamir. For example, a sequence of shots dwells on Saddam Hussein and his army. He stands among his soldiers (voice-over: 'He appears more confident and arrogant than usual') and his soldiers promise they will fight to the end (the camera switches to a scene of Iraqi soldiers dancing and singing 'We shall fight to the death'). This sequence is cut and replaced by a close-up of the Israeli flag. The camera quickly moves away from the flag (in a zoom-out) and switches to Yitzhak Shamir. The voice-over says: 'In reply to Saddam's threats, the government of Israel announces that in case of an Iraqi attack, Israel will retaliate.' The Israeli flag reappears on the screen and the camera pans back to Shamir. This time, he is being interviewed and speaks of the right of self-defence. His words are illustrated by shots of war weapons such as missile launchers, tanks and warplanes. Thus the editing reconstructs the conflict as one between Yitzhak Shamir and Saddam Hussein and gives Shamir the support of the state apparatus and the army.

In most cases a shot of Saddam Hussein is followed by one of Yitzhak Shamir, and those of Shamir are preceded or followed by footage of defence forces, soldiers or weapons. These are usually photographed in motion – the soldiers are marching, the missiles are being launched, the planes are taking off. Although the Israeli army is not actually fighting, its dynamism on screen gives the impression of action, and the editing of the film characterises this action as the outcome of the prime minister's words and decisions. In this way the impression is that of real warfare led by two leaders who have actually sent their armies to fight against each other. The might of the Israeli army is further magnified because, as stated, it is characterised as standing up not only to Saddam Hussein but to all the enemies of the past, as well as those of the present.

The documentary film *Nachash Tzefa* set out to create dramatic effects. It thus begins with one dramatic event and ends with another, and switches, as it progresses, from one drama to another. It intensifies the dramatic effect by creating confrontations between leaders and between their armies by invoking blood and corpses, and by making sudden switches from dread to great rejoicing, and from destruction to vengeance. Since these dramatic effects are consistent with those constructed in the speeches of Shamir and other leaders, the drama presented in the film served the dominant ideological narrative.

THE EFFECT OF THE RIGHTIST-JEWISH NARRATIVE ON THE PUBLIC

The speeches of Israeli leaders during the Gulf War were characterised by a national pathos that usually accompanied the rightist-Jewish narrative. However, in newspaper articles and topical reports, and in street interviews with passers-by, this pathos is rarely evident. Thus, a gap was created between the rightist-Jewish narrative espoused by the leadership and the reality of the war as experienced by the populace. During the two months of the Gulf War Iraqi missiles were directed at, and fell on, various populated parts of Israel. The threat that these might contain a poisonous gas forced virtually the entire population of the country to spend hours in rooms 'sealed' against the penetration of gas. The hours spent in such close quarters drew families, neighbours and friends together, but the experience did not create a sense of national unity or the usual patriotic wartime morale.

Moreover, the Gulf War could not be regarded as one for liberation from a tyrannical despot or a 'war of the sons of light against the sons of darkness', both because the enemy was too remote and because the war was being fought by others. It was also exceedingly difficult to characterise the war as one of an isolated nation against a broad, hostile front when Israel and this broad front were on the same side. Even Israel's defence doctrine, according to which neither alliances nor diplomacy, but only the Israeli army, can defend the country from its enemies, was fractured, since the Israeli army was not sent out into the field at all. In addition to this, the leadership's attempt to 'bill' the United States financially for remaining passive further damaged the nation's and the army's self-images as an active and dynamic force, and undermined the national pride that had been so potent a factor in the narrative. Even the image of a fatherly leadership disintegrated as it became evident that this leadership was unable to provide the public with clear and inarguably correct instructions on how to behave. Some of its positions, such as the policy of non-retaliation, were not made at the decision-taking level at all, while others were adopted by lower echelons such as *Haga*, the Civil Defence, which advocated the use of sealed rooms.[14] The fact that the members of the political leadership rarely addressed the public directly during the war, relying on IDF spokesman Nahman Shai to 'stand in' for them, further weakened their power and authority. The 'national hero' of the Gulf War was thus Nahman Shai, who projected an intellectual, non-macho persona. And it was Shai, rather than Shamir, who successfully embodied the paternal, concerned-for-the-public image – but in TV-celebrity style, not in the image of a leader-of-the-people.

The government's power and authority deteriorated, especially after the war, when it became known that the gas masks would have been ineffectual, and as the confusion and lack of information that prevailed in the hours following the missile strikes were revealed. The description of these hours by a radio broadcaster interviewed for the film *Sha'anan Si* (Peak Lethargy) attests to this:

> We'd been left in the dark.... Anyone you approached knew nothing or wasn't telling. I could have ordered warplanes to strike Iraq. The powers granted me, a simple radio announcer, were suddenly vast. The power given to someone who shouldn't have power – who after all is just a mouthpiece – was unlimited.[15]

The rightist-Jewish narrative had been losing a lot of its relevance and appeal since the Lebanon War. The Gulf War served to accelerate this process.

THE BROADCAST NEWS

During the war televised news broadcasts were notably suitable for expressing the government's rightist 'ideological drama', mainly because Israel's two television stations were unified into one national network. In addition, by their very nature news broadcasts are based on conflicts and deviations from the norm, and their time frame inhibits detailed descriptions of situations or in-depth analyses of causes, trends and results. Consequently, television news tends to provide climaxes rather than processes, events rather than contexts, struggles between protagonists rather than clashes of interests and abstract forces: 'The more tumultuous, visual and dramatic a conflict is, the better suited it is to the news.'[16]

The dramatic structure of the rightist-Jewish narrative could have provided good material for televised news, just as it did for Yarin

Kimor's film. And yet, the televised newscasts actually tended to play down highly dramatic elements, or even to keep them out of sight. This was partly owing to the fact that both the journalists and broadcasters and their audience were ambivalent about the pathos expressed by the national leaders. Moreover, the establishment itself was presenting two conflicting demands – the first, to intensify the crisis and highlight the national drama, and thus express the rightist ideological narrative; the second, to minimise the crisis and play down the drama, in order to calm the public. The television reports responded to the second demand – either because it corresponded more closely to the journalists' way of thinking or because it expressed the public's own leanings. However, the task of soothing the public was contradictory to the presentation of blatantly dramatic televised newscasts that would have expressed the government's rightist-Jewish ideological narrative. The newscasters thus refrained, during the Gulf War, from doing what Kimor did in his film after it was over.

It is interesting that the televised reports not only refrained from reconstructing the dramatic narrative of the right, but actually gave expression to a type of narrative based on a constructive, step-by-step endeavour rather than on vengeance and war. The reader will recognise this as the structure of texts of the Labor movement and its affiliates in the pre-state *Yishuv* period, as expressed in the movement's leaflets and posters (discussed in Chapter 1). Into this constructive-endeavour mould, the Gulf War reportage injected new elements of the 1980s 'personal narrative', which was centred around the routine of daily life, consumerism and normality.

STRUCTURE

Unlike Kimor's film, which begins and ends with antipodal peaks of destruction and redemption, death and celebration, the newscasts begin and end with the comfortable normality of daily routine and everyday activities, or with the likelihood of these returning shortly. The dramatic news event – siren, missile barrage or destruction and damage – is not glossed over but is inserted discretely into the middle of the report, between a pleasant beginning and a happy ending. For example, a news report filmed after the first missile strike begins with an interview with Shlomo Lahat, the mayor of Tel Aviv, who says:

> Thank Heaven, the damage is less than I expected. There's no

> reason to get excited, no reason for panic. A house was destroyed? That's not so important; [the owner] will get a new and more beautiful house in its place. You've got to continue living and smiling.

The report switches from the interview with the mayor to interviews with people whose homes had been damaged or destroyed by the missiles. They describe the sirens, the blast of the missile as it struck, and the panic that gripped them. The reporter corroborates their words by showing clips of the site hit by the missile and describing the 'clouds of dust that are still rising from the explosion'. The report does not close on the note of destruction, however, but of reconstruction: 'Emergency teams went into action at once and reached the spot immediately. In this sense, we see that the rear is well-prepared. The emergency system functioned like a well-oiled machine.'

The accepted norm in television reports is to use the authorities to provide the background for the events and to explain them after this priming.[17] In the Gulf War newscasts, this form served the additional need to begin and conclude the reports on a note of peace and secureness. A report about emergency operations in Tel Aviv's Ichilov Hospital following a missile attack begins: 'The hospital was prepared and ready. The workers, the medical staff – doctors and nurses – arrived early in the morning, equipped with their gas masks.' The camera sweeps across the teeming hospital waiting room, pans crowds of people as if 'searching' for something specific in the tumult, and zeroes in on the doctors. As the camera focuses on them, the whiteness of their uniforms 'illuminates' the surrounding chaos. After offering a general description of the hospital, the report continues with interviews with the injured, who describe their traumatic experiences ('There was a tremendous noise; I was thrown about ten metres into the air.' 'Everything was full of blood.'). Behind them and busy with their care of other patients are the doctors, who serve as a soothing backdrop to the grim descriptions. The report ends with an interview with Mayor Lahat, who promises the victims new homes. Thus, the report that begins with a 'happy end' (the hospital was ready, everything went according to plan, doctors and nurses were on hand) also ends with one (promises of new and better houses). This happy end, supported and confirmed by political leaders, mayors and doctors, is intended to look more stable and certain than anything that threatens it.

Wherever a report cannot end with an interview with an official representative, that role is filled by an ordinary citizen who expresses the current national imperatives. One news report, for example, begins with the following words: 'Shortly after the missile attack security men reach the area that was hit.' The camera pans the destruction, focuses briefly on the security men, and then switches to interviews with residents of the destroyed houses: 'What have our children done to deserve such a fate?' and 'We're living in terror.' The discourse is painful and moving, but towards the end one of the by-standers seizes the microphone and changes the tone: 'There's no panic. Show some nice shots. Give Israel some encouragement.'

The structure of these reports is effectively delineated by comparing how the same documentary material is filmed and organised by different bodies. On 22 January 1991 Israel Television presented three reports of the same Iraqi missile attack. The first was by Israeli Television itself, the second by a team of the Israeli army's spokesman, and the third by CNN. The Israeli Television and army spokesman's reports begin with shots of rescue teams and ambulances, accompanied by appropriate texts (delivered by news announcers):

> Many teams were ordered to the spot and arrived within minutes of the call. Civil Defence and [the emergency medical services] also arrived in a flash.... As you can see in these scenes, numerous rescue teams are here, and they are doing wonderful work.

The shots themselves show destroyed balconies and building wreckage, but the report ends with lengthy panoramic shots of the rescue teams at work. In general, the report tries to present an overall view of the rescue operation. Several close-ups focus more on labels or symbols than on people, that is, on police and medics' insignias or the Star of David emblem on the rescue workers' uniforms.

The CNN shots of the same event tend to seek out the personal human-interest items from among the rescue teams, police and soldiers, and to focus on them – a man carrying a little girl on his shoulders, youngsters running about in pyjamas, confused children, a woman in panic. The shots tend to linger on close-ups of such details as an uprooted tree, a shattered cooking-gas cylinder, a burst water tap. Here too, as in the Israeli Television and IDF footage, rescue teams fill the screen, but the CNN camera finds and highlights the people and the metonymic details that exemplify the human drama.[18]

The Israeli reportage thus delimits the devastation and emphasises the rescue work rather than the grim human drama on which the

American clip focuses. Kimor's film, discussed above, is motivated by the same imperative – to present and intensify the drama. However, the drama with which Kimor's film deals is a collective drama, not a personal human one, thus corresponding to an Israeli national narrative rather than to the personal viewpoint that motivates the CNN report.

The structure of the Israeli television reports also evokes a mood of stability, security and calm by mixing or reversing the order of the events, or by repeating them. Security personnel or visiting officials are shown at the scene of a missile attack at the beginning of the report, before the event itself is described, and again following the description, thus giving the viewers the impression they had been there all the time. One such report opens with a demolition squad examining a fallen missile and ends with police closing off the site, while another begins with civil defence forces and ends with a group of soldiers. Another report opens with a shot of a little girl asleep, describes the missile landing on her house, and ends with the same shot of the sleeping girl. The reporter explains that the child was sleeping in her home when 'the missile awakened her, and now she continues sleeping in a hotel'. The missile attack is thus characterised as a passing event that has not succeeded in changing the normal situation.

The fact that the missiles could not be filmed as they fell, and that the actual hit could only be described as a flashback, or as reported by the victims, helps create the desired structure. The trauma is presented only once, as a recollection and therefore something out of the past; calm and quietude are shown as part of the present, and this is repeated at the most significant points of the report, the beginning and the end. The destruction and damage thus seem to be unimportant, trivialities of the past, and somewhat unreal or abstract when contrasted with the permanence of daily life that is shown, in real time, on the screen.

The reports also use visual compositions, landscapes or lighting in order to delimit the trauma within a frame of security and calm. A common formula consists of a transition from low-angle shots to eye-angle shots and back again. One typical report begins with a view of the sky, in which Israeli warplanes appear. The camera then 'comes down to earth' in order to show local Arabs expressing solidarity with Saddam Hussein. Then it rises again, showing television antennae and a soldier standing on the roof of a building. The sky, the army and the air force provide a 'frame' of security around an event that is liable to shatter this security. The camera's sweep from the ground to the sky also instils a feeling of control of space in a report that describes a threat to such control.

Many reports end with shots of the seashore, pigeons taking flight from puddles in a town square, a view of the coastline from Jaffa, or the approaching dawn. Their goal is the same. The cinematic and literary conventions for a happy ending (the sea, flying pigeons, dawn) suggest a culmination of peace and tranquillity even though the scenes and the accompanying texts actually attest to the opposite: the beaches are deserted, the pigeons fly freely around the square because the people who usually throng it are at home in their sealed rooms. The transitions from night to dawn and from cityscape to uncluttered beach also endow the report with a dynamism that the events themselves cannot provide.

Many of the same scenes that appeared in the televised newscasts during the war were used in *Nachash Tzefa*, but the structure of Kimor's film gave them a different function. For example, scenes of Palestinians in the territories were utilised to symbolise the broad anti-Israel front and were therefore usually paired with Saddam Hussein's threats and actions. In the structure of the television reports, these shots of Palestinians were used to symbolise the army's ability to restore and maintain order, and were therefore inserted between shots of soldiers in action.

The return to an everyday life of constructive endeavour after its disruption by enemy actions had been a conspicuous theme in the narrative of the Labor movement during the *Yishuv* period, when it also reflected that organisation's policy of *havlagah* (self-restraint) and non-retaliation. During the Gulf War the news reports used this narrative, for it was more suitable for the purpose of keeping the populace calm than the rightist-Jewish narrative. The return to the old Labor narrative, unintentional though it may have been, reinforced the ideological and political positions of the left. In addition, the injunction of this narrative to maintain daily routines despite the warlike situation corresponded to a central element of the personal narrative of the 1990s.

Since the theme of television reports in general is conflict, the normal routine of life and work in Israeli towns, especially in Tel Aviv, had never been the subject of television reportage. This changed during the Gulf War when the prosaic events of daily life – the bustle in the vegetable market, shopping, a morning walk along the shore – were viewed as a departure from the norm. Routine thus became a news item. The Gulf War invested television news with an element that, before the war, had been dealt with only in the personal narrative that turned routine daily life into its main subject.

CITIZENS AGAINST AUTHORITY

Just as the television reports did not articulate the destruction-to-redemption structure of Shamir's speeches, so too they refrained from expressing another struggle that he portrayed in them, that of freedom fighters against tyranny. A real struggle for power was taking place between America and Iraq, and it was extensively filmed and broadcast by the American CNN.[19] The Israeli broadcasts concentrated, rather, on the anxious anticipation of the missile attacks and descriptions of their aftermath, and did not extend the drama to the source of the missiles, Iraq, and to its leader, Saddam Hussein. This had a strange result: the conflict described in the Israeli reports was one of an anonymous force against luck, fate or a miracle, and the contestants were not Saddam Hussein versus George Bush, but the Scud missile versus the Hand of God. This merged with a conflict between Israel's citizens and authorities, which was usually expressed as a clash between contradictory explanations of how a catastrophe was handled. By beginning and ending with interviews of municipal and government officials, the reports portrayed the establishment authorities as those who ensured the order and calm that prevailed before the missile strike and who would see to their resumption. Often, however, their versions of the events ran counter to those of the civilian victims of the attack, who complained of the authorities' incompetence and relied instead on miracles and luck. Thus, the conflict portrayed by the Israeli television reports is neither the one that Shamir articulates in his speeches nor the global conflict of the Gulf War and Israel's place within it; it is a conflict between Israeli citizens and Israeli authorities.

On one of the first days of the war, for example, a missile landed on an abandoned and unused air-raid shelter. The residents of the neighbourhood had decided to use another nearby shelter and were saved. The report of the event begins with an interview with Mayor Shlomo Lahat, who says:

> You can count on the Tel Aviv Municipality. We took care [of you] and have been planning for five months, and such events are not chance. … We must continue to live and to smile and to obey the instructions of its *Haga*.

The report then moves on to the destruction and focuses on a group of residents. One of them tells the story from his perspective:

> Yesterday we decided to use the [more distant] shelter in case of a missile attack. Some people here have no shelter at all. They confirmed for us that there's a shelter [there] and that everything's all right. We got this confirmation by chance, not from the authorities in charge.

One woman describes how they went to sleep in the shelter, how they were about to leave it, and how, at the last minute, the siren went off, the missile fell, and they were saved. The residents point out that their houses are not reinforced, that there are no shelters in their immediate neighbourhood and that they now have nowhere to go because all their windows and shutters have been shattered. The reporter insists: 'All in all, it was a miracle?' They admit that it was just that: 'We had a God-given miracle. We sat down and read Psalms.' At the end of the report, in keeping with the custom, the interviewer returns to Mayor Lahat and says in a questioning tone: 'It was quite a miracle that the residents preferred one shelter and not the other.' The mayor replies that the closer shelter was not in use: 'It's no accident that they were not there. It was shut. We closed shelters that are out of service and do not provide protection. You can count on Tel Aviv City Hall.' Thus the residents, who took the initiative to use another shelter, attribute their survival to a miracle. Lahat attempts to take credit for it and to attribute their survival to the municipality.

The conflict here is not between Israel and the enemy (this report, like most others, does not even mention Iraq and Saddam Hussein); it is between two interpretations of the forces of 'evil' and 'good' that take part in the struggle – the Scud and the miracle by one reading, and the Scud and City Hall by the other. Thus, although the purpose of the televised reports was to substantiate and confirm the authorities' ability to prevent destruction by the missiles, or to repair it, what actually emerged from them was a conflict between civilians and authorities. In the final analysis, not only did the television reports express narratives that differed from those of the political establishment, they also undermined the validity of the establishment's authority that they had set out to reinforce.

PERSONAL DOCUMENTARIES

The rightist-Jewish narrative thus failed the 'test of the public' and was unable to capture the television screen during the Gulf War. However, it had already lost much of its power before the war, during which time two other narratives had already gained considerable strength and were thus ready to spearhead a struggle against it. During the war itself, these narratives served as the basis for attacks directed against the rightist-Jewish narrative. Street posters, graffiti, the press (in its satirical columns) and popular television programmes ridiculed and parodied it, and exposed the disparity between it and reality. These and other texts helped the revived constructive-endeavour narrative of the Labor movement on the one hand, and the personal narrative on the other, to make growing inroads in Israeli society.

The personal narrative was not completely new. It had appeared already in the 1960s when it expressed the decline of nationalistic ardour and Israel's transition into an individualistic, consumer-oriented, bourgeois society. It was then expressed in a sophisticated form in *belles-lettres* and cinema. In the 1980s and 1990s, however, it was much more disconnected from the Israeli political reality. It neither sought nor found values or a source of power in the nationalist narratives, of the right or of the left; it sought alternatives to them, even though these might be in the worlds of fantasy or reverie (as discussed in Chapters 6 and 7).

Many texts based on the personal narrative are confined to an Israeli town or neighbourhood which, steeped in American cultural values, ignores, or refuses to relate to, the national political reality.[20] The Gulf War forced this narrative into a debate with the nationalist narratives, especially the rightist-Jewish one, which these texts tried to topple. The film *Sha'anan Si,* for example, begins with a shot of a man standing in an air-raid shelter and singing: 'This shelter is ours. It belongs to one nation. God loves this shelter and will guard it forever.' The song is suddenly interrupted and the film moves on to a scene of a deserted town at night, photographed from a travelling vehicle with the noise of a siren in the background. The national and divine promise, parodied in the song, is immediately punctured by dread and anxiety – night, a deserted city, a siren's wail.

Similar parodies filled the pages of the press and appeared on street posters. A photograph of people gazing skyward, for example, was captioned: 'We're not Patriots. We're afraid of the heavens.' There is a double word-play in this example: 'Patriots' refers both to loyalty and to the American-sent 'Patriot' anti-missile-missiles pointed skyward, while 'afraid of the heavens' is the Hebrew idiom for 'God-fearing'. The scene itself was a parody of an earlier double-entendre morale-boosting poster 'We're all Patriots'. This poster had been parodied once before, when somebody added to it the graffito 'Shoot down the copywriter'.

The final scene of the film *Sha'anan Si* ends in much the same way as the television reports ended – with the Israeli flag, the symbol of national stability and security. In the film, however, the flag appears only in the margin; the rest of the screen is totally dark. In the background, the end of an interview is heard: 'It reminded me of summer. We were by the sea. Last summer. And then I suddenly understood: where is that summer that we spent by the sea? Where is that summer and where are we?'

The accepted symbol of national security and stability has thus been shifted to the fringe of the screen and dwarfed by the darkness, thereby losing its significance. Ridicule of the national symbol was a common element in other texts during the war. An example of such ridicule is an illustration in the satirical section of the newspaper *Davar*, which depicts a landmark Tel Aviv theatre as a coffin draped in the Israeli flag.[21] In other caricatures gas masks are placed on the flag and the Star of David, while in journalistic articles the flag is set in the context of nostalgic films. The journalist Tamar Gelbetz writes:

> What are all these flags? Shredded by the wind, all over town? Like on that Independence Day in 1963 when [President] Yitzhak Ben-Zvi died. At half-mast. Soon we'll begin seeing everything in black and white, like in the [old] newsreels.[22]

Sha'anan Si uses similar parodies and integrates them in a structure that replaces the national narrative with the personal one. It begins with the theme of unity and redemption and ends with a symbol of national pride and patriotism, outwardly copying the comforting frame within which the news reports of the war events were presented. Not only is this frame now presented as a parody, it is immediately replaced by elements of the personal narrative. The song of redemption and national unity at the beginning of the film gives way to sounds expressing the fears of the people confined to their shelters; the flag at the end is overwhelmed by nostalgia for the Tel Aviv seashore, a well-known symbol of freedom, leisure, and *joie de vivre*. Both fear and nostalgia exist now only on the individual plane, here dissociated from any national significance. The recurrent shots of gloomy night evoke dread, but it is a personal dread, unlike the national dread that is elicited by scenes of the *Intifada* in Kimor's film *Nachash Tzefa*. The way it copes with this is also different from that of the television reports: the night remains black until the very end; no dawn illuminates it; no mayor or prime minister ends it.

The film *Ha-yozma Ha-tzarfatit* (The French Initiative) by Ron Katznelson and Eitan Dotan is structured in a similar way. Many of its scenes use motifs that were used in the television reports, but their meaning is now reversed. For example, in one scene pigeons are splashing in a puddle in a deserted town square, a motif very common in the television reports. In this film, however, the camera does not follow the pigeons' flight into the sky in order to provide the 'happy end'; it remains focused on the now deserted puddle.

Both *Sha'anan Si* and *Ha-yozma Ha-tzarfatit* express anxiety by using a very broad range of cinematic devices. In *Shana'an Si* the nocturnal journey through a dark, deserted town is a recurrent motif and is accompanied by threatening sounds such as moaning wind, falling rain and the yowl of distant cars. The view of a shelter filmed through a wide-angle lens gives the impression of a huge space, empty and threatening, and the unstable shaking of a shoulder camera calls to mind the trembling of a frightened hand. *Ha-yozma Ha-tzarfatit* uses many familiar cinematic conventions to create the same sense of terror – for example, drums rumbling in the background; shots of marching feet (actually of shoppers in a supermarket); views of long, dark corridors; terror-stricken faces reflected and distorted in windows; lengthy close-ups of a gas mask. In both films the anxiety and terror are not compressed into a stable and soothing structure as in the television reports, and they do not progress in the direction of national catharsis, as in *Nachash Tzefa*. They are invoked repeatedly as motifs that echo only themselves. Neither film attempts to alleviate anxiety or to present it as a transitional stage leading towards redemption. The films confront the apocalyptic structure of destruction and redemption, and present only an enormous anxiety without relief – the fear of disaster without redemption.

During the Gulf War many parodies targeted the much-repeated dramas of destruction and redemption and the struggle of forces of light against forces of darkness. This was usually done by reducing the drama to a context of entertainment and by presenting it as a picture, a film or a radio broadcast. The drama of redemption is seen by the journalist Ya'ir Lapid as 'part of a speech at a school graduation ceremony'.[23] It is cast in the framework of a radio broadcast by another journalist, Eli Shai, who describes

> a hidden desire to put the radio on one clear night, sometime around one of the [Jewish] holidays, and hear the final, closing

> announcement: '… This is the Voice of Israel from Jerusalem. And here is the news. There is much commotion around the approaches to the city and its outskirts as far as Sha'ar Hagai. Our reporter was told that, any minute now, the convoy of the Messiah-Son-of-David will pass by on its way to the Temple Mount.'[24]

The films create similar parodies but use them to transmute the national, apocalyptic drama into a personal, human one.

While during the Gulf War the television news reports focused on the conflicts between Israeli citizens and the authorities rather than on the Gulf War itself, the 'personal' films turned this struggle into the main topic of a debate between the personal and the national narratives, especially the rightist-Jewish narrative. One of the people interviewed in *Sha'anan Si* speaks to the camera:

> This war is a series of humiliations in which all of a sudden you have to rely on the IDF. Or listen to the IDF spokesman. Or rely on the army, which is an organisation I've been sceptical about all my life.

The television set alongside him is on and is 'competing with him' for the audience's attention as American soldiers can be seen advancing towards their targets in Iraq. The interviewee continues speaking while the scene on the television set in the background changes and Israeli Foreign Minister David Levy appears in a special televised interview. The audience of *Sha'anan Si* does not hear Levy's words in the interview, but those of 'their' interviewee who continues to speak to the camera:

> I'm trying to find constellations so I won't be alone. We all have to give up this idea of our individuality and become a herd.… Nahman Shai has a very soothing effect on me. That's what's humiliating about it; it robs us of our freedom.

In *Ha-yozma Ha-tzarfatit* a background of radio broadcasts accompanies all the events seen on the screen. The radio voices provide, for instance, commentaries, a report on French attempts at mediation, a description of preparations for the war and of the waves of bombing over Kuwait. All these seem divorced from the pictures, which focus on objects – worried people, a stray cat, empty streets. These pictures evoke a reality that appears to be totally unrelated to the global initiatives and measures that are taking place far away. The structure of the film puts these two domains into direct confrontation, when, for example, the radio announces a 'reliable commentary' by a lieutenant-colonel and the film itself presents commentaries by ordinary people interviewed on the street, or when lingering shots of representatives of the army, uniformed soldiers, are seen, while on the radio the army officer is unable to answer questions about how to protect oneself in case of a gas attack.

Whenever the public authorities appear in these films, they are shown to be detached from the man in the street. In *Ha-yozma Ha-tzarfatit*, Tel Aviv Mayor Shlomo Lahat explains: 'The situation in Tel Aviv is that we're prepared. We're calm. We're not worried.' The shot of City Hall Square, where Lahat makes these statements, does not substantiate his words. The camera sweeps the large and empty square and then lingers on two heaps of sand in the middle of the square that look like the unfinished preparations for some construction work. The next scene simply contradicts Lahat's words completely. A woman walking in the street with her dog admits: 'Yes, I am really very scared. Of what? Of being caught in the street without a gas-mask, or simply of being caught up by the war itself. It's very frightening.'

The wartime press, street posters and some television programmes abounded with puns on the country's leadership. For example, since the Hebrew term for lifeguard is the same as that for saviour, the frequently seen beach sign 'Ein matzil', which means 'No lifeguard [on duty]', resurfaced as 'There is no saviour', which is another meaning of the expression. In the television entertainment programme *Zehu Zeh*, the comic actor Shlomo Bar-Abba promised: 'You'll see, Begin will yet return to power. He'll bring in Ben-Gurion and create a National Unity Government and we'll be able to sleep in peace', when Begin was ill and no longer able to lead the country and Ben-Gurion had long since died.

In addition to parodies on the nation's leadership, others ridiculing the Israeli army appeared in graffiti and on street posters. For example, a poster rehashing the motto 'Bravo, IDF!' reminds the public that the army does not deserve its customary kudos this time. *Ha-yozma Ha-tzarfatit* inserted both kinds of parodies into the struggle between citizens and authorities, and between the personal and the national narratives. It was composed of footage taken by an Israeli photographer for a French film company which had asked him to photograph Israel's preparations for the war. The company's faxed requests are presented in the film, verbally and word for word, and are accompanied by suitable footage. In many cases the requests are treated with irony. This is often directed at the way the French perceive the war, but also at the way the Israelis cope with it. One of the targets of this irony is the Israeli army.

For example, the French faxed a request for footage of IDF soldiers in action. The film shows bored soldiers patrolling a totally empty market, switches over to a closed window shutter and a wailing cat, and then back to the soldiers. In another shot, the camera pauses at one of the water-valves of the gas-decontamination showers outside a Tel Aviv hospital. The valve, painted bright yellow and red, looks alive. Behind it an IDF soldier with a submachine gun is standing, blurred but visible. The camera pans the soldier's body from bottom to top, but neither adjusts the focus nor reaches his head. It is the valve, in its entirety, that remains in focus throughout. The headless soldier looks pitiable, marginal and unimportant. Elsewhere in the film, the camera completely ignores a woman soldier explaining the use of the atropine hypodermic syringe and remains focused on the intent and panic-stricken face of the woman listening to her. The French asked for soldiers in action; the film gives them shots of blurred, faceless soldiers, and of soldiers who have nothing to do. Thus, by using contrived, selected and edited footage, the film 'rebels' against the French. But it also 'rebels' against the Israelis by mocking the televised reports in which soldiers in action were frequently shown as a sign of control and as a means of calming the populace. In mocking the French requests, it also mocks the Israeli situation; instead of authority and order, it presents confrontations between citizens and civil and military authorities, between national narratives and the personal one.

CRITICISM OF THE PERSONAL NARRATIVE

As the new personal narrative coalesced and struggled for its place against the national narratives, it was already being criticised in the name of the very same political reality that it tended to spurn. Michal Peleg's documentary *Tel Aviv Neged Ha-zman* (Tel Aviv: Biting Time) is an example of the latter. It consists of interviews with young Tel Avivians who have turned their backs on both rightist and leftist versions of Israeli history. They are forced to grapple with this history when it penetrates the safety of their ivory towers in the form of the Gulf War. The historical and political events leading up to the war do not interest them. Itzik, one of the interviewees, explains: 'I wasn't astounded when the *Intifada* broke out. I wasn't astounded when it continued … as long as it didn't affect me personally.… I believed that if I was really lucky, I wouldn't be affected.' His girlfriend Daniella says:

> Everyone sees Arabs now and then. They're the ones who build your houses for you. They're the ones who paint your houses, who clean up your streets, who wash the dishes in restaurants. You can't help but see them, but you're really not seeing them. In the long run, none of this bothers me. What bothers me much more is whether I have a pimple on my face or whether I've put on weight.

These young adults, who do not live within the 'history of *Eretz Yisrael*', are not even comfortable with its geography. Daniella says:

> If Herzl had set up Israel in Africa, I wouldn't have had any problem with that. The fact that we're here seems to me the worst possible hole in which to be in the whole world. For all I care, it could have been any place.

Instead of the entire geographical area of Israel, they narrow their sphere of interest to one place, Tel Aviv. They agree that 'If you're an Israeli anyway, the only bearable place to be in this country, the only place that gives the illusion of normal life, is Tel Aviv.' They defiantly add their voices to the attempt to turn Tel Aviv into a centre of culture and values, an alternative to the country's other areas and centres (for example, Jerusalem, kibbutzim). Tel Aviv – a cosmopolitan hedonistic city with a strong tendency towards American culture and the routine of daily life – is a geographical representation *par excellence* of the personal narrative. Tel Aviv, writes one columnist,

> was created from the dunes, and it is Israeli. Not Jewish. Not People of Israel. Just Israeli. It has no past to speak of. Its future, too, won't be anything special. It won't be a light unto the nations, and it won't be the capital of the world.[25]

Consequently, as another columnist explains,

> our loyalty to Tel Aviv is not so different from our loyalty to Maccabi Tel Aviv [a sports team]. When they bring home the

> cup, we leap into the water-fountain, and when they lose to the Czechs, we start getting interested in American football.[26]

The war, which threatens their personal, localised narrative, causes them to cling to it even more vehemently. Itzik, interviewed in the film immediately after a missile attack, complains:

> Tel Aviv was a different place. A bit European. Now what kind of Europe is it that's being hit by missiles? I hope we can still, once again, get back to the illusion of this normality. But I doubt it very much.

Young people in other places make similar remarks. A third Tel Aviv columnist admits:

> Do you want the truth? The truth is like this: we're scared to death. Don't forget that we don't have this agreement that the collective settlements or the green extremities of the country have. We – get ready to laugh – haven't really promised anyone anything.... All in all, all we wanted was to live near the ice-cream parlours and pizza shops and bus fumes, ... and where you can see good movies.[27]

The attempt to adhere to the personal narrative during the war, despite the pressures to relate to the national narrative, brings the principal elements of this narrative into sharp view, particularly its characteristic lack of political involvement. Itzik admits that

> During the war, I thought it would leave me with a trauma because they really didn't prepare us for the suddenly very likely possibility that the quietest and most normal place in the country would become a target for missiles.

The interviewer interrupts him with 'But what has changed in the city?' to which he answers:

> Oh, you must mean the Arabs – and believe me, for a long time I didn't even notice that they'd disappeared. In fact, just a few weeks ago it suddenly occurred to me that the Arabs are white. They're the ones who sweep the streets and build our buildings. It suddenly occurred to me – now let's say I became

> aware – that the new 'Arabs' are the Russians, and the former Arabs just like disappeared somewhere. I think it's partly because I'm apparently a very representative Tel Avivian, and when they were here, they didn't really concern me; and now that they're gone, I don't really miss them very much. All I do is lead my own life. As long as the grocery store is open and the pub is in business and I leave in the morning and find the number five bus where it was yesterday, then all the rest doesn't really bother me. And all of that survived the war.... The next war will surprise us exactly as this war did. As far as I'm concerned, Tel Aviv is the place where missiles simply don't fall. I'm denying that missiles ever fell here, and if there are missiles [again], I simply won't understand where they came from. It will seem like the first time.

The structure of *Tel Aviv Neged Ha-zman* reflects what the interviewees say, but also judges them by linking them with the political reality they try to ignore. The film opens with footage taken in January 1991 during the war – Tel Aviv by night, missiles landing, the destruction, the silent deserted streets – and at the end returns to these scenes and expands them. The bulk of the documentary, filmed in June 1990 and shown between the two war sequences, consists of a juxtaposition of interviews with young Tel Avivians (plus earlier scenes of them dancing on the seashore, in pubs and in discotheques), and interviews with slum-dwellers and Palestinian Arabs (filmed in the small living-rooms or kitchens of tenements in south Tel Aviv). The film ends with a long after-the-war sequence of celebrations and dancing, accompanied by interviews with the young Tel Avivians who had forgotten or repressed their memories of the trauma they had experienced.

Thus the film portrays Tel Aviv life as one of uninterrupted entertainment and pleasure, while its sequential structure creates circles within circles: the scenes of the slums and Palestinian Arabs are 'enveloped' by those of the Tel Avivian good life of dancing and pleasure, which is in turn 'surrounded' by the war scenes. Thus the film characterises the hedonistic culture as a bubble attacked by an external reality in the form of war and assaulted by an internal reality in the form of the social groups at whose expense, to a great extent, such entertainment becomes possible.

ADVERTISING

During the Gulf War advertising was in the doldrums. There was little demand for most consumer goods or for the advertisements designed to promote them. To pull through this war-induced recession and keep their businesses alive, the advertisers thought up the idea of using manufacturers' patronage (and their money, at reduced rates) to advertise patriotic announcements intended to 'fortify national morale'. The result was a wave of posters and heroic and patriotic advertisements that reinforced the national narratives in their rightist-Jewish version.

This narrative was evident in the dramatic structure of the 'patriotic' announcements and posters that depicted national unity, might and indestructibility in the face of an enemy who would be annihilated 'in blood and fire'. As in Shamir's speeches, these posters also used many traditional sources to express the national view – familiar quotes from the Bible ('Be strong and of good courage and do not fear'; 'Fire and brimstone on Saddam [Sodom] and Gomorrah'); references to Jewish holidays ('Sa-*dam* [blood], frogs, lice', a pun on the Ten Plagues enumerated at Passover); national watchwords ('The whole world shall see that we're here and shall not budge'); popular songs ('We Have No Other Tel Aviv' – a play on a well-known popular song - 'I Have No Other Country'); wordplays ('We're all Patriots'; 'May Sa-*dam* [his blood] be on your head'); and so on.[28]

Along with these patriotic slogans, some posters, revived the narrative of the *Yishuv*-period Labor movement, thus taking the same direction as the television reports. This is especially conspicuous in Bank Hapoalim advertisements such as the neatly rhyming 'The *meshek* is the *neshek*', which means 'The economy is the weaponry', but brings to mind the early agricultural development of the country because *meshek* also means a farm. This slogan not only repeats a similar one from the *Yishuv* period, it also summarises the Labor movement attitude behind it – the belief that victory will be achieved by construction, creative endeavour, industry and toil, no less than by struggle and war. Other slogans that appeared are: 'We shall continue to work and we shall win'; 'We must continue to build'; 'We must dream of the future'; and 'Each building is a strategic asset'.

The last example quoted is accompanied by an illustration that identifies its time frame: houses and factories loom upwards and are depicted in diagonal lines, illuminated from a low angle, and all is spread over hills and amid trees, an exemplification of the socialist-realist art of the pre- and early-state years. The *Yishuv* period and the Labor movement ideology are thus combined into a message that befits a war in which the possibility of taking up arms does not exist. Implicitly, however, it resurrects the same ideology that had been fashioned, 50 years before, as an answer to similar constraints.

Most of the advertisements used combinations, particularly of the nationalist-rightist and personal narratives. On the one hand, they continued to address the consumers and to urge them to tend to their personal needs and desires, but along with this they tried 'to sell' national pride and beliefs. To do this they spoke to the consumers in two different languages, culled from the two narratives. This combination of nationalism and consumerism was very common in the political discourse of the 1970s and 1980s (as discussed in Chapter 4). During the war, however, the context of consumerism contributed to the devaluation of the national narratives, and of the rightist-Jewish narrative in particular.

In one advertisement the sentence 'There is nothing like Tel Aviv in the whole world' is printed on a flag of Israel fluttering in the breeze. The text and the flag express the view of Jewish singularity and superiority and the ability of Tel Aviv to represent this. In this way it incorporates Tel Aviv into the rightist-Jewish narrative. However, the sentence and the flag on which it appears are draped over half of the body of a seductive model in order to promise a 'selection of knits and winter models at bargain prices'. The city of Tel Aviv thus reverts to the personal narrative from which it had been 'extricated' and returns to the promises of sex, consumer goods and pleasure that characterise it. America plays a similar double role in an advertisement in which a picture of a woman bearing aloft the torch of liberty half-hides an open refrigerator. The torch symbolises the valour of the American forces; the refrigerator symbolises the good life that this valour assures.

In another example, a Zionist stand against the enemy serves as a motive for buying an apartment: 'A Zionist phenomenon. / Now is the time to purchase an apartment. / Saddam Hussein will no longer tell me what to do with my life.' A mortgage-bank advertisement plays on the national narrative in a similar fashion: 'Each apartment is a flag. / We must continue to build. / We must continue to dream of the future.' However, this pitch then switches from the national narrative to the personal one: 'There is no reason to let this war stop our dreams of a quality of life that includes a lovely, spacious apartment.'

Dreams of a high 'quality of life' and of a lovely spacious apartment had been embedded in the national dream for many years. In the Gulf

War they succeeded in outweighing this dream, and to some extent in supplanting it.

NOTES

1. W. Dorman, 1991; W. Beeman, 1991.
2. E. Katz, 1992.
3. When the actual fighting in Iraq began, the vast majority of the public (94 per cent according to the polls) supported 'the way the government [was dealing] with the current situation'. This support, and with it approval of the government's positions, weakened as the war went on.
4. Izhar Harari, Knesset session of 22 May 1967; Yitzhak Rafael, Knesset session of 22 May 1967; Levi Eshkol, Knesset session of 12 June 1967; and Arie Ben-Eliezer, Knesset session of 12 June 1967, respectively.
5. Conference of United Kibbutz Movement members, 11 September 1948; opening session of the Zionist Executive, 24 August 1948; responses given in the Zionist Executive session of 24 August 1948; conference of United Kibbutz Movement members, 11 September 1948, respectively.
6. See also Chapters 3, 4 and 5.
7. Yitzhak Shamir's speech in the Knesset, 4 February 1991.
8. D. Shmuel, 1948; M. Megged, 1975; D. Ben-Gurion, radio greeting for Rosh Hashana (New Year) on 24 September 1948; Ben Gurion, opening of the meeting of the Zionist Committee, 1948. And see the analysis of the War of Independence press in Chapter 2.
9. Yitzhak Shamir, television interview; speech in the Knesset, 4 February 1991, respectively.
10. Yitzhak Shamir, television interview.
11. Yitzhak Shamir, speech in the Knesset, 3 April 1991.
12. See Chapter 3.
13. Yitzhak Shamir, television interview.
14. On the disarray in *Haga* (Civil Defence), see R. Tzeror, 1991; see also M. Niv, 1991.
15. From the film *Sha'anan Si*.
16. T. Liebes, 1992(a). See also Liebes, 1992(b); I. Lapidus, 1991.
17. Liebes, 1992(b).
18. This CNN footage deals with an attack that took place in Israel. The scenes from Iraq and the battlefields are different in nature.
19. Only a few television reports attempt to create some identification between the IDF and the American armed forces. For example, a report on Israeli air force activity begins by praising the American army: 'They did it better than anyone could have imagined. They simply took over the world championship.' From the American army, the report switches to the Israeli air force ('The [Israeli] Air Force did not rely on today's world champions') and describes its state of alert. A warplane is readied for take-off as the camera hums. A pilot climbs into the warplane, and the effect is heightened by the low-angle photography used. The plane takes off and is filmed in the sky. The footage of the take-off gives the impression of uninterrupted activity while, in fact, there was no action at all.
20. Among them, films such as S. Gabison's 'Shuru' (1990) or A. Menachemi and N. Yaron's 'Tel Aviv Stories' (1992), and books such as Y. Katsir's, 'They Closed the Sea' (1990) or G. Taub's, 'What Would've Happened If We'd Forgotten Dov?'. All these were especially popular among young Israeli adults.
21. *Davar Aher*, 15 March 1991.

22. T. Gelbetz, 1991.
23. Y. Lapid, 1988.
24. E. Shai, 1988.
25. G. Hovav, 1988: 68.
26. G. Nitsan, 1991.
27. Gelbetz, 1991: 68, 69.
28. See B. Doner, 1991.

CONCLUSION

In the elections of June 1992, after a decade and a half of Likud government, a majority of the voters of Israel voted for the Alignment, which established a new governing coalition headed by Prime Minister Yitzhak Rabin and Foreign Minister Shimon Peres. Fifteen months later, this government and the Palestine Liberation Organisation signed a Declaration of Principles for the establishment of peace, thus beginning the Oslo process.

The political changes that had led to this were neither sudden nor surprising. There had been a gradual transformation in Israeli society during the 1980s, engendered by disappointment with the outcome of the Lebanon War, an increasing weariness with the protracted *Intifada*, disenchantment with national slogans and ethnocentricity, and fatigue with the country's long history of wars – not to mention the longing for normality and the pleasures of a newly affluent society. During the 1980s, these feelings and desires were expressed in the country's *belles-lettres*, cinema, theatre and the press. They then expanded into a broad range of texts of both the elite and the popular cultures.

The Gulf War sharpened this trend and brought the latent cultural controversy into the open. The debate between the rightist-Jewish narrative and other narratives could now infiltrate into the political and cultural centres of Israeli society. The disparity that developed between the heroic rhetoric of the rightist-Jewish narrative on the one hand, and the non-heroic reality of the Gulf War on the other, had prepared the grounds for change. When it came, however, this change was fragile and partial. The narrative of the right, reinforced by several large-scale terrorist attacks in Israeli cities, gained strength as the Oslo process moved forward. But even the government of the right, which returned to power in the elections of 1996, a few months after the assassination of Prime Minister Yitzhak Rabin, did not halt the peace process. Ehud Barak of the Labor movement,[1] who was elected prime minister in 1999, was publicly determined to continue it. The narratives of 'a people that dwells apart' and of 'destruction to redemption' thus lost their primacy in Israeli society.

In each of the wars between Israel and the Arab countries – 1948, 1956, 1967, 1973 and 1982 – and earlier during the Disturbances, people had been asked to rally around the prevailing ideologies and stand behind the country's leaders, and to express their solidarity with the fighters and the nation at large. To do this, narratives that had been built up in previous wars were utilised, but were modified and adjusted each time to the new conditions and the different wars. Through these narratives a dialogue was conducted between the nation's leaders and the media that served them, and the public, which usually stood behind the leadership during times of crisis. The extent to which the political centre succeeded in establishing these narratives in the culture after each war was determined by their interrelationship with other narratives and by their status in the culture. While it is generally accepted that wars affect and expedite social processes, the specific social processes which are catalysed by each particular war depends on the circumstances and nature of the historical event itself and on the character of the culture and the socio-political situation in which it unfolds.

Before Israel's independence, various versions of the few-versus-many narrative were dominant in the *Yishuv*. This narrative merged well with the *Yishuv*'s ideals of universal humanism and Zionist socialism, which also gave it national, social and moral justification. The 1930s were years of considerable tension between Jews and Arabs in Palestine, of increasingly virulent anti-Semitism in Europe and of the polarisation of inter-party struggles in the *Yishuv* itself. The few-versus-many narrative proliferated during this decade because it formed a framework for these ordeals and inspired faith in their eventual positive outcomes. While this narrative retained its prominence in the reportage of Israel's War of Independence, another appeared alongside it. This second narrative stressed the Jewish people's – and Israel's – place as one of the nations of Europe and a partner in its culture. It presented Israel's war against the Arabs as one of an enlightened west-European culture against a primitive and cruel east-Asian one. This narrative actually combined within it both the narrative of the Jewish people as 'one among the nations of the world' and that of the struggle between West and East. It thus enabled the Israeli soldier to view himself as a warrior in the great and strong army of the Allies, and to view the Arabs as a weak and isolated enemy.

With the years, these narratives shifted gradually to the margin and their place was taken by others that filled various different roles in the new Hebrew-Israeli culture. The most central of these was the narrative that depicted Israel as 'a people that dwells apart'. While during the period of the *Yishuv* this narrative had been perceived as one that depicted the Jews of the Exile, after independence was achieved, and particularly after the Six Day War, it was perceived as the story of Zionism and the state of Israel. And although it was dominant mostly in circles of the political right, it appeared in the subtexts of what were ostensibly expressions of the political left or centre. Nevertheless, like its predecessors, this narrative, too, was but one among many that could be found in different texts. As the struggle between the Israeli left and right sharpened, so too did the debate between the 'people that dwells apart' narrative and others, such as the local-personal, Zionist-socialist and universal-humanist narratives.

The Gulf War was the testing ground, so to speak, where the various narratives that had prevailed in Israel's culture throughout its short history coalesced, crystallised and clashed. There is a fine line that leads from the 1991 Gulf War to the agreement for peace concluded in Oslo in 1993. An analysis of the wartime texts reveals this line, for they constituted the arena in which the struggle between the narratives took place. This struggle appeared in many verbal and visual forms – speeches, news reports, *belles-lettres*, documentary films, journalistic articles, cinema and advertisements. The course of the war did much to determine which narratives would gain in strength and which would be pushed to the margins. The struggle, however, is far from over. The polarisation in Israeli society – between right and left, Ashkenazi and Sepharadi, religious and secular, rich and poor – increased in the second half of the 1990s. The familiar, well-rehearsed narratives continue to serve in the struggle between these poles, but it is the nation's on-going history, including both its internal strife and its external hostilities, that will determine which of these will dictate the character of Israeli society in the future.

NOTES

1. Now combined with other like-minded parties and called One Israel.

BIBLIOGRAPHY

Ahimeir, A. 'The Desert and the Garden of Eden', *Doar Ha-Yom* (newspaper), 4 September 1929. (In Hebrew.)

——. 'Posters from "The Toughs"', *Hazit Ha-'Am* (newspaper), 5 September 1933. (In Hebrew.)

——. 'Revolutionary Zionism' (Tel Aviv: The Committee for the Publication of Ahimeir's Works, 1966). (In Hebrew.)

——. 'Alliance of the Toughs', Vol. 3 (Tel Aviv: The Committee for the Publication of Ahimeir's Works, 1972). (In Hebrew.)

Alter, R. 'Images of the Arab in Israeli Fiction', *Hebrew Studies*, XVIII (1977), pp. 60–9.

——. *Necessary Angels* (Cambridge, MA: Harvard University Press, 1991).

Althuser, L. *Lenin and Philosophy and Other Essays* (London: New Left Books, 1971).

Amihai, K. S. G. 'Concerning a Clear Conscience and Clean Hands', *Al Ha-mishmar* (newspaper), 6 June 1948. (In Hebrew.)

Amikam, Y. 'When I Saw the Civilians Leaving in an Orderly File, I Realised There Was Another Way to Fight a War', *Yedioth Aharonoth* (newspaper), 2 July 1982. (In Hebrew.)

Amit, M. *The History of Classical Greece* (Jerusalem: Magnes, 1984).

Angenot, M. 'La lutte pour la vie: migration et usages d'une idéologeme', *Communication, colloque sur 'La locution'*, October 1984.

——. 'Pour une théorie du discours social: Problématique d'une recherche en cours', *Littérature*, 70 (May 1988), pp. 82–98.

Arbel, N. 'Ready for Battle Overnight', in Y. Wallach, 'A State Rises in the Storm of War, 1947–1950' (Tel Aviv, 1981). (In Hebrew.)

Arikha, Y. 'Paths in the Upper Galilee', *Gilionoth*, 4, 9 (1936), pp. 205–9. (In Hebrew.)

Aryeh, Y. 'Eight Days of Battle for Beit Yosef', *Davar* (newspaper), 4 June 1948. (In Hebrew.)

Azariah, R. 'I Was With the Fighters for the Liberation of the City of David', *Ha'aretz* (newspaper), 24 May 1948(a). (In Hebrew.)

——. 'How Katamon and Its Monastery Were Conquered', *Ha'aretz*, 9 May 1948(b). (In Hebrew.)

Bachar, A. 'At Six After the War', *Yedioth Aharonoth*, 16 June 1982. (In Hebrew.)

Band, A. 'Popular Fiction and the Shaping of Jewish Identity', Wilstein Conference on Jewish Identity in America, University of Judaism, Los Angeles, 4–7 June 1989.

Bargad, W. 'The Image of the Arab in Israeli Literature', *Hebrew Annual*

Review, 1 (1977), pp. 53–65. (In Hebrew.)

Barthes, R. *Mythologies* (New York: Hill & Wang, 1982).

Baruch, A. 'A Visit to Occupied Tsemah', *Davar*, 25 May 1948. (In Hebrew.)

——. 'God Accepts What You Have Done', *Yedioth Aharonoth*, 13 August 1982(a). (In Hebrew.)

——. 'The Players Are Pointing at You, Dear Brigade Commander', *Yedioth Aharonoth*, 6 August 1982(b). (In Hebrew.)

Bar-Yosef, Y. 'There's a Strength in Negba That Will Endure Forever', *Al Ha-mishmar*, 27 July 1948. (In Hebrew.)

——. 'What Kind of War Is This?', *Ba-mahane*, 16 June 1982. (In Hebrew.)

Bar-Zohar, M. 'At the Approaches to Beirut', *Yedioth Aharonoth*, 16 June 1982. (In Hebrew.)

Basok, M. 'The Likud Has Launched a War on the Israeli World of Creative Endeavour', *Al Ha-mishmar*, 4 December 1989. (In Hebrew.)

Bass, S. 'The Farmer from Motsa', 'Great Moments', 'Winds of August in Jerusalem', *Gilionoth*, 2, 8 (1934), pp. 165–8. (In Hebrew.)

——. 'Last Stop in Canaan', *Gilionoth*, 1, 3 (1934), pp. 246–8. (In Hebrew.)

Beeman, W. 'Renewed Debate: Covering the Aftermath of Victory', in C. Wakeman (ed.), *The Media and the Gulf: A Closer Look*, Conference Proceedings (Berkeley, CA: Graduate School of Journalism, 3–4 May 1991).

Ben Dov, N. 'In the Opposite Direction' (Tel Aviv: Hakibbutz Hameuhad, 1995). (In Hebrew.)

Ben-Ezer, E. 'Shadow of Orchards and a Volcano', *Moznayim*, 5–6 (October–November 1983), pp. 57–9. (In Hebrew.)

Ben-Gurion, D. Opening Session of the Zionist Executive, 22 August 1948. (In Hebrew.)

——. Broadcast on the Occasion of the Jewish New Year, 24 September 1948. (In Hebrew.)

——. 'From Class to People' (Tel Aviv: Davar Press, 1933). (In Hebrew.)

——. 'Discipline' (Tel Aviv: Davar Press, 1935). (In Hebrew.)

——. 'The Sinai Campaign' (Tel Aviv: Am Oved, 1959). (In Hebrew.)

Ben-Ner, Y. 'After the Rain' (Jerusalem: Keter, 1979). (In Hebrew.)

——. 'Lebanon from a Man's Height', *Ma'ariv* (newspaper), 18 June 1982. (In Hebrew.)

Ben-Porat, Z. 'Represented Reality and Literary Models: European Autumn on Israeli Soil', paper presented at the ICLA Conference, Munich, 1986.

Ben-Shaul, N. *Mythical Expressions of Siege in Israeli Films* (New York: Edwin Mellen Press, 1997).

Ben-Yeruham, H. 'Beitar Book', Vol. 1 (Jerusalem and Tel Aviv: The Committee for Publishing 'Beitar Book', 1969). (In Hebrew.)

——. 'Beitar Book', Vol. 2 (Jerusalem and Tel Aviv: The Committee for Publishing Beitar Book, 1976). (In Hebrew.)

Benjamin, A. (ed.). *The Lyotard Reader* (Cambridge: Basil Blackwell, 1989).

Bourdieu, P. *Question de Sociologie* (Paris: Les Editions de Minuit, 1980).

——. *Ce que parler veut dire* (Paris: Fayard, 1982).

Carlibach, E. 'The Earth Moves as You Approach Tulkarm', *Ha-mashqif* (newspaper), 14 May 1948. (In Hebrew.)

Cohen, G. 'Where Is Mr Peres Flying?', *Yediot Aharonoth*, 25 July 1986. (In Hebrew.)

Daromi, P. 'An Outing in Jaffa', *Ha-mashqif*, 2 May 1948. (In Hebrew.)
Dayan, U. 'Ricochets', *Ma'ariv*, 30 July 1982. (In Hebrew.)
Derrida, J. *De la Grammatologie* (Paris: Minuit, 1967).
Domb, R. *The Arab in Hebrew Prose* (London: Vallentine Mitchell, 1982).
Doner, B. 'Real Time in the Gulf War – Graphic Texts' (Tel Aviv: Museum of the Arts, 1991). (In Hebrew.)
Dorman, W. 'Redefining Censorship: The Control of Access, Information and Public Opinion', in C. Wakeman (ed.), *The Media and the Gulf: A Closer Look*, Conference Proceedings (Berkeley, CA: Graduate School of Journalism), 3–4 May 1991.
Elon, A. 'Those Who Broke Through,' *Ba-mahane*, 17 June 1948. (In Hebrew.)
Erez, Y. 'Beirut and What Next?', *Ma'ariv*, 18 June 1982(a). (In Hebrew.)
——. 'Golani Brigade, Company 3', *Ma'ariv*, 27 July 1982(b). (In Hebrew.)
——. 'The Man Who Defeated the Missiles', *Ma'ariv*, 25 June 1982(c). (In Hebrew.)
——. 'The Battle for the Road', *Ma'ariv*, 30 July 1982(d). (In Hebrew.)
——. 'The 70-Kilometre War', *Ma'ariv*, 23 July 1982(e). (In Hebrew.)
——. 'A Desk of Lebanese Sand', *Ma'ariv*, 11 June 1982(f). (In Hebrew.)
Even-Zohar, B. 'System, Repertoire', in N. Gertz, 'Literature and Ideology in Eretz Israel in the 1930s' (Tel Aviv: Open University of Israel, 1988). (In Hebrew.)
——. 'The Emergence of Native Hebrew Culture in Palestine 1882–1948', *Studies in Zionism*, 4 (1981): 167–84. (In Hebrew.)
——. 'Polysystem Studies', *Poetics Today*, 11, 1 (1990).
Feldman, Y. 'The "Other Within" in Contemporary Israeli Fiction', *Middle East Review* (autumn 1989), pp. 53–60.
Fichman, Y. 'Actions and Days: The Rehearsal', *Moznayim*, 1, 2 (1934), pp. 111–12. (In Hebrew.)
Foucault, M. *Histoire de la Folie à l'Age Classique* (Paris: Gallimard, 1972).
Freelance reporter. 'On the Roads and in the Villages These Days', *Ha-mashqif*, 23 May 1948. (In Hebrew.)
Fridman, M. 'Three Days and a Child', Lecture at the Open University of Israel, 1987.
——. 'The Arab in Israeli Cinema', Lecture at Tel Aviv University, 1988.
Gelbetz, T. 'We Are All Ants in a Convoy', in R. Tzeror (ed.), 'People Died of Fright' (Tel Aviv: Peratim, 1991), pp. 65–81. (In Hebrew.)
Gelblum, A. 'Patrolling the Jordan Front', *Ha'aretz*, 28 May 1948. (In Hebrew.)
Gertz, N. 'Hirbet Hiza'a and the Morning After' (Tel Aviv: Hakibbutz Hameuhad and the Porter Institute for Poetics and Semiotics, 1983). (In Hebrew.)
——. 'Literature and Ideology in Eretz Israel in the 1930s' (Tel Aviv: The Open University of Israel, 1988). (In Hebrew.)
——. 'Changes in Ideological Models', *Semiotica* 86, 3/4 (1991), pp. 247–75.
——. 'A Different History', in N. Ben-Dov (ed.), 'In the Opposite Direction' (Tel Aviv: Hakibbutz Hameuhad, 1995). (In Hebrew.)
Gil'adi, D. 'In Rosh Ha-'ayin – Wellspring of Hope for the Waters of Redemption', *Ma'ariv*, 14 July 1948. (In Hebrew.)
Gitlin, T. 'Redefining Censorship: The Control of Access, Information and

Public Opinion', in C. Wakeman (ed.), *The Media and the Gulf: A Closer Look*, Conference Proceedings (Berkeley: Graduate School of Journalism, 3–4 May 1991).

Goldstein, A. 'With the Fighters at Sha'ar Ha-gai on the Way to Jerusalem', *Ha-mashqif*, 31 May 1948. (In Hebrew.)

Greenberg, G. 'Orthodox Jewish Theology, 1945–1948: Responses to the Holocaust', in *Remembering for the Future* (Oxford: Pergamon Press, 1988).

Grossman, D. 'The Smile of the Lamb' (Tel Aviv: Siman Keriyya and Hakibbutz Hameuhad, 1983). (In Hebrew.)

——. 'See Under: Love' (Tel Aviv: Hakibbutz Hameuhad, 1986). (In Hebrew.)

Guri, H. 'A Journey to God's Mountain', in A. Cohen, 'A Man in War' (Tel Aviv: 1975). (In Hebrew.)

——. 'Tidings of the Lepers', *Yedioth Aharonoth*, 9 July 1982. (In Hebrew.)

Haber, E. 'Streets of Fire', *Yedioth Aharonoth*, 6 August 1982. (In Hebrew.)

Hadari-Remedge. 'Time Heals Everything', *Ha'aretz*, 3 July 1982. (In Hebrew.)

Hagedarati, Y. 'With the First Ringing Offensives in the South', *Ha-boqer* (newspaper), 14 May 1948(a). (In Hebrew.)

——. 'I Saw Negba Firm and Taut', *Ha-boqer*, 9 June 1948(b). (In Hebrew.)

Hanani, Y. 'Three Fingers', *Gilionoth*, 5, 2 (1937), pp. 142–6. (In Hebrew.)

Harshav, B. 'The Resurrection of Eretz Israel and the Modern Jewish Revolution', in N. Gertz (ed.), 'Points of View: Culture and Society in Israel' (Tel Aviv: Open University of Israel, 1988). (In Hebrew.)

Hazaz, H. 'Drabkin', *Knesset*, Vol. 3 (1938(a)). (In Hebrew.)

——. 'The Great Sojourner', *Moznayim*, 7, 3 (1938(b)), pp. 289–300. (In Hebrew.)

Hever, H. and Moshe, R. 'The Battles and Killing Never End' (Tel Aviv: Hakibbutz Hameuhad, 1983). (In Hebrew.)

Hirsch, E. 'Mr Mani', *Ha'ir* (newspaper), 4 May 1990. (In Hebrew.)

Hovav, G. 'The Way from Jerusalem', *Politica*, November (1988), pp. 30–1. (In Hebrew.)

H. S. 'The Inhabitants of Ramle Have Tired of the War', *Ma'ariv*, 13 July 1948. (In Hebrew.)

Jabotinsky, Z. 'In the Storm' (Jerusalem: Ari Jabotinsky Publications, 1943). (In Hebrew.)

——. 'Speeches: 1905–1926' (Jerusalem: Ari Jabotinsky Publications, 1947). (In Hebrew.)

——. 'Speeches: 1927–1940' (Jerusalem: Ari Jabotinsky Publications, 1948(a)). (In Hebrew.)

——. 'On Literature and Art' (Jerusalem: Ari Jabotinsky Publications, 1948(b)). (In Hebrew.)

Kaes, A. 'The Holocaust and the End of History: Postmodern Historiography in Cinema', in S. Friedlander (ed.), *Probing the Limits of Representation* (Cambridge, MA: Harvard University Press, 1992).

Kaplan, S. 'Negba – An Example and a Lesson', *Al Ha-mishmar*, 29 June 1948. (In Hebrew.)

Kastel-Bloom, O. 'Hostile Surroundings' (Tel Aviv: Zemona Bitan, 1989). (In Hebrew.)

Katz, E. 'The End of Journalism', *Journal of Communication*, 42, 3 (1992), pp. 5–14.
Kenan, A. 'Holocaust 2' (Tel Aviv: Hotza'a Meyuhedet, 1975). (In Hebrew.)
——. 'Express a Lamentation for Tyre', *Yedioth Aharonoth*, 18 June 1982. (In Hebrew.)
Kimmerling, B. 'A Rear-Guard War for External and Internal Hegemony', *Politica*, March (1991), pp. 9–18. (In Hebrew.)
Kovner, A. 'Face to Face' (Merhavya, Israel: Sifriat Poalim, 1953). (In Hebrew.)
Kritz, R. 'Perspectives on the Literature of the War of Independence', in Y. Wallach (ed.), 'We Were Like Dreamers' (Tel Aviv: Masada, 1985). (In Hebrew.)
Kronfeld, C. *Modernism/Theory/Category* (Berkeley: University of California Press, forthcoming).
Lacan, J. *Ecrits 1* (Paris: Seuil, 1966).
Lapid, Y. 'Mug [Murder] Shot', *Politica*, November (1988), pp. 22–5. (In Hebrew.)
Lapidus, I. 'Reporting the Middle East: An Overview', in C. Wakeman (ed.), *The Media and the Gulf: A Closer Look*, Conference Proceedings (Berkeley: Graduate School of Journalism, May 3–4, 1991).
Levi, I. 'Letters of Sun, Letters of Moon' (Tel Aviv: Keter, 1991). (In Hebrew.)
Levi, S. 'Captives of a Fiction', *Moznayim*, 5–6 (October–November 1983), pp. 70–3. (In Hebrew.)
Liebes, T. 'See [It] on Television', *Politica*, May (1990), pp. 20–4. (In Hebrew.)
——. 'Decoding Television News: The Political Discourse of Israeli Hawks and Doves', *Theory and Society*, 21 (1992(a)), pp. 357–81.
——. 'Our War/Their War: Comparing the Intifadeh and the Gulf War on U.S. and Israeli Television', *Critical Studies in Mass Communication*, 9 (1992(b)), pp. 44–55.
Liebman, C. and Don Yehiya, E. *Civil Religion in Israel* (Berkeley and Los Angeles: University of California Press, 1983).
Lior, G. 'Captain Yohanan Tried to Console the Lebanese [Man]', *Yedioth Aharonoth*, 23 June 1982. (In Hebrew.)
Litani, Y. 'To Beirut and Back', *Ha'aretz*, 21 June 1982. (In Hebrew.)
Lotman, J. 'On the Reduction and Unfolding of Sign System', in H. Baran (ed.), *Semiotics and Structuralism* (New York: Art & Science Press, 1976).
Lotman, J. *et al.* 'Theses on the Semiotic Study of Culture', in Th. Sebeok (ed.), *The Telltale Sign* (Liss, Netherlands: Peter de Ridder Press, 1975).
Lyotard, J. *The Differend* (Minneapolis: University of Minnesota Press, 1983).
——. *The Post-Modern Condition* (Minneapolis: University of Minnesota Press, 1984).
Mastboim, Y. 'The Jewish Sheikh Munis', *Davar*, 3 June 1948. (In Hebrew.)
Megged, M. 'Dangers' (Tel Aviv: Sifriat Poalim, 1975). (In Hebrew.)
Meiron, M. 'I Was Placed [There] to Do as Told', *Yedioth Aharonoth*, 15 June 1982. (In Hebrew.)
Michelson, M. 'How I Downed Four MiGs', *Davar*, 18 June 1982. (In Hebrew.)
Miron, D. 'Four Facets in Contemporary Hebrew Literature' (Jerusalem and Tel Aviv: Schocken, 1975). (In Hebrew.)

——. 'If There Will Be No Jerusalem' (Tel Aviv: Hakibbutz Hameuhad, 1987). (In Hebrew.)
——. 'The Face as Viewed in the Tray', *Yedioth Aharonoth*, 22 and 28 April 1988. (In Hebrew.)
——. 'Facing the Silent Brother' (Jerusalem: Keter, 1992). (In Hebrew.)
——. 'Behind Each Thought There Is Another One', in N. Ben Dor (ed.), 'In the Opposite Direction' (Tel Aviv: Hakibbutz Hameuhad, 1995). (In Hebrew.)
Morahg, G. 'Reality and Symbol in the Fiction of Yehoshua', *Prooftexts*, 2 (1982), pp. 179–96.
——. 'New Images of Arabs in Israeli Fiction', *Prooftexts*, 6 (1986), pp. 147–62.
Morris, B. *The Birth of the Palestinian Problem, 1947–1949* (Boston: Cambridge University Press, 1987).
Mossinsohn, Y. 'Blue Jeep', in 'The Road to Jericho' (Tel Aviv, 1960). (In Hebrew.)
Nir, R. and Roeh, I. 'Intifadeh Coverage in the Israeli Press: Popular and Quality Papers Assume a Rhetoric of Conformity', *Discourse and Society*, 3, 1 (1993), pp. 47-60.
Nitsan, G. 'Heat-wave Booty', *Hadashot* (newspaper), 8 February 1991. (In Hebrew.)
Niv, M. 'The First Night of the Missiles', in 'About the Confusion in Civil Defence' (1991), pp. 49–55. (In Hebrew.)
Oren, E. 'We're Going Up to A-Ziv', *Ma'ariv*, 22 July 1948. (In Hebrew.)
'Our Correspondent'. 'Jabaliya and Tel-Arish are Abandoned', *Al Ha-mishmar*, 10 May 1948. (In Hebrew.)
Over Orach (A passer-by). 'On the Roads and in the Villages these Days', *Hamashkif*, 23 May 1948. (In Hebrew.)
Oz, A. 'My Michael' (Tel Aviv: Am Oved, 1968). (In Hebrew.)
——. 'Unto Death (Tel Aviv: Sifriat Poalim, 1971). (In Hebrew.)
——. 'A Perfect Peace' (Tel Aviv: Am Oved, 1982). (In Hebrew.)
——. Series of lectures on 'Hirbet Hiza'a' (unpublished), Ben-Gurion University of the Negev. (In Hebrew.)
Peli (Fichman). 'The Eternal Rehearsal', *Moznayim*, 5, 2 (1937), pp. 149–52. (In Hebrew.)
——. 'On the Edges of the [Tent] Flap: Ebbing Bonfires', *Moznayim*, 7, 3 (1938), p. 413. (In Hebrew.)
Perry, M. 'The Israeli–Palestinian Conflict as a Metaphor in Recent Israeli Fiction', *Poetics Today*, 7, 4 (1986), pp. 603–21.
Rabinov, Y. 'The Night Ploughman', *Gilionoth*, 5, 5 (1936), pp. 390–2. (In Hebrew.)
Rahav, A. 'My First War', *Ma'ariv*, 25 June 1982. (In Hebrew.)
Ramras-Rauch, G. *The Arab in Israeli Literature* (Bloomington and Indianapolis: Indiana University Press, 1989).
Rosen, J. 'Reporting and Hi-Tech War: Combat as Spectacle', in C. Wakeman (ed.), *The Media and the Gulf: A Closer Look*, Conference Proceedings (Berkeley: Graduate School of Journalism, May 3–4, 1991).
Rotem, A. 'Even When They're Dead They Look Better Than Us', *Davar*, 21 December 1986. (In Hebrew.)
Said, E. *Orientalism* (New York: Vintage Press, 1979).

Sebeok, T. 'The Doctrine of Signs', *Journal of Social and Biological Structures*, 9, 4 (1986), pp. 345–64.

Segev, T. Untitled article, *Ha'aretz*, 18 June 1982. (In Hebrew.)

Sha'anan, A. 'The Literature of Struggle: Fate and Rebellion' (Tel Aviv: Sifriat Poalim, 1976). (In Hebrew.)

Shaham, N. 'The Gods are Lazy' (Merhavia, Israel: Sifriat Poalim, 1949). (In Hebrew.)

Shai, E. 'Alternative Journalism, or Cock-a-Doodle-Doo Media', *Politica*, November (1988), pp. 12–17.

Shaked, G. 'A New Wave in Hebrew Literature' (Merhavia, Israel: Tel Aviv, Sifriat Poalim, 1971). (In Hebrew.)

——. 'The Arab in Israeli Fiction', *Modern Hebrew Literature*, 3 (autumn 1989), pp. 17–21.

——. 'Hebrew Literature 1880–1980 (Part IV)' (Tel Aviv: Keter and Hakibbutz Hameuhad, 1992). (In Hebrew.)

Shamas, A. 'He Mixed Up His Roles', in R. Schorr and O. Lubin (eds.), *Avanti Popolo* (Jerusalem: Kinneret, 1990). (In Hebrew.)

Shamir, M. 'The Three-Sided String' (Tel Aviv: Sifriat Poalim, 1967). (In Hebrew.)

Shamir, Y. 'Saddam Hussein's Aggression and Menace to World Peace', speech in the Knesset, 49–1, in *Documents* (Ministry of Education and Culture, Information Centre, 1991). (In Hebrew.)

Shavit, Y. 'From Majority to State' (Tel Aviv: Yariv-Hadar, 1978). (In Hebrew.)

——. 'The Mythologies of the Right' (Tel Aviv: Beit Berl, 1986). (In Hebrew.)

——. 'Ideology, World View, and National Policy: The Case of the Likud Goverment 1977–1984', *Jerusalem Journal of International Relations*, 9, 2 (1987).

Shimshoni, A. 'With the Conquerors of Tantura', *Ha-boqer*, 26 May 1948. (In Hebrew.)

Shmeterling. 'Sights of Summer', *Gilionoth*, 2, 9 (1935). (In Hebrew.)

Shmuel, D. 'Seventy-Three Hours on the Latrun Front', *Ha-boqer*, 10 June 1948. (In Hebrew.)

Shohat, E. *Israeli Cinema* (Austin, TX: University of Texas Press 1989).

Siah Lohamim. 'Soldiers Talk about the Six Day War: 1968' (Israel: Young Friends from the Kibbutz Movement, 1968). (In Hebrew.)

Smilansky, Y. 'Illustrated Postcards from Lebanon', *Davar*, 13 August 1982. (In Hebrew.)

S. N. 'We Returned to Base Safely', *Ha'aretz*, 9 April 1948 (from *Ba-mahane*). (In Hebrew.)

Special reporter. 'The Third Week of the War', *Ha-boqer*, 4 June 1948. (In Hebrew.)

Steinman. 'In the Shadow of Edom', *Moznayim* (1937), pp. 129–33. (In Hebrew.)

Talmi, E. 'In Occupied Acre', *Davar*, 28 May 1948. (In Hebrew.)

Talmi, M. 'In the Areas of the Beaten Enemy', *Ba-mahane*, 22 July 1948. (In Hebrew.)

Tavor-Bannet, E. *Structuralism and the Logic of Dissent* (Urbana and Chicago: University of Illinois Press, 1989).

Tavor, E. 'Lebanon: Surrealistic Pictures', *Yedioth Aharonoth*, 2 July 1982. (In Hebrew.)

Tzanin, M. 'A Day in Abu Kabir', *Davar*, 25 May 1948. (In Hebrew.)

Tzeror, R. (ed.). 'People Died of Fright' (Tel Aviv: Peratim, 1991). (In Hebrew.)

Tzifroni, G. 'At Night the Fighters Crossed the Vale of Hinnom', *Ha-boqer*, 26 May 1948(a). (In Hebrew.)

——. 'Thus the Jewish Fighters Conquered Katamon', *Ha-boqer*, 9 May 1948(b). (In Hebrew.)

——. 'Victory at the Southern Approach and the Northern Approach to the City', *Ha-boqer*, 7 June 1948(c). (In Hebrew.)

Valentine, A. 'Alef-Gimmel Tank – Afternoon Prayers', *Ha'aretz*, 20 August 1982(a). (In Hebrew.)

——. 'Square of the Partings, *Ha'aretz*, 9 July 1982(b). (In Hebrew.)

Wakeman, C. (ed.). *The Media and the Gulf: A Closer Look*, Conference Proceedings (Berkeley: Graduate School of Journalism, May 3–4, 1991).

Walter, Y. 'A Baby Girl on the Damascus Highway', *Ma'ariv*, 2 July 1982. (In Hebrew.)

Weiss, S. 'The Upheaval' (Tel Aviv: Am Oved, 1981). (In Hebrew.)

White, H. *Tropics of Discourse* (Baltimore and London: Johns Hopkins University Press, 1978).

Ya'ari, Y. 'The Hero', *Davar*, November 1933. (In Hebrew.)

——. 'The Bird's Nest', *Davar*, December 1934. (In Hebrew.)

Yambour, Y. 'In the Courtyard of Negba on the Thirtieth Day', *Al Ha-mishmar*, 16 June 1948(a). (In Hebrew.)

——. 'On the Roads of Israel in the Days of the Cease-Fire', *Al Ha-mishmar*, 5 July 1948(b). (In Hebrew.)

Yehoshua, A. B. 'Facing the Forests' (Tel Aviv: Hakibbutz Hameuhad, 1968). (In Hebrew.)

——. 'Early Summer, 1970' (Tel Aviv: Schocken, 1972). (In Hebrew.)

——. 'Nine Stories' (Tel Aviv: Hakibbutz Hameuhad, 1972). (In Hebrew.)

——. 'The Lover' (Jerusalem and Tel Aviv: Schocken, 1977). (In Hebrew.)

——. 'Mr Mani' (Tel Aviv: Hakibbutz Hameuhad and Siman Keriyya, 1990). (In Hebrew.)

Yehoshua. 'Six Days of Battle at Yad Mordechai', *Davar*, 28 May 1948. (In Hebrew.)

Yemini, Y. 'The Town of Tsemah is in the Hands of the *Hagana*', *Ha'aretz*, 13 May 1948. (In Hebrew.)

Yerushalmi, Y. H. *Zakhor: Jewish History and Jewish Memory* (Washington: Washington University Press, 1982).

Yizhar, S. 'Paths in the Fields', *Gilionoth*, 7, 5-6 (1938), pp. 362–406. (In Hebrew.)

——. 'A Night Without Gunfire', *Gilionoth*, 9, 4-5 (1940), pp. 282–323. (In Hebrew.)

——. 'Hirbet Hiza'a' and 'The Prisoner ', in 'Four Stories' (Merhavia, Israel: Sifriat Poalim, 1949). (In Hebrew.)

Zerubavel, Y. *Recovered Roots* (Chicago: University of Chicago Press, 1995).

INDEX